D1049863

To my dear, dear
mother, Ruth, whose
strength and courage have
shown me how to face
challenges in my life. Thank
you for your continuing love and
support... you have always been
there for me. I love you, Mom!

'Sis
2/99

As good teachers weave the fabric that joins them with students
and subjects, the heart is the loom on which the threads are tied,
the tension is held, the shuttle flies, and the fabric is stretched
tight. Small wonder, then, that teaching tugs at the heart, opens
the heart, even breaks the heart—the more one loves teaching,
the more heartbreaking it can be. The courage to teach is the
courage to keep one's heart open in those very moments when
the heart is asked to hold more than it is able so that teacher and
students and subject can be woven into the fabric of community
that learning, and living, require.

—PARKER J. PALMER, *THE COURAGE TO TEACH*

A Tapestry *of* Knowledge

A Tapestry *of* Knowledge

Weaving Classroom Portraits:
A Reflective Collection of Inquiry and Dialogue

Written by Virginia Beach City Public School Educators
Virginia Beach City Public Schools
Timothy R. Jenney, Ph.D., Superintendent

Compiled and Edited by Leanne K. Self

Published by The Virginia Beach City Public School System
2512 George Mason Drive
Virginia Beach, Virginia 23456-0038

Printed in the United States of America

Letton Gooch Printers, Inc.
700 West 21st Street
Norfolk, Virginia 23517

First Edition
Volume One

ISBN 0-9666992-0-3

Front Cover Art by Cindy Copperthite, 1998
"Time Spirit" Tapestry, 1997, mixed media collage

Book design by Susan Carson
Produced by Brett Riordan

Body copy typeset in Goudy Old Style
Additional copy typeset in Avenir and Franklin Gothic

Documentation Style: Modern Language Association of America
MLA Style Manual and Guide to Scholarly Publishing, 1998.

Table of Contents

Collaborative Teaching *(continued)*

Assessment: Looking In and Beyond

Student-Centered Learning: Our Subjects, Our Souls

About the Editor

Acknowledgements

Dedication

This book is dedicated to students – past, present, and future – students who inspire and teach us daily, and who enliven our classrooms by being part of a brilliant, diverse tapestry of cultures and stories.

WORDS FOR TEACHERS

About eight of them entered my high school classroom kicked out
of school at least three times
kicked out of their homes more than that.
Richard entered class with a swagger,
his cut off baseball bat slung by his side,
Ready.
Sherri sat in the back of the classroom
so she could prop her head against the bulletin board,
seems two children by sixteen was too much to handle—
her eyes lulled by the lure of sleep.
A wad of money fell from Chris's pocket—
too much money for a kid his age,
his morning highs, his clouded eyes.
Nobody talked to him much,
not even his parents who told me he was retarded,
not at all like his older brother,
even when I showed them his poetry,
his gift.

Another school year I was discussing existentialism
and Camus' intent in *The Stranger* when it occurred to me
the only real strangers were my gifted students.
They had forgotten what was "in" learning,
forgotten everything except GPA's and SAT's
and a resumé that boasted of community service.
They had perfect attendance,
participated in every club, in every fund raiser.
Still, in spring, they trudged around school
with dead eyes and bodies,
their clothes disheveled, their eyes bloodshot from lack of

sleep,
their backpacks slung over their shoulders
like a question mark:
Is this life?

Still, they dragged themselves up
to wear the faces to meet the faces that they meet.
And with that Prufrockian smile
they pushed forward into the Myth of Perfectibility.
They stopped briefly to see their reflections in the mirror,
a reflection of a former self when twice upon a time
they had but one face.

But Shawn remained in love with learning,
used books to release his soul;
His mother told him he would be a failure,
so Shawn fought back by dreaming.
His valedictory speech was full of the musings
of a small boy who once was at peace
with himself and his dreams,
a young man comfortable with risk,
who flew airplanes, and trudged up steep mountains to converse
with the village people of Spain.

Soon, other students awakened. But the year was hard.
William cheated his way through straight "A's" and
I caught him copying a disk.
Tamika was afraid to go home with anything but an A,
her alcoholic mother living through her child,
beating sense into her,
wanting more than an empty house full of nothing.
And my true intellect Justin, so
accustomed to playing the intellectual bantering game that he
couldn't handle a challenge anymore.
He failed the first semester
and had to make an A to graduate.
In his final portfolio, he said:
"This is the class that taught me once again what it feels like
to strive and work hard for an accomplishment I'll be proud of."

And so these are our students.
Students who face shattered lives and dreams,
who have created an armor of anger and apathy to shield
themselves from fear and rejection,
hundreds of soldiers at war with themselves and with us.

May we love them still for their justice and courage and
desperate loves.
May we understand their pain and the pain they can inflict on
others.
May we love them by making demands upon them
even when they test—test deadlines, test class rules, test
patience.
May we teach them the beauty of a rhetorical question,
to value differences in others,
to appreciate the fruits of hard work and a dedication to dreams.
May we teach them with compassion,
Still.

—LEANNE SELF

Gratitudes

This book, written, compiled, and edited in one brief year, is a symbol of what can happen when educators believe furiously in a dream, and when they have the support and encouragement necessary to bring that dream to fruition.

I am grateful to the extraordinary educators who contributed to this book by giving of their time and expertise to publish their stories, their research, and their reflective moments in the classroom.

I am also especially grateful to teach in the Virginia Beach City Public Schools where the Superintendent, Timothy R. Jenney, Ph.D., possesses the vision and progressive leadership to allow a book such as *A Tapestry of Knowledge* to become a reality.

While it is impossible to thank all the individuals who have contributed in some way to the creation of this book, I would like to extend a special thanks to the following individuals for their love of the classroom, their teaching expertise, their insights, editorial suggestions, and keen eyes:

Dr. Mark Gulesian, Professor of English Education, The College of William and Mary - Manuscript Selection Board and Editorial Board;

Dr. Lelia Christenbury, Professor of English Education, Virginia Commonwealth University - Manuscript Selection Board;

Mrs. Mary Barnes, retired English Supervisor, Virginia Beach City Public Schools - Editorial Board;

Ms. Beverly McColley, librarian, Norfolk Academy - Writing Consultant;

Mrs. Betty Smith, retired English Department Chairperson, Ocean Lakes High School and former Language Arts Coordinator, Virginia Beach City Public Schools - Editorial Board and Writing Consultant;

Kathy Phipps, Assistant Superintendent, Department of Media & Communications, Virginia Beach City Public Schools, and her entire staff for their continued support, encouragement, and willingness to share ideas;

Bonnie Fischer, Public Relations Coordinator, Department of Media and Communications, Virginia Beach City Public Schools - Editorial Board and Writing Consultant;

Nancy Soscia, Special Assistant, Department of Media & Communications, Virginia Beach City Public Schools - Art Selection Board;

Yolanda Jones-Howell, Special Assistant, Department of Media & Communications, Virginia Beach City Public Schools - Editorial Board and Marketing Director;

Jeff Barba, Video Production Specialist, Video Services Department, City of Virginia Beach - Editorial Board;

Anne Wolcott, Art Coordinator, Virginia Beach City Public Schools - Art Selection Board;

Donna Schuler, Executive Secretary to the Superintendent, Virginia Beach City Public Schools;

Heather Strickland, Secretary, Governmental Services, Virginia Beach City Public Schools;

Jody Blaufus, Secretary, Office of Media and Communications, Virginia Beach City Public Schools - Special Assistant to Ms. Self;

And finally, to the readers of this book. My hope is that you will know what is possible in this tapestry of knowledge we call the classroom.

—LEANNE SELF

A Tapestry *of* Knowledge

t he right time, place and people need to be present to take what is only a concept, and bring it to fruition. This book, A Tapestry of Knowledge, is such a literary piece, one conceptualized long before it became a reality. The text of these enlightened ideas evolved through the careful tutelage of entrusted professionals who believed in the worth of intellectual property. I think it is noteworthy that the success of this project is as much in the process of its development as it is in the results of scholarly effort. Though I have twenty-five years of experience, I still marvel at the talent I encounter within our profession.

Knowledge is, of course, the cornerstone of technical advantage. But true competence exists when teachers demonstrate their genius through the transmittal of that knowledge to children. The enthusiastic and demanding expectation of a caring and competent teacher is, to be sure, a valued memory each of us possesses. In this age of technology and with the speed in which we process information, some may question the wisdom of a yearlong effort to capture lessons on paper. However, literature of old and that generated new, whether it is transposed to CD or to video, still must be written first. I can think of no better way to preserve the intellectual knowledge of those teachers than to record for posterity their documented success.

There is certain satisfaction when one relates the methods of, and their resultant reward for, successful teaching. When talented teachers teach, children exhibit a glowing persona, the delights of which are nurtured and shared as if it is theirs to own as a mentor. The act of mentoring is to shape and convey knowledge to those less learned, and I would maintain that every one of the thirty-seven educators profiled in this text has served as a mentor in multiple ways to countless children. Great teachers are mentors in every definitional aspect, and I cannot emphasize enough the lack of quality role models today. So to memorialize them through the print medium is at least one way to signify their importance.

I trusted in Leanne and her creative talents to produce a work of pride and promise. That has happened. From the art teachers who provided marvelous illustrations to the classroom teachers, demonstrating example after example of remarkable effort, we are complete–by way of a team and by way of a dream. A Tapestry of Knowledge was in my mind's eye, but it was only through exceptional people that it became tangible. To say thank you is perhaps much too simplistic. Nonetheless, as inadequate as any expression of appreciation may be, let me simplistically say, "Well done!"

—TIMOTHY R. JENNEY, SUPERINTENDENT

Preface

f or the history teacher the world is seen in landmark dates and historical movements; for the science teacher the world is a challenging hypothesis; for the art teacher the world becomes an art studio, a palate of color, shape, and play of light. For the English teacher the world, the classroom, is a writer's workshop, a paintbrush, a quill pen and reams of paper, a poem nearing its completion. The educational metaphor for this anthology is a tapestry—a finely threaded, multicolored intricate design, full of depth and perspective and thematic consistency. This tapestry tells a story as most tapestries do, and through their prose these skilled weavers, these educators, unravel the meaning of their journeys to discover and rediscover the art of what it means to teach.

Together, we ask questions: What would happen if we allowed students to tell their stories? if we modeled a positive sense of community in the classroom based on mutual respect? if diversity became a source of inspiration instead of alienation? and if educators learned to tap the unlimited potential of our class leaders making them facilitators and critical thinkers?

As educators, how do we show our students who we are and allow them to experience our disciplines in a personal and intellectual way with the same urgency of that poem nearing its completion? How do we know how children comprehend what they read until we allow them to see it—like poems on paper—until we allow them to hear it like the sounds and meter of a cascading stanza?

While studying the Romantic poet, William Wordsworth, at Oxford University this past summer, I had the opportunity to visit the Lake District in northern England and contemplate Wordsworth's depiction of the influences of light and dark on the landscape and ponder his theory of the sublime. Like a well-written poem, or a perfect classroom lesson full of passion and vitality, I breathed in England's landscape. In Cumbria, I followed one of Wordsworth's private walks along the edges of stone-walled fields that later I would describe to my students in

September when we studied Wordsworth's autobiographical poem, *The Prelude*. Behind Wordsworth's cottage, I sat atop Rydal Mount, the church bells ringing through the deep ravine that leaned into the valley—a dramatic swathe of wild heather, the old woody scent burning the morning haze. What set this beauty apart for me was the absolute variety of terrain, like students in a classroom, actually. I looked out and in one sweeping glance I saw Wordsworth's poetic inspiration; the jagged cliffs appeared angry, the rugged rock bold and broken—shards of limestone scattering the green. Other cliffs were cushioned by vibrant green moss, seats of velvet within the mountain's side. Rivers of fern gave the mountain a lacy feathering that softened its monstrous presence. It bore veins of muddied rust that twisted up and down, around and through the earth. Atop Rydal Mount, a jagged pattern was etched. This scene I took back to my English classroom; the experience first became an introductory lesson to memoir, then it became the stimulus for writer's workshop and a discussion of descriptive writing evoking tone. And finally, my experiences on the side of this mountain inspired me to create a lesson on Romanticism and the contrasting philosophies of the Nature Poets, both British and American.

Upon my descent from Rydal's summit, I found my way back to Wordsworth's private garden, imagining the year 1848, imagining him pacing back and forth, back and forth, wearing the path thin in front of his stone writing cabin. All in an effort to discover the poem, the poem that hides because it is too painful, too beautiful, too much of the imagination to commit to paper; that same pain writers speak of when they discover the courage to publish the stories of their lives. They realize they can't take it back. Just as courageous teachers who publish their deepest fears, concerns, and reflective moments in the classroom can't take them back.

"Poems hide in the bottoms of our shoes," states Naomi Shihab, "we must live in a way that lets us find them…" and that lets us find our students. Certainly, hidden treasures are within them—their pasts and their present learning experiences that oftentimes speak of cultural stereotype, pain, success, and failure. How many Davids and Dans and Heathers have we seen, too comfortable with hiding? And what happens to the English as a Second Language student who hides merely because he is afraid? Doesn't he know how his cultural stories enrich? Like characters hiding in the darkest corners of a stage, our students are hiding in our classrooms, our stages, waiting to be discovered.

Educators mine for diamonds. We search for the at-risk, the gifted, the culturally diverse, polishing and teaching in a way that helps us discover our students' learning styles. Teaching becomes an odyssey of courage, and like Sisyphus we push the boulder, struggle with our own realities and those of our students to demonstrate how, like unwritten poems, unwritten lives, and unwritten beginnings, tentativeness is welcome. Until we do, we have no idea the roads our students will be able to travel.

Through the articles in this anthology, veteran teachers, prospective teachers, and parents will realize a sense of the familiar, a "shock of recognition," much like the soul of a poem. This anthology presents a myriad of grade levels, disciplines, and areas of expertise. Readers hear from the curriculum specialist, the speech pathologist, the school psychologist, and the classroom teacher.

Chapter one deals with the art of reflection. Educators look critically at teaching methodology and offer personal essays that address issues in education or essays that reveal influences on teaching. This chapter takes a close look at how educators use reflection in the classroom as a way to evaluate teaching strategies and as a process that has changed approaches to teaching.

Entitled "Collaborative Teaching," chapter two critically examines how educators benefit from working closely with colleagues. Educators share their research concerning problem-based learning, the effectiveness of simulating the corporate world through business education, the benefits of multidisciplinary projects, the importance of integration, and the success of providing increased stability for first and second graders through the process of looping.

Chapter three concentrates on assessment. Educators look at a variety of means to assess student progress and mastery. Educators pose questions: What types of assessment are actively employed in the classroom? How do educators collect and assess data to draw connections about how students learn? How have those conclusions shaped the way educators develop future lessons?

The final chapter, "Student-Centered Learning," emphasizes how educators promote critical thinking and encourage active leadership among students. Educators share how they develop, create, and assess learning during collaborative projects.

As educators, we can reshape reality. How many times have we asked our students to travel with us outside the four walls of our classrooms to re-imagine a time when…or recall a memory about…or become the character of…yet how many times have we walked down the halls of our own school buildings to see students in classrooms slumped over their desks with dead eyes? If only they would listen to the poems that hide in the bottoms of their shoes…like knowledge…like periods of history waiting to be discovered…like mathematical equations waiting to be solved…or like traveling to foreign countries to learn and speak different languages. Classrooms are powerful places and educators feel at home in the chalk dust, in the sound of pencils scratching across paper, in the soft watercolors lining shelves of an art studio, even in the sound of squeaking desks when students squirm over the excitement or agitation of an idea or a challenge.

Unlike any other anthology, *A Tapestry of Knowledge* weaves colorful vignettes of those powerful classrooms. And underneath the prose difficult questions arise: What would our classrooms be like if we worked cooperatively as well as independently? if we discovered the poetic refrains that exist among various disciplines to encourage our students to connect layers of meaning? "To be great is to be misunderstood," according to Ralph Waldo Emerson. Could this misunderstanding occur when we label our students learning disabled? discipline problems? intellectually and artistically gifted? Maybe the answer lies not so much in becoming great, but in valuing the various degrees of greatness that exist within our teachers, our students, and our school systems. As Yale President A. Bartlett Giamatti reminds us: "The purpose of education… is to lead us to some sense of citizenship, to some shared assumptions about individual freedoms and institutional needs, to some sense of the full claims of self as they are to be shared with others"(McMannon 6).

Will this book provide all the answers? Certainly not. But it will pose the questions aimed at discovering some of the solutions. And even if the process of looping, or the benefits of integrating disciplines, cooperative learning, applied problem-solving techniques are not new, what this book will offer is validation— that publication is a valuable means of collaboration, that the process of how students learn and how teachers teach is more important than what they teach and how quickly they cover the curriculum. Self-renewal demands continual reflection and educational theory without reflective practice remains just that, theory. This book will present a community of educators who have developed and incorporated unique, philosophically sound strategies. The teacher will be recognized as a scholar and will teach with the focus on the kind of reflection-in-action that combines knowing with artistry. Developing inspired teachers evolves from sharing a belief system and communicating a vision to our students. We must constantly seek answers to our questions then "constantly reexamine our answers—in order to renew not only our educational system but also our teacher education programs and even our nation" (McMannon 1). We spend years teaching students to know their own minds and that same act must be something we value in ourselves.

At a time when many are losing hope in the future of public education because of claims that students are unprepared, that teachers are unmotivated and unenlightened, the Virginia Beach City Public School System offers the reader a glimpse at what is working. The reader hears and sees the students in this book, students who revel in the knowledge and enthusiasm of teachers. These educators embrace not only student questions but their own. They communicate the techniques and methodologies they incorporate in the classroom and critically examine how these teaching techniques demonstrate student mastery of curriculum objectives.

When the fury of the classroom ends for the day and the chalk dust has settled, what remains? What will our students remember? What skills and insights will they take with them to the next grade level or through the graduation line in June? Maybe we will never know where our influence begins and ends, and that fact must confirm for us that each day in the classroom must be a journey for our students. As educators, we must create lessons that allow students to respond in ways that feel comfortable to them at first—then, we must challenge them to move forward intellectually—and always we will meet, even surpass, our objectives, just as a poem surpasses reality and lingers in the air a moment after the last phrase is uttered.

Maybe that is what William Wordsworth meant when he discussed the careful crafting of a brilliant piece of poetry inspired from the English landscape as "emotion recollected in tranquility" or what Parker Palmer means when he describes the crafting of a brilliant lesson as charting the inner landscape of the teaching self: "to chart that landscape fully," he explains, "three important paths must be taken—intellectual, emotional, and spiritual—and none can be ignored. Reduce teaching to intellect, and it becomes a cold abstraction; reduce it to emotions, and it becomes narcissistic; reduce it to the spiritual, and it loses its anchor to the world. They are all interwoven in the human self and in education at its best" (Palmer 4). Therefore, according to Socrates this teaching self involves assisting the inquiring mind so the learner discovers knowledge; for Comenius in *The Great Didactic*, teaching, like farming and healing, becomes a cooperative art; and for Plato the teacher's art is the same as the physician's. So maybe the stuff of pure poetry, of great classrooms, and great teachers is almost indescribable. Almost...

—LEANNE SELF

Ed Obermeyer

Frag Scene, 1997

Transformation
of Paintings into
Digital Media

*Ed Obermeyer is concerned with communicating to his audience
and his students an awareness of the fragility of the rain forest.
His keen understanding of the vast array of plants and animals
inhabiting the rain forests is based on research as well as personal
experiences in Costa Rica. By combining and layering airbrush
and paintbrush techniques in his large canvases, Obermeyer
achieves a striking realistic effect within fragmented compositions.
Multiple views of the same subject at different levels of magnifica-
tion give the viewer a wide variety of visual surface qualities to
explore. This image was created by Obermeyer using Adobe
Photoshop, KPT Bryce, and Ray Dream Studio.*

*"Working in a cubist fragmented format on my original paintings,"
explains Obermeyer, "I wanted to create a piece that emphasized
this quality. The graphic creates a sensation of wonder and beauty on an infinite horizon. The fragmented pieces are from my
original painting,* Dendrobates Auratus (The Green and
Black Poison Frog), *found in Costa Rica."*

Ed Obermeyer

Biographical Information

Ed Obermeyer is a teaching artist who has been teaching in the Virginia Beach Public Schools for twenty years. Currently, he teaches at Larkspur Middle School. Recently acquiring his M.A. from Virginia Commonwealth University with a concentration in painting and graphic design, he explored in his thesis the transformation of paintings into digital media. His work has been exhibited in numerous local galleries including the Contemporary Art Center of Virginia where his larger fragmented canvases are displayed—the focus consistently on the relationship between his personal research in Costa Rica and the delicate relationship between nature and technology.

Art Education Statement

"I believe in teaching by example. My goal is to share my talent and experience with the students and teachers at my school through interdisciplinary curriculum planning and the teaching of art as an aesthetic component of daily living.

Motivating students is the key to unlocking learning potential and I try to do this by creating lessons that utilize the latest technology, as well as leading by example. I am an art maker and an art teacher and this means a great deal to students. Students are encouraged to take risks and do so willingly by receiving positive reinforcement and constructive criticism. I not only teach art, I teach students to think, observe, appreciate, and respect the world around them. It is a classroom atmosphere where the teacher and students lead by example."

Chapter 1
Reflection: Our Inner Journeys

"When the great things disappear, when they lose their gravitational pull on our lives, we fall out of the communal orbit into the black hole of posturing, narcissism, and arrogance."

—PARKER PALMER, THE COURAGE TO TEACH

...And the great stuff of education hinges on our ability and our responsibility to reflect actively on what we do in the classroom, how we do it, and why.

*a*s an English teacher and an avid collector of books, I recall a reflective essay by Virginia Woolf that has inspired me in promoting the art of reflection in my classroom: the essay is entitled "The Fascination of a Pool." Woolf contemplates: "But if one sat down among the rushes and watched the pool—pools have some curious fascination, one knows not what..." perhaps its fascination is that it holds "in its waters all kinds of fancies, complaints, confidences, not printed or spoken aloud, but in a liquid state, floating one on top of another, almost disembodied..." and beneath the surface "went on some profound under-water life like the brooding, the ruminating of a mind."*

It is not too fanciful a notion, too literary, too romantic, too philosophical or poetic, to remember why we are drawn to the rhythmic lure of the sea, why we spend time creating ponds in our backyards, or why we remain fascinated with watching fish in aquariums. What draws us to the water's edge? to the mirror?

How are these moments analogous to the art of reflective practice in the classroom? How will reflective practice transform the teaching/learning experiences for our students and ourselves? What is the profound value of thinking about the act of thinking? Too often, do educators use the convenient excuse that they do not have enough time to reflect deeply? Do we fall into the trap of concentrating more on doing, on meeting specific learning objectives more than we spend contemplating how we are meeting those objectives and why? Does the product—the test score, the comparative analysis with other school districts, the competition with other countries, take precedence over the process of learning in our classrooms? Do we teach students to value what is in learning or do we teach "at" them?

When I think of my own teaching experiences, I guess I did not fully understand the value of reflection until I was asked by my fiction writing professor to reflect about my own composing process. And all of us in the class had the same questions even in gradu-

ate school. What does Dr. Clair mean by reflecting through a process paper? What format will it take? We were a group of English teachers working on a master's degree and were accustomed to research, to literary analysis, poetry explications, personal essays, and reaction papers. We prepared for seminar discussions and debates but had never been asked to discuss our individual composing processes. Being teachers ourselves, we had to laugh. Just like our students we complained that it was enough having to write three twenty-page short stories that we'd eventually slice to eight pages—all in six weeks.

But then something happened to us as we became comfortable with the sound of our own thoughts. The process paper became a writing diary, and we progressed as writers and teachers of writing much more quickly because we did not just generate material or hack out parts of a short story. Rather, we became concerned with finding the heart of the story. We became intimately involved with the actions and inactions of our major and minor characters; we realized the importance of precise detail in painting for the reader a crumbling medieval castle, a yellow-fogged evening at dusk, or a churning, rustic surf. We studied the process of creating a story—how we were moving our sentences and how that movement either enhanced or distracted from the tension of the piece.

We were reborn as writers and teachers. Sure, we had been teaching the art of showing detail for years, and the value of varying sentence structure had always been a part of the English curriculum; but somehow as we wrote, discussed, and reflected as students ourselves, we realized for the first time the powerful impact reflection could have on our students' academic achievement and personal fulfillment.

After completing my summer study at the Breadloaf School of English, I took my personal experiences as a writer back to my classroom. I reshaped my lesson plans to embrace reflection each day, each class, each assignment. I noticed my students became engaged with every aspect of the subject; they assumed active ownership. I made certain that student voices and uncertainties were valued. I wrote with them, and about them, in my teaching journal. I reflected on the specific strengths and weaknesses of my lessons. Students struggled with their own questions as I did; they reshaped their sentences paying close attention to sound and movement. They welcomed publishing sessions where they discussed the progression of multiple drafts and their progress as writers.

Teaching the process of self-examination is not easy; it is a patient, consistent nudging, more like a pushy invitation; it is real, dramatic, satisfying, risky. One needs only to listen to students to hear the power of reflection and its relationship to learning. In February, my student Heather wrote: "My second draft is much improved. I narrowed my topic to concentrate on one major focus. My paper right now is competent and meets the assignment but does little more." And that same student in June wrote of the place of writing in her life: "One thing I've learned as a writer this year—a simple lesson actually, but one that took me a while to learn—real is good. Back in September, I didn't even think about syntax. I didn't even know what the word meant. Now I can bend it and shape it to my will. In September, I was a quick essayist who said what had to be said and then quit. Now, writing is an art form, like painting or acting. I write to understand what I'm thinking. Real writing is a course in introspection."

Real teaching is introspection in action. Finally, my students understood what I meant when I quoted V. S. Pritchett's definition of a good story—that it is "something glimpsed from the corner of the eye, in passing." The moment is illuminated like classroom moments when we create opportunities for reflection. This growth, both my students' and mine, I attribute to this power of reflection.

The educators presented in this chapter specifically, as well as the educators featured in this book, are reflective practitioners who personally communicate the vital connection that must exist between reflective practice and pedagogical decisions. They watch their students carefully—their expressions—the way they react to new learning situations—the way they appear bored with some teaching techniques and not others. In this chapter the reader will discover educators, master weavers, who believe that students need to be valued, challenged, and empowered.

Through the personal essay or through a critical analysis of what happens in their classrooms, educators share personal stories about being an African American during integration, about witnessing potentially great teachers and students slip through the cracks of our educational system because their intellectual needs were not recognized or learning styles identified. One teacher, for example, finds that teaching letters in isolation does not help her students achieve literary growth, so she finds a way to incorporate problem-solving skills to enhance reading instruction. Another teacher, aware that having students copy from a board makes them passive learners, has created multimedia presentations that incorporate reflective inquiry. And still another teacher, who observed that it is not enough merely to teach the content of the curriculum, has discovered ways to validate student worth.

Chapter one focuses on teachers who ask themselves tough questions: How do I know if I have met my objectives for this lesson? or if my students have really mastered the material? If I did not meet my objectives, if students did not reveal mastery of the information, why? How will I present, teach, and facilitate so students remain excited about learning? What introspective questions do I need to pose about the ways I involve my students in the lesson or the methods I use to assess them? What changes will I make in my presentation? Did I meet the needs of all of my students or just a select few?

Reflection can occur in a variety of ways—by experiencing parenthood, by attending an educational workshop, by retelling negative educational experiences, or by simply watching students. The teachers in this chapter present their questions and struggles so the reader becomes intimately involved with issues that affect the classroom directly. These teachers have faced what we all have faced—students who oftentimes forget the value of learning as a process.

Reflective teachers are innovative. Reflective teachers watch other teachers close-ly. Reflective teachers read widely and critically. Reflective teachers reenvision the class-room daily. Reflective teachers create reflective students. Reflection is what draws us together when we rethink ourselves.

—LEANNE SELF

Pushing the Rock

by Tom Markham

do you ever feel like you are pushing a rock uphill? Sometimes, do you think that the rock just will not budge, no matter what you do? I am one of those rock pushers, too. I teach Spanish I. Sometimes I teach French I. Then sometimes I also teach Spanish II. But even after twenty-three years in the classroom, I am still at the beginning. It's a new day, a new year; it's creation all over again. It's like Sisyphus, the mythological king of Corinth, who was condemned to roll a huge rock up a hill in Hades only to have it roll down again upon his nearing the top…in perpetuity. His task never ceased. His conflict and his turmoil were never mitigated. His efforts never reached fruition. I am Sisyphus…back at the beginning once again.

At the beginning of each school year, I have my students write about beginnings in their journals. As I reflect on those entries now, I realize typical among student experiences was the uncertainty associated with beginnings. One young man wrote about Spanish I: "When you begin a foreign language, you are totally lost. With Spanish it felt difficult, and many times I felt frustrated with the fact that I couldn't understand what was going on. It is not only with a foreign language, because beginnings are difficult in anything I do. I feel frustrated, helpless, and completely lost and have no idea where to start." His sentiments were my own. When I encounter the rock at the bottom of the hill, he does too. When I use every resource I can muster to push it to the top, so does he.

So does another student who writes about learning how to learn. She explains, "The hardest part of learning a new language is learning how to learn a new language." Her point is a long-standing one. How do you best learn about something you cannot speak or understand? What experiences help you learn the material better? For both of us, they raised Sisyphus-related questions. What tools work best for moving the rock up the hill together? What strategies are most efficient? As I reexamined student writings dealing with beginnings, I noticed that most of the students used analogies to accomplish their task.

For example, one fourteen-year-old girl, an accomplished violinist, drew upon her musical experiences to explain how she learned how to learn Spanish. She explained that each time she looks at a new piece of music she feels defeated. She stares at the page. She convinces herself that the challenge is too great and her abilities too small, despite her previous successes. Then, with courage she sight reads the piece. She recoils from harsh sounds, sits back and looks at the music. Eventually, she finds her self-confidence again, convinced that her knowledge of musical theory will dispel her original self-doubt. "Soon everyone realizes that people start new things every day," she explained. "Nobody has the same life every day. Something always happens, small or large, and you can't control it."

Her point about each day's uncertainties is one worth pondering for a teacher who aspires to be a facilitator of student learning. My students do not live in the same world in which I lived as a student. They are bombarded with a postmodern cacophony of sights and sounds and experiences that cause school to have a different priority for them than it had for me. How can they focus on the educational tasks at hand when they find distractions everywhere around them?

Many students may not ever find in school the satisfaction that leads to life-long learning. So how does a teacher show them that education is a journey and not just a destination? How can teachers help students embrace their personal responsibilities for their own learning? As a facilitator, it is not enough for me to teach the information from the curriculum; I must show my students in both word and deed that I feel the same apprehension.

Another student wrote, "The hardest part of learning a new language is learning how to learn a new language." Her point is a long-standing one. How do you best learn about something you cannot speak or understand? What experiences help you learn the material better?

They must see that my learning and my attempts at improving my teaching do not stop. For example, Matamoscas, matar (swat) mosac (word), was a delightful revelation to me when I first saw the flyswatter technique used at a conference of the Foreign Language Association of Virginia. The first time the students see me lift the flyswatters to give an explanation, however, their eyes become huge. I can almost hear them thinking, "Oh, no! What's coming next? Who's in trouble now?" But when they divide themselves into teams for the blue or the green flyswatter and then line up to swat (matar) the word (mosca) at the board that answers my clue, they become excited not only for themselves but also for their teammates. Usually, they do not even realize they are performing a vocabulary review or a grammar drill. It is still great fun for my students, and we continue to revisit this activity from time to time, sometimes with more sophisticated linguistic variations as the students advance in their language skills.

Another teaching strategy I use in the classroom provides transition between the end of one school year and the beginning of another. The vacation letter I sometimes assign at the end of Spanish I, I use initially as an ice breaker at the beginning of Spanish II. Again, I discovered another idea by learning from another educator; this time I found the activity reading a French teacher's article in a state foreign language journal. For Spanish II students, a scavenger hunt for information found in their classmates' letters helps them review Spanish I and get acquainted with new classmates. When we use the letters again later in the year to introduce the preterite verb tense, they have a real sense of the sequence of tenses and the need to expand their learning beyond the present tense! I push the rock. They push the rock.

However, that challenge never stops me from trying that much harder and like Sisyphus, I push the rock again, this time with renewed strength.

There is no peak, no culminating point at which we can claim that our task is finished, that our rock is at the top of the hill forever, that we have gained complete knowledge. I tell my students often that I am frightened and nervous in my endeavors, but that I am confident that we can move forward together. We can push the rock. We can create synergy.

This synergy is addressed by another student as he writes in his vignette about the nervousness he experienced beginning Spanish I: "It was… intimidating on the first couple of days, but it was also fun to learn some interesting vocabulary in the new language. After the first two days, I actually began to look forward to coming to Spanish class. On my first day, I was blown away by the awkward vocabulary and pronunciation. I went home and studied because I was afraid that I wouldn't catch on." But catch on he did, and he came to excel as a Spanish student.

Eventually my students move on to another teacher and another school, and I am gratified to learn from their parents, their high school teachers, and the students themselves of their continued success as they pursue all educational challenges. Their task, that of learning, is never finished. Yet some modicum of apprehension does continue for me as a teacher of foreign languages. I fear that I cannot keep the lessons fresh and inviting. I try that much harder, and I push the rock again. However, that challenge never stops me from trying that much harder and like Sisyphus, I push the rock again, this time with renewed strength. What keeps me striving? questioning? reflecting? if it is not simply my desire to help students continue to realize their potentials?

So, as I plan to embark on a trip to Spain, France, and Italy in about five weeks with two Latin teachers from my school and a group of approximately fifty Latin students, Spanish students, and their parents, I am reminded once again of the importance of life-long learning. These students will look for "the Latin connection" in the history, the architecture, the art, and the Romance languages that they will encounter; their lives will change forever. New doors will open. Connections will be made. Possibilities will be seen.

> How much better it is to teach, to really teach, for twenty-three years than to teach one year twenty-three times.

Soon September will signal the beginning of a new school year and a new horizon. Students without prior knowledge of Spanish will arrive with their own apprehensions and expectations. I will try again to cajole, tease, and nudge them toward success, all the time wondering if I am giving them enough to accomplish my high expectations and fearing that my reserves of energy, knowledge, and my "bag of tricks" will be depleted before I reach my goal of helping students recognize and reach their own potential. But I draw on self-knowledge and the recollections of my former students to know that success can be reached. Some students will become proficient language learners, and if past experience holds, some will even come to incorporate that proficiency into their professional lives. We will push the rock… together. We are Sisyphus.

Noted French writer and philosopher Albert Camus tells us to "Imagine Sisyphus happy." This existential dilemma has a lesson for me. I've come to view Sisyphus' work in a different light; he is happy doing the perpetual task of pushing the rock. The condemnation to push forward without ever reaching the top is not a punishment. It is a beginning.

And even after all these years of teaching, I am still at the beginning. But it is never the same beginning as before and it gives me joy to know that my work is always dynamic, never static. How much better it is to teach, to really teach, for twenty-three years than to teach one year twenty-three times.

About Tom Markham

"There is a quote that is attributed to Confucius: 'To learn, and when the right time comes, to try out what one has learned; is this not indeed pleasure?' To my mind this is indeed a pleasure for both the learner and the teacher, and it is a pleasure 'devoutly to be wished.' It is a pleasure for which I strive to contribute in my daily interactions with students."

Tom Markham has taught in the Virginia Beach Public School System for the past twenty-three years. Currently, he teaches Spanish at Kemps Landing Magnet School where he was named the 1998 Teacher of the Year. Also in 1998, Mr. Markham was selected as one of five finalists for Virginia Beach Citywide Teacher of the Year. Tom Markham holds a B.A. in Modern Languages (Spanish and French) from the College of William and Mary and an M.B.A. in International Management and Finance from Old Dominion University. Active in the American Council of Teachers of Foreign Languages, the American Association of Teachers of Spanish and Portuguese, and the Foreign Language Association of Virginia, Tom continues to be a frequent presenter on the local, regional and national levels. He is also an advocate for gifted and talented education.

From Teacher To Parent and Back Again:
A Lyrical Journey

by Barbara Kennedy

I've always wanted to be a teacher. As a child, I'd play for hours in the cinder-walled, chalk-cloud-filled basement classroom world I created. I didn't have too many friends at first, but I had my dreams. And I was a great teacher in that basement. I always knew the answers, always had the unruly children under control, and I could always reach every student. I could recreate any classroom's floor plan, designing a masterpiece of flexibility and function. I taught spelling for hours, math for minutes. The sequential order of things fascinated me, the detailed lesson plans, lunch at 11:53 a.m., fresh paper and pencils. I remember the feel of that chalk in my grasp as I used my teacher voice to guide my imaginary students. It waltzed along the slate scribbling word after important word. Sometimes, even now, I hear the same chalkboard waltz in my class, see my hand guiding it along. It's harder to hear, now, but I've never forgotten.

I've learned volumes from my teachers through the years. From my fourth-grade teacher, Mrs. Crosen, I learned that teachers can be young and fashionable. I watched her pass my class on a daily basis, heard the click, tap, click of her heels on the aging linoleum. Though she wasn't my teacher that year, I could picture her blonde flip, Mary Quant style, as she stood in front of the class using the new, technologically advanced chalk holder. I was still playing jacks, listening to Gary Puckett and the Union Gap's "Young Girl," but I knew style when I saw it. And I can still transport myself to that time of playing, wishing, and dreaming every time I hear that song.

That same year, as a lip-gloss-wearing, oh-so-mature, sixth grader, I would sit on the edge of my neighbor's bed and listen to "Windy" by the Association. Miss McCartney, whom I did have that year, taught me that having a "mean" teacher meant being challenged, not tortured, that it was okay to wear comfortable shoes, and that a teacher who sees potential is priceless. When I hear "Windy," I still think of her.

By the time I had eighth-grade English, I was listening to Jackson Browne's "Doctor My Eyes" and discovering that lyrics were poetry, that bad singers can write great songs, and that radio personalities control air play. Mr. Williams taught me that it was okay to laugh in class; that real world issues are addressed in old, dusty literature; and that seeing things in a way that challenges preconceived notions is not a bad thing.

I still wanted to be a teacher. Even when adolescence struck and I tried to diversify, "I want to go to college and be a marketing executive, renowned actress, famous writer, and, oh yeah, a teacher!" I wanted to be Mrs. Crosen, Miss McCartney, and Mr. Williams, all rolled into one. I wanted to tell them, to show them, that the subjects they taught, important as they were, paled in the shades of meaning they brought to my life. I knew I could honor them by being the best teacher I could be, and I strived for that when I began teaching.

> And I was a great teacher in that basement. I always knew the answers, always had the unruly children under control, and I could always reach every student.

But life changed. Marriage. Motherhood. Chalkboard waltzes turned into baby powdered lullabies and I was mesmerized.

I stayed home with our two young sons because I wanted to teach them. I wanted my children to learn right from wrong, fairness, and sharing before I sent them off to school. My kids weren't going to be like some of the wild ones I remembered, not if I could help it.

And then a revelation occurred. I would be sending my children to a teacher who would teach, nurture, and love them, or not. Our sons would be learning from their teachers as I had learned from mine and as my students had learned from me. This time, I'd be the parent looking in. This time, my sons would be the ones watching the chalk dance across the board. Would I be as effective a parent as I was a teacher? Could I practice what I had preached for so many years? Who was I, really? Teacher? Parent? Where would this journey take me? How much remained of the teacher I used to be? How much of me? What would I be like as a teacher when I went back?

What came to me, as answers, were snippets of lyrics and songs that whisper and scream to me about life, kindness, and humanity. I no longer hear "Windy" or "Young Girl," the time traveling songs of my youth. But I do hear lyrics of a favorite artist who helped me through tough times. Haunting songs about life and living, about power and influence, about teachers, mothers, and children, and about how I want a teacher to treat my own children. The lyrical glimpses have transformed me from teacher to parent and back again.

"She must be somebody's baby, she's got to be somebody's baby..." (Browne 1982).

All children come from parents. Did I realize that before I had my own? Of course I did. But to think that each child I teach is as treasured as the babies I held in my arms. That every day some parent is worried that I may not do my job with care and sensitivity and knowledge, as I have sometimes worried for my sons. Cyrilla Hergenham, an award-winning teacher in Catonsville, Maryland, sums up the teacher's role in this way: "I have come this far in my education because I have been lifted up on someone else's shoulders. This is how I see my role as teacher. I lift up my students so they can see into the horizon. I do this knowing that they will have a vision farther than mine" (Boyer 46).

Sadder still, I know some children aren't treasured; some parents don't care. Children are told to shut up, to go away. And then there are children who want to go away, but can't. Children who will get attention any way they can. Children who wish their parents wouldn't try to buy their love. Don't they deserve to be "somebody's baby"? I don't want to look into my class to see "only" students, to love "only" the lovable. They all go home at night with our words and deeds in their minds, no matter whose babies they are. The school, according to Ernest Boyer, should be "a communicative place where the emphasis is on the integrity of ideas, not the authority of an office. The climate is collegial. Everyone in the school speaks and listens carefully to each other, creating a relationship of trust among the principal, teachers, students, and parents!" (21) This school, this communicative place, should not dramatize our students' failures but embrace their strengths.

"Don't confront me with my failures, I have not forgotten them" (Browne 1973).

The mother in the grocery store screams names at her little girl yelling, "What's wrong with you?" Yet this same mother will wake up one day and wonder why she has no relationship with her daughter, why her daughter is distant, even hostile. Where did she go wrong?

Another scene. A teacher, who knows

> Miss McCartney, whom I did have that year, taught me that having a "mean" teacher meant being challenged, not tortured, that it was okay to wear comfortable shoes, and that a teacher who sees potential is priceless.

better, shouts and threatens her class into behaving, and wonders why the lessons don't work. Why do students who obviously don't understand the lesson refuse to raise their hands? She states, "What do you mean, you don't understand. I just taught that." And that same teacher, who fears her weaknesses will be discovered and criticized, doesn't hesitate in pointing out her students' mistakes. Don't most of us know where our failures are? Do children need to consistently be reminded of their weaknesses in the name of education? Or can we find a way to teach from their strengths? What do our classrooms say about us? Do we really believe that we learn from our mistakes or do we expect perfection the first time? If we, as educators, were constantly confronted with our failures, what would that do to us? To our children? To wishes and dreams?

"We want to play, just a little bit longer... We want to stay, just a little bit longer" (Browne 1977).

I see teachers stuck in the preparation mode, parents pushing, leading the charge. It's a problem even in the elementary grades now. We must work very hard. Kindergarten is preparing you for first grade. First grade is preparing you for the second grade... and heaven help you if you're not prepared for middle school! Of course, I know the importance of being ready for the next challenge, but do we really have to talk about it so much? Let's just get them ready. I worry that all the talk takes away from the excitement and thrill of being a kid. How much can you enjoy where you are if you're never allowed to be there? And how long does it last, anyway?

> **Mr. Williams taught me that it was okay to laugh in class; that real world issues are addressed in old, dusty literature; and that seeing things in a way that challenges pre-conceived notions is not a bad thing.**

"Nothing survives, but the way we live our lives" (Browne 1976).

Parents and teachers don't always stop to remember that we are giving our children lifetime memories right now. I realized this one day when our older son was about four. I was reminiscing about my childhood and began to consider what memories I was creating for him. Would he remember Mom and Dad in front of the TV or playing and reading with him? Would he see work as a joy or as painful drudgery? Are our intentions mirrored by our actions? Will he have a Mr. Williams in his life to imitate? Would his teacher (will I?) remember to smile each day, or send him away with a sarcastic comment? What can we, as educators, as parents, do about it? Most teachers will never realize the impact of their influence on children. And we won't know whether they learned all of what we were teaching on a given day. We can, however, remember the children we were, hear the classroom waltzes we heard, remember the influences we felt. We have the power just once, but it lasts a lifetime.

"....between the time you arrive, and the time you go, there lies a reason you were alive, but you'll never know" (Browne 1974).

I have come to believe that the songs we carry in our hearts have touched and will continue to touch lives, and that the difference between the parent and the teacher within me is nothing and everything.

Works Cited

Boyer, Ernest. *The Basic School.* Princeton, New Jersey: The Carnegie Foundation for the Advancement of Teaching, 1995.

Browne, Jackson. "These Days." *For Everyman.* Elektra/Asylum Records, 1973.

Browne, Jackson. "For a Dancer." *Late For the Sky.* Elektra Asylum Records, 1974.

Browne, Jackson. "Daddy's Tune." *The Pretender.* Elektra/Asylum Records, 1976.

Browne, Jackson. "Stay." *Running on Empty.* Elektra/Asylum Records, 1977.

Browne, Jackson. "Somebody's Baby." *The Best of Jackson Browne.* Elektra Entertainment Group, 1997.

About Barbara Kennedy

"Education is not the filling of a pail, but the lighting of a fire."

—WILLIAM BUTLER YEATS

Currently, Barbara Kennedy is the gifted resource teacher at Independence Middle School in Virginia Beach; however, her experience ranges from teaching Language Arts at Green Run Elementary to teaching social studies at Kemps Landing Magnet School. A graduate of James Madison University, the Eastern Virginia Writing Project, and the College of William and Mary, Mrs. Kennedy shares her teaching expertise by presenting numerous workshops for the Virginia State Parent Teachers Association and presenting for the 1997 Association for the Education of the Gifted conference.

Learning from Inclusion: Perspective of the Educators

by Carolyn Thompson

her face appears eager, but is she capable of sustaining the pace? She seems to understand, but is she truly comprehending? Her blue eyes dart about the room while the content is offered. Does this mean she is searching for someone or something to validate her thoughts? So Amy waits and tentatively poses a question. Are her peers about to ridicule her as she poses her question? Is the teacher's response to her query understood? What can the teacher do to establish meaning for her? Furthermore, what can Amy possibly offer this class? Diagnostically she demonstrates restricted ability to express her meaningfulness both orally and, more importantly, in written form, which is the mainstay of English classwork. How can Amy or any student with a learning disability succeed in a regular education content class?

The sustained academic rigor of the general education classroom is formidable. Expectations are driven by standards of learning as well as school curriculum issues. For the cognitively challenged student, however, the academic arena poses demands that are, at times, insurmountable. The learning impaired student struggles with dissecting, devouring, and divulging the material presented within the general education classroom. Words spoken by the teacher may merely rebound off the tympanic membrane without signaling the brain to integrate this information, in short, in one ear and out the other.

> Her blue eyes dart about the room while the content is offered. Does this mean she is searching for someone or something to validate her thoughts?

As we observe Amy, we notice that she often nods in agreement with the teacher and with the information proffered; however, her written notes as well as oral responses contradict this: partial words, mere initial sounds and/or sketchy, unmeaningful words are hastily scattered on her paper. What does the educator do? What will work for this student?

For the past three years in the ninth-grade English classroom and for two years in twelfth-grade English, two regular education English teachers and a speech/language pathologist have sought and fought to make the content of those English classrooms accessible to learning disabled students. Despite our wish for a recipe that consistently solves each challenge and event, we have learned that feedback from one another tempered with immediate student monitoring is the only method that works. As a result, not only do lessons change from year to year, but lessons change daily.

Because of the specific accommodations afforded the special needs student, these English classrooms have evolved as best practices. When material is presented, each English educator understands that every student experiences success when content is clarified, made functional, and made parallel with everyday experience. When learning disabled students cannot remain seated, we all move—students and teachers. For example, doing a walk-about (where small groups of students rotate stations within the classroom in order to complete a chart, add pertinent information, or extract data necessary for a presentation) allows physical movement not only for the student who cannot focus beyond a fifteen-minute period, but for all students. If visual presentations of a piece of literature clarify the printed as well as the spoken word, we all see the graphic representation. Drawing the characters of *The Odyssey* or scenes from *Beowulf* brings the text to life; and as one student in English 12 succinctly states, "Now I know what happened because I see the text in the illustrations." These quick sketches connect the printed text to the stronger visual image, thus creating the "Ah-ha!" of learning. In addition, oral presentations become an option for the student who views written assignments as limiting. Oral presentations allow the student to concentrate more on communication skills and less on the strict rules of grammar, syntax, and coherence.

For the cognitively challenged student, however, the academic arena poses challenges that are, at times, insurmountable. The learning impaired student struggles with dissecting, devouring, and divulging the material presented within the general education classroom.

When students in English 9 are unable to tease out the elements of a short story, we devise lessons that reduce the cognitive aspects of the reading process. This strategy makes plot identification, characterization, setting, and point-of-view achievable. For example, since most of the students are familiar with the tales of "Little Red Riding Hood" and "The Three Little Pigs," these stories serve as a template for mapping the elements of a short story. We use the same principles when we ascertain if the class understands the moral lesson inherent in more demanding literature, Chaucer's "Pardoner's Tale." Or with, for example, Aesop's fables because they tap prior knowledge and can serve as a stepping stone for another class assignment requiring the development of a cartoon strip and related text that demonstrates an underlying moral. Balancing an assignment with what students can do versus what the assignment requires is pivotal to a higher linguistic task.

Reducing cognitive aspects of assignments helps Amy, or any student, connect daily tasks to prior information. By using illustrations as she composes or orally responds, Amy creates anchors of meaning. She can refer to these stable pieces of information as often as she needs to do so because she uses her sketches to comprehend the highly linguistic and cognitively demanding task of reading, in this case, *The Odyssey*. Now, she responds with assuredness and recalls previously discussed events because the plot in this epic now meaningfully overlaps with the printed text. Amy answers questions

> **As Roman Jacobsen profoundly stated, "Language without meaning is meaningless."**

that once were baffling. She refines her work because meaningfulness has displaced confusion.

This observation concludes that the learning environment is crucial to a student with a disability; the methods and strategies for assuring academic success must be on-going and varied. Because of this varied instruction in inclusion classrooms, peer acceptance will develop over the course of an academic year because all students learn to trust and risk in this unique learning community.

As educators, we, too, must be intricately woven into the fabric of the English classroom. Our goals for each student become as individualized as the myriad of personalities and learning styles present. The challenge comes from teasing out the best in each learner and in encouraging a positive dynamic among all students in the classroom. Each day this dynamic centers on success.

Yes, those blue eyes continue to struggle, but the rewards Amy experiences continue to be demonstrated in her daily successes. Currently, she is achieving well beyond expectations in English 10. Picturing the semantic relationships of various pieces of literature remain constants in her learning methodology, but now she is confident and embarks enthusiastically on the journey. The regular education classroom held Amy to high expectations, but it wasn't until she understood the meaningful connection to words printed on the pages in her literature book and the spoken words heard during lectures that learning actually occurred.

We certainly do not have the key to creating the ideal learning environment; nonetheless, what we do have is the desire and willingness to aspire to that lofty goal of success for all. We approach each day anew. We readily accept the challenge that language learning presents for our disabled students. Content must not act as a barrier to knowledge but must be addressed creatively and honestly, because to present content without providing a means wherein our students have an opportunity to learn is foolhardy. As educators in the classroom, we must actively create a responsible partnership in this inclusive environment. And as Roman Jacobsen profoundly states, "Language without meaning is meaningless."

About Carolyn Thompson

"'Teaching is like learning to tango.' The 'dance of learning' requires attentive watchfulness integrated with steps that bridge to successive levels of comprehension. Each twist and turn necessitates reflective monitoring to ensure that both partners are on the same 'dance floor.' Working in partnership, each member of the class achieves only when the rhythm becomes internalized. The finished product is derived from the quest along with the hours of practice."

Carolyn Thompson has been a speech/language pathologist in the Virginia Beach City Public Schools since 1980. Currently, she teaches at Ocean Lakes High School and is part of an English 9 and 12 inclusion team participating in a research project with The College of William and Mary. In 1991, Carolyn was named Virginia's Outstanding Speech/Language Pathologist by the Speech-Language Hearing Association of Virginia and also selected as 1995 Ocean Lakes High School Teacher of the Year. Receiving her B.A. in Speech Correction from The College of New Jersey and a Master's degree from Columbia University in Speech/Pathology, Carolyn continues to be recognized for her research regarding inclusion methodology. Her publications include "Given the Opportunity" and "Yes! We're Getting It Together," both of which appeared in the *Pragmaticism Methodology Newsletter*, as well as "Establishing Meaningfulness for Michael" in the *Journal of the Speech-Language Hearing Association*.

Using Exemplary Teaching and Pop Music to Enhance Learning

by Robert Jones

n early thirty years ago, as a new teacher, my concerns were similar to most new teachers today. How would I make my subject relevant? I knew students would be motivated through a dynamic lesson, yet I also knew a gap existed between what I saw as adequate and exemplary teaching. And I wanted to be an exemplary teacher. Even though in the beginning I wasn't sure of exactly *how* I wanted to present a lesson, I was sure of the characteristics displayed by exemplary teachers. Exemplary teachers:

- become student advocates rather than student adversaries;
- realize the best classroom management technique is a well-planned, well-presented lesson;
- create student centered classrooms and a positive learning environment based on mutual respect;
- model behaviors they want students to demonstrate;
- encourage and facilitate emotional and academic success in their students;
- set high expectations and consistently motivate and challenge students to become lifelong learners;
- remain open-minded and able to view all situations not only from the teacher's perspective but from that of the parent, administrator, and, most importantly, the student.

Exemplary teachers create original lessons that dazzle their students; they vary teaching techniques and styles. As a beginning teacher, and now as a thirty-year veteran, the questions still remain the same: How will I dazzle my students? What will motivate young people and spark their interest in a world beyond school? Young people enjoy sports, games, and music, so how will I incorporate these outside motivators in my social studies classroom? How will I move my students into higher levels of learning and thinking?

For me, music became the answer. As a professional musician, I have found music to be a very underutilized medium in the classroom—not only can music easily be incorporated into various academic subject areas but the possibilities are limitless! For example, a song like "The Shortest Story" by Harry Chapin which deals with the problem of world hunger could be used to introduce a social studies unit on third-world nations, and yet that same song could be used in a health class as an introduction to a discussion on the value of proper nutrition. As a culminating activity based on a lesson of First Amendment rights, "The Shortest Story" could also be used to encourage students to compose original songs, raps, or letters to the editor expressing their concerns on a given issue they found especially compelling. Because I have used this song to teach such a lesson on First Amendment rights, I have found that students not only make valuable personal connections, but they also realize the impact and importance of individual freedoms. For example, one student who parodies modern life, begins her rap about the year 1986:

"Eighty-Six Blues"
Oh mama, got dese eighty-six blues, the days r dull, can't find the fuse.
Preppies, punkies, no friends of mine! I think I'll tie dye my Calvin Kleins!
Yeah, we've lost the beat, Jack Kerouac! Help us Elvis, please take us back...

In addition, another song such as "The Russians" by Sting could be used to introduce a unit on the cold war or begin a philosophical discussion on pacifism. One can even trace our changing values through popular music. In the 1950s Elvis sang "Love Me Tender," by the early 1960s, the Beatles sang "I Want to Hold Your Hand," and by the late 1960s, the Rolling Stones were performing "Let's Spend the Night Together," even though Ed Sullivan made them revise the lyrics to read, "Let's Spend Some Time Together" when they performed on his program. For educators, music can be used as a tremendous primary source since it so often reflects and even shapes public opinion. It's not a coincidence that "I Am Woman" by Helen Reddy hit #1 on June 24, 1972, at the peak of the Women's Movement in the U.S. or that "In America" by the Charlie Daniels Band hit #11 on May 21, 1980, as the first post-Vietnam War patriotic song which helped launch the Reagan era, or that "Highwire" by the Rolling Stones was the first song to question Desert Storm.

> As a beginning teacher, and now as a thirty-year veteran, the questions still remain the same: How will I dazzle my students?

However, at no other time did music do more to reflect public opinion than during the Vietnam War. Because I taught a U.S. history course, I had the opportunity to explore the effects of the Vietnam War in depth. As I contemplated the unit, I knew I wanted to create an introductory activity that would go beyond taking notes—one that would engage my students and peak their interest. Serving as a resource for this unit, I reflected on my days as a college student during the Vietnam War and recalled how, as a student and a professional musician, my impressions of the war were influenced dramatically by the music of the era. How could I intertwine my first-hand knowledge of the time period with the objectives of my curriculum? What additional objectives did I feel were critical?

I decided I would have my students discover and experience the same feelings I had in the 1960s by designing lessons that included an analysis of song lyrics, as well as activities that would teach students to draw connections with how public perception shapes the influence of popular music on our society. I also felt I could further emphasize that point by making additional comparisons to another historical period, World War II.

> **As I contemplated the unit, I knew I wanted to create an introductory activity that would go beyond taking notes— one that would engage my students and peak their interest.**

I began the lesson by informing students that the lesson would involve traveling through time to view two different periods in our U.S. history. The first era we would explore would be World War II. Because I wanted to challenge my students to think critically and to synthesize characteristics from World War II, I asked them to predict through several "What if " questions. I asked them to imagine being eighteen years old during the war: "What are your feelings regarding the war?" I asked. "If you were an eighteen-year-old young man, would you enlist in the armed forces?" After students had several minutes to reflect and adopt another perspective, I brought them back to the focus of my introductory activity—the impact of music in shaping and reflecting public opinion.

Now, I told them, imagine again you are an eighteen-year-old teenager at the time of World War II and you are listening to the radio. This is what you might hear: I then play the "Boogie Woogie Bugle Boy" by the Andrews sisters which is light, bouncy, and upbeat, and then I ask students if listening to the song aroused any feelings that could be related to the war. A frequent response from my students was "It sounds like fun." I noticed after playing the song that nearly all students felt positively about the war. Next, I briefly described three other songs that were popular during World War II: "Der Fuhrer's Face" by Spike Jones, "Accentuate the Positive," by Bing Crosby, and "Praise the Lord and Pass the Ammunition," by Kay Kyser. We discussed as a class specific characteristics of these songs and drew comparisons.

Now my students were ready to travel to the next historical era we would be studying and again imagine themselves as eighteen-year-olds, but this time during the Vietnam War. Once again that eighteen-year-old teenager might turn on the radio, but instead of hearing "Boogie Woogie Bugle Boy," that same teenager might hear "War" by Edwin Starr. I played the song for my class and drew their attention to certain lyrics: *"war, what is it good for... absolutely nothing... good for... nobody but the undertaker..."* After playing the song again, I asked my students "how" and "if" this song might affect their attitudes concerning the war and enlisting in the armed forces. This dilemma aroused a lively class discussion as nearly every student internalized the sense of fear and frustration in the song. Next I played "Fixin to Die Rag" by Country Joe & The Fish with lyrics including, *"Well it's one...two...three...what are we fightin for, don't ask me, I don't give a damn, next stop is Vietnam and it's five...six...seven...open up the pearly gates, there ain't no need to wonder why, whoopee we're all gonna die...come on mothers throughout the land...be the first one on your block to have your kid shipped home in a box."*

> This dilemma aroused a lively class discussion as nearly every student internalized the sense of fear and frustration in the song.

Students responded to these graphic images with comments like, "No wonder people were against the war," and "I look at the twenty-one songs listed on our handout, but only one, 'The Ballad of the Green Beret' portrays war in a somewhat positive light (Appendix I)." After another brief discussion, students were encouraged to think of current songs that reflect public opinion. Soon, we were comparing and contrasting these songs and evaluating their impact on society. Now, students were anxious to discover the historical background of the period which caused these songs to be written because they examined how their own music reflected societal beliefs. Students were now ready to begin our study of the Vietnam War.

One of the real advantages of a lesson like this is the potential for additional parallel studies. For example, the next series of lessons might focus on the influence of other media like television on the Vietnam war, since it was the first "television war." This same lesson might also be adapted to other subject areas. For example, in my civics class, I might use the lesson as an introductory study of the influence of media on politics or propaganda techniques, or the creation of political cartoons on presidential decision-making. Other Vietnam lessons involving music might include:

- having students write a song or poem about the Vietnam War as seen from the point of view of a student demonstrator, a foot soldier, or a parent; or
- reading descriptions of the Boston Massacre and Kent State

Massacre, showing Paul Revere's engraving and playing the song "Ohio" (Appendix 2). Then, having students discuss whether the depiction was accurate or not. Students then analyze whether the word "massacre" served as an accurate or inaccurate label for what occurred at the Boston Massacre and Kent State. Students write poems, songs, raps, or letters from the point of view of a national guardsman, a college student, a British soldier, or a colonist.

Because students need to draw generalizations and make comparisons between historical periods in order to participate in this point-of-view activity, higher level thinking is emphasized. Students publish their writing and my classroom comes alive with discussion and debate; students evaluate, criticize, dispute, and defend their opinions by offering specific details to support their generalizations.

Music is so much more than just a beat to dance to. Music showcases many of the most outstanding writers, poets, and historians. For educators, music is too important a resource to be ignored, and it is a resource that exemplary teachers should use to help students make a personal investment in learning and to help them make valuable connections with other disciplines. This creative, multidisciplinary approach to teaching revitalizes the classroom again and again. And, after thirty years of teaching, I am still discovering new songs and new ways to make learning meaningful for my students.

> **Music is so much more than just a beat to dance to. Music showcases many of the most outstanding writers, poets, and historians.**

Appendix I

Music of the Vietnam War

1. "War" - Edwin Starr (original) or Bruce Springsteen
2. "Fixin' to Die Rag" - Country Joe and the Fish
3. "The Ballad of the Green Beret" - Sgt. Barry Sadler
4. "Goodnight Saigon" - Billy Joel
5. "Bummer" - Harry Chapin (strong language)
6. "Foreign Policy" - Buckinghams
7. "Give Peace a Chance" - Plastic Ono Band (strong language)
8. "It Better End Soon" - Chicago
9. "Monster" - Steppenwolf
10. "Happy Xmas (War is Over)" - John Lennon
11. "Revolution" - The Beatles
12. "Ohio" - Crosby, Stills, & Nash
13. "For What It's Worth" - Buffalo Springfield
14. "Student Demonstration Time" - Beachboys
15. "Universal Soldier" - Donovan or Glen Campbell
16. "Unknown Soldier" - Doors
17. "We Gotta Get Out of this Place" - Animals
18. "Eve of Destruction" - Barry McGuire
19. "Dawn of Correction" - Spokesmen
20. "Born in the U.S.A." - Bruce Springsteen
21. "Zor and Zam" - Monkees
22. "Progress Suite" - Chad & Jeremy
23. "Long Time Gone" - Crosby, Stills, & Nash
24. "Volunteers" - Jefferson Airplane
25. "Running" - Anne Murray
26. "Still in Saigon" - Charlie Daniels Band
27. "Nineteen" - Paul Hardcastle Group
28. "I Don't Want to be a Hero" - Johnny Hates Jazz

Using Music to Introduce Major Themes: A Multidisciplinary Approach to Teaching

TITLE	ARTIST	TOPIC
"War"	Bruce Springsteen	War
"The Shortest Story"	Harry Chapin	World Hunger
"Scarecrow"	John Cougar	Plight of Farmers
"Luca"	Susan Vega	Child Abuse
"Sun City"	Artists against Apartheid	South Africa
"Russians"	Sting	Disarmament
"At 17"	Janis Ian	Difficulty of Teen Years
"Save the Whales"	Country Joe and the Fish	Ecology
"War Song"	Culture Club	War
"Ohio"	Crosby, Stills, Nash & Young	Kent State
"Fixin' to Die Rag"	Country Joe and the Fish	Vietnam
"Bomb Iran"	Vince Vance	Iranian Hostages
"Hair Spun of Gold"	Janis Ian	Growing up too Fast
"Revolution"	Beatles	Revolution
"Pride"	U2	Martin Luther King, Jr.
"The Night that Made America Famous"	Harry Chapin	The American Dream
"Indian Sunset"	Elton John	Native Americans
"Indian Reservation"	Raiders	Native Americans
"Second Wind"	Billy Joel	Teen Suicide
"Leningrad"	Billy Joel	Cold War
"This Note's for You"	Neil Young	Corporate Sponsors
"Beds are Burning"	Midnight Oil	Aborigines
"Downeaster Alexa"	Billy Joel	Watermen
"Blue Sky Mine"	Midnight Oil	Miners
"We're all in the Same Gang"	East Coast Rap All Stars	Gang Violence
"Another Day in Paradise"	Phil Collins	Homeless
"Hell is for Children"	Pat Benator	Child Abuse
"Man in the Mirror"	Michael Jackson	Humanity
"Right Here Right Now"	Jesus Jones	World in Change
"Winds of Change"	Scorpions	World in Change
"Open Letter to a Landlord"	Living Colour	Urban Life

About Robert Jones

"Teaching is a performing art, and the quality of that performance varies from teacher to teacher. One sign of an effective teacher is to have the same enthusiasm at last bell Friday in June as first bell Monday in September. My goal is to reach every student, to turn them on to learning, and to keep them excited."

Robert Jones has been teaching in the Virginia Beach City Public School System since 1973 and began his teaching career at Virginia Beach Middle School. Currently, he teaches social studies and also serves as Curriculum Coordinator and Grade Level Chairperson at Kempsville Middle School. Having received his B.S. and M.S. degrees from Old Dominion University, he serves as adjunct faculty member in the School of Education, Department of Curriculum and Instruction. A frequent presenter at various Virginia Beach elementary and high schools regarding innovative teaching techniques, Mr. Jones is also a presenter at Hampton University in Hampton, Virginia. He has been listed in Marquis *Who's Who in America, Who's Who in American Education,* as well as *Who's Who in the World Council of Social Studies.* In 1981, Mr. Jones was named Outstanding Social Studies Educator at Old Dominion University, in 1986 was named Virginia's Social StudiesTeacher of the Year, and in 1991 was named Kempsville Middle School's Teacher of the Year.

Reflections on Fate

by Wendy Lewis

during my last summer's vacation, I took the time to read the best-selling novel by David Guterson, *Snow Falling on Cedars*. Like many English teachers, I suppose, I can't seem to read a book for mere pleasure. As I read this novel, I found myself making connections with the characters, highlighting their observations, especially those I thought were particularly meaningful because they were based on themes that I teach in my classes.

The first lines that I highlighted were Ishmael's, who is a well-read, cynical journalist, and his encounters with American literature in college. Ishmael felt particularly bothered by the conclusion of Nathaniel Hawthorne's *The Scarlet Letter* because "the woman (Hester Prynne), after all, deserved better" (Guterson 32). These are my sentiments, and those of my students, each year when I teach *The Scarlet Letter*. I knew as soon as I read those lines that I was hooked on this book and attached to Ishmael.

> I realized when I came to the end of the novel that the point of the book is that man does have a measure of control over fate... and that control is most effectively managed through reason.

As I kept reading, I noted that many of the portions of the novel I was underlining centered around the theme of fate. To me, the hopelessness of controlling one's fate is reflected in the jail scene involving Kabuo Miyamoto, on trial for the murder of a local fisherman, when the narrator comments, "Perhaps it was now his fate to pay for the lives he had taken in anger. What a mystery life was! Everything was conjoined by mystery and fate" (Guterson 169).

Later, when Ishmael talks to Hatsue, Kabuo's wife and Ishmael's first and only love, he realizes that "there were things [fate] beyond anyone's control" (Guterson 326). Though circumstances appeared hopeless, I realized when I came to the end of the novel that the point of the book is that man does have a measure of control over fate... and that control is most effectively managed through reason.

From this stated theme about fate and reason, my mind quickly went to my English 12 classes that would be starting in less than a month. The theme of fate explored in *Snow Falling on Cedars* related directly to Thomas Hardy's character,

Tess, from the novel, *Tess of the d'Urbervilles,* who like Hester Prynne, certainly "deserved better." Though *Tess* is one of my favorite novels, I had not taught it in several years and recalled I always taught it near the end of the school year when many of my seniors, as they so aptly put it, were "over school" and found it difficult to sustain the intricacies of a Victorian novel. At that time, it seemed more logical to move chronologically through the literature. That meant starting with the Anglo-Saxon heroic epic, *Beowulf,* and ending the year with *Tess.* It suddenly occurred to me a better idea would be to teach *Beowulf,* incorporating into the lessons personal and analytical essays, and then end the study of the Anglo-Saxon period by incorporating a companion study, *Tess of the d'Urbervilles.* Would it work? I knew I had to give it a try, so during that week of summer vacation I sketched my first quarter's unit, a unit I hoped would be a refreshing change for my students and for me!

I realized the unit would fulfill several of the state's Standards of Learning (SOL) objectives as well as many of the Virginia Beach City Public Schools' specific requirements to meet those objectives. The students would "build knowledge of literary terminology, forms, and vocabulary in context" (SOL 12.4); "analyze the development of British literature" (SOL 12.7) by recognizing "major literary forms and techniques" (SOL 12.7.1); recognize "the characteristics of major chronological eras" (the Anglo-Saxon and the Victorian periods) (SOL 12.7.2); and relate these works and their authors "to major themes and issues of their eras" (SOL 12.7.3). The students would also "use the writing process involving prewriting, writing, revising, editing, and publishing" (SOL 12.12 and all of its enablers); and would "communicate ideas in writing using correct grammar, usage, and mechanics" (SOL 12.14).

They had no trouble at all doing this; in fact, I could not get many of them to stop writing.

September came and went and after my students read and discussed *Beowulf* and examined the Anglo-Saxon belief in the power of "Wyrd," or fate, I asked them to think about the power of fate in their own lives. I wrote the following two quotes taken from *Snow Falling on Cedars* on the chalkboard for my students to use as writing prompts: "What a mystery life (is)! Everything (is) conjoined by mystery and fate" (Guterson 169); and "There are things (in life) beyond anyone's control" (Guterson 326). I asked my students to ponder the words and then apply them to their own lives, writing entries in their journals under the heading "Fate." They enjoyed the writing assignment because it related directly to them, and most eagerly shared their reflections with their peers. My students enthusiastically volunteered to publish their journal entries because we had not approached literature as a "neatly codified and packaged truth of knowledge from which we may formulate truth" (Probst 27). Instead, I became sensitive to student responses and reminded myself that reading involves "drawing on past experiences with life and language as the raw materials out of which to shape the new experience symbolized on the page" (Rosenblatt 26).

According to Louise Rosenblatt, reader response theorist, "the reader brings to the literary work personality traits, memories of past events, present needs and preoccupations, a particular mood of the moment, and a particular physical condition. These and many other elements in a never-to-be-duplicated combination determine his response to the peculiar contribution of the text" (Rosenblatt 31). Teaching, then, must become a matter of improving the "individual's capacity to evoke meaning from the text by leading him to reflect self-critically on this process (26). So, my students were free to decide how they would respond. And decide they did! The following journal excerpts reveal the depth of thought from several of my students. Brett writes:

> Nothing can match the grip with which fate holds on to us; not money, not power, not even the weapons created by man can hold a person so strongly as can fate. Most of us have been taught that we control our own destinies, but when we are faced with sudden accidents, such as car crashes or plane wrecks, we begin to question why this happened. When the basic principles of the world we live in confront us with a kaleidoscope of life and death, happiness and sorrow, we begin to understand that we cannot control the future.

And Ann writes about fate playing a major role in who she is today. She writes impassionedly about the physical and emotional abuses she suffered as a child, about the horrible situation of her family's house burning down, and about the happy times surrounding the recent birth of her baby sister. What particularly amazed me, and her peers, was her acceptance of all—the good and the bad. As she reflected on all of these happenings, she wrote:

> I like to believe that the things I had no control over were all part of God's plan, or Fate, as some would call it. Fate played a major role in making me who I am today. Despite a few complexes and scars, Fate has made me a stronger person and has shown me that I can handle and cope with whatever life dishes out.

Another student, Donna, writes about a friend's unplanned pregnancy and its effects on changing her life. To my surprise, she attributed all of this to fate, writing: "It must have been her fate to get pregnant at this time in her life." Like many of her peers, Donna wrote about what we do have control over but choose to think we do not.

This examination of fate's role in my students' lives prepared the class for the reading of Thomas Hardy's *Tess of the d'Urbervilles*. When I had taught this novel in the past, I had not discussed the theme of fate prior to the students' reading. This time I hoped the personal connection would give them an incentive to read and that they would question what would happen to Tess as well as analyze and explore how fate directed Hardy's story.

I was pleasantly surprised to read their reflective responses that challenged their former attitudes.

After I presented a brief review of Hardy's philosophical beliefs and themes, my students plunged into the novel. When they completed their reading, I asked them to ponder the same two quotations I had written on the board several weeks earlier during our study of *Beowulf*. They had no trouble at all doing this; in fact, I could not get many of them to stop writing. Most were very angry at what had happened to Tess throughout her life and attributed these things to the powers of fate; things happened to her that were beyond her control.

It was now time to make my point and get my students to realize that they do have a good deal of control over their lives. I put the quotation from Nels Gudmondon, the defense attorney in *Snow Falling on Cedars*, on the board underlining the portion that contained the essence of what I wanted them to realize: "There are things in this universe that we cannot control, and then there are the things we can. Ensure that you do nothing to yield to a universe in which things go awry by happenstance. Let fate, coincidence, and accident conspire; human beings must act on reason" (419).

I then asked them to apply this quotation to Tess: Was everything that happened to her really out of her control? They agreed that fate and coincidence played an active part in her life, but I asked them to consider some of the following questions as well: Did Tess simply succumb to the powers of fate, or did she make decisions to take charge of her life to change her life's circumstances? What could she have done differently? Was it really fate that caused her death? After examining these questions, writing their responses, and sharing them with their classmates, the students began to see that Tess actually had more control over her life than many of them had previously believed.

Now my students were ready to revisit their own writing. I asked them to return to their "Reflections on Fate" entries in their journals, and to do some thought revision based on these new quotations and observations. "What aspects of your lives did you think were attributable to the whimsical moods of fate when they really were within your ability to change them?" I asked. I was pleasantly surprised to read their reflective responses that challenged their former attitudes.

Donna, who had previously written about the unplanned pregnancy of a friend, now realized that her friend made a choice, not based on reason, and that she was in many ways responsible for her situation.

When my student Ann revisited a previous journal entry, she merely confirmed what she knew all along. She writes: "Fate does play a role in everyone's life, but I believe that you alone have control over your career path, your grades, and the friends you choose to chill with. Don't waste time trying to control your future in areas you have no control over because all you're doing is overlooking the things that you can control." Colleen writes: "If fate gives you something that makes your life difficult, burdensome, or even sometimes unbearable, then you can try your hardest to make it better." She continues to discuss a severe learning disability that makes getting good grades extremely difficult for her and then concludes, "I could have used my learning disability as an excuse to make barely passing grades, not to work hard, and to just slide through school; instead, I work very hard to try and make good grades. Although I do not get straight A's, I know that I try my hardest to get the best grades that I know I can get."

Finally, Mark concludes his new essay by stating that "Life is a series of ups and downs, rises and falls, a constant battle for survival (for some) and for some peacefulness. Thus, we need to let the uncontrollable be the uncontrollable, control what we can, and live life to its fullest."

My English 12 students shared, revised, and edited their writing throughout the quarter and by the end of the grading period had not only written final drafts of a personal essay that explained how the universal truths explored in literature related to their own lives, but also were able to compose an analytical essay addressing Hardy's stance on fate as well. Most importantly, by the end of the first quarter, I was confident that I had come a long way in helping my students to realize that they do have control over many aspects of their lives. They, in turn, were much more excited about their new observations and their means of expressing them. My students had mastered the curriculum objectives and had come to a

> I was confident that I had come a long way in helping my students to realize that they do have control over many aspects of their lives. They, in turn, were much more excited about their new observations and their means of expressing them.

better understanding of themselves as a result, and seniors who normally were "over school," now enjoyed a Victorian novel and wanted me to recommend other Hardy titles. And, as fate would have it, I will be teaching Charlötte Brontë's *Jane Eyre* next, where we will examine yet another Victorian commentary on the theme of fate—this time through the eyes of the main character, Jane, who, like Tess, definitely "deserved better."

Works Cited:

Guterson, David. *Snow Falling on Cedars*. New York: Vintage Books, 1995.

Probst, Robert. "Adolescent Literature and the English Curriculum." English Journal 76 (198): 27.

Rosenblatt, Lousie. *Literature as Exploration*. New York: Modern Language Association, 1991.

Virginia Beach Public Schools. Department of Curriculum and Instruction. *Standards of Learning*. Virginia Beach, VA: Virginia Beach City Public Schools, 1997.

About Wendy Lewis

"Teaching is one of the most important contributions that one can make to society today. To influence students' lives in a positive way that they will always remember and to foster in them a love of literature and writing and a sense of its importance in understanding themselves and their fellow human beings is truly one of the most rewarding jobs that one can have."

Graduating Summa Cum Laude, Wendy Lewis received a B.S. in Secondary English Education from Old Dominion University in 1983. In 1986, she received the Virginia Beach Jaycees Outstanding Young Educator of the Year award. Graduating once again Summa Cum Laude in 1990, Ms. Lewis received her M.A. in English from Old Dominion University. She has been teaching eleventh-grade honors English and senior English at Kempsville High School for all of her fourteen years in education. Active in curriculum development, Ms. Lewis incorporates the Paideia Method of Socratic questioning in her classes and is highly interested in research addressing learning styles. Her professional affiliations include: NCTE, VATE, VBATE, NEA, VEA, and VBEA. At Kempsville High School, Ms. Lewis has served on various curriculum and instruction committees and most recently was selected as a member of the Faculty Planning Council.

A Hidden Treasure

by Beverly Wooddell

Summer ended, September arrived, and school preparation was well under way. Soon the room would be filled with eager faces ready to soak up knowledge. The door opened and a family walked into my classroom. I thought, "Oh no! another interruption; I'll never get things done." The time kept ticking away faster and faster. I stopped, mustered up a polite smile and said, "Hello." One of the ladies spoke, "Hi, I'm sorry to come in and disturb you, but we are here to see what my son's new school is like." I introduced myself and welcomed Henry, the young man who would soon be one of my fifth-grade students. He was a handsome eleven-year-old young man with brown wavy hair and beautiful dark, piercing eyes. He stood quietly, very hesitant and extremely uncomfortable with the focus that was being put on him.

I soon learned why the family was so eager to visit my elementary school. Henry's mother said he always struggled in school, hated his last teacher, made poor grades, always seemed to be in some sort of trouble, and did not want to be in school. Period. I thought, "Oh great! I get all of the challenges—a nonmotivated student and a troublemaker." I was very nervous about what contribution Henry would make in my class. But I forced a smile and commented that this year would be different with a new school and a new teacher. Then, I proceeded to tell him what I had in store for my students. We would have an assortment of activities which would include re-enactment groups, storytellers, living history presenters, role playing, oral presentations, and speeches. We would read exciting books and write on a variety of topics. Language arts and social studies would come alive, I told him. The more I talked, the more the whole mood of our conversation changed. The family seemed relieved and so did I. However, I'm not so sure I had Henry convinced, but he did manage to force a smile, seemed a little less uncomfortable, and responded quietly and politely, "Yes, Ma'am. See you next week, bye." After he left, I kept wondering if I could produce the great results I had talked about. Would I make a positive mark on

> The more I talked, the more the whole mood of our conversation changed. The family seemed relieved and so did I. However, I'm not so sure I had Henry convinced...

Henry's life, or would he perceive me as "mean and uncaring" as he did his previous teachers?

School began and Henry seemed to adapt well to my class. He began to love learning. He listened intently, nodded approval, and willingly shared his ideas with other classmates. He appeared more comfortable with himself, his peers, and me. Though his grades were average and his writing below average, it became less of an effort to collect Henry's homework and I saw slow, but gradual improvement on a daily basis. I liked him and he appeared to like me. I saw great potential in him, yet knew the rewards would appear only with perseverance — both mine and Henry's. I would talk to him and ask his opinion of certain lessons. After listening to him, I modified Henry's assignments at first, but then, when I saw his confidence improving, I would move toward more challenging tasks, especially where writing was concerned. I would challenge him with brainstorming and reshaping activities and his learning progress continued. The perseverance worked because Henry refused to be absent even when he was sick. He absorbed every new piece of information like a sponge. Most importantly, his self-confidence blossomed. The secret of my success with Henry was a combination of mutual trust and concern. I knew the motivation was within Henry all along but just needed to be ignited.

Looking back over my year with Henry, I realized the highlight involved the DARE essay, seeing his voice on paper. All my students were required to write an essay for the DARE (Drug Abuse Resistance Education) program discussing the importance of being drug free. After my students handed in their essays, I selected the top five. Surprisingly, the one essay that stood out among the rest was Henry's! His essay expressed words straight from his heart: his words spoke of his dream of becoming an Air Force pilot, a goal which drug abuse could destroy; then he wrote of his desire to be a good role-model for other students. He wanted to give other students hope. In his essay, he wrote, "I want to live a healthy life and don't want to do anything to ruin my life. I will try to give other kids the same message and try to keep them on the right track."

I submitted the essays to the DARE officer and Henry's received the first-place award. I was elated—and could hardly wait to announce the winner to my class. However, when I did, Henry sat in shock. All he could say was, "You're kidding! You're kidding. Right, Mrs. Wooddell?"

> He absorbed every new piece of information like a sponge. Most importantly, his self-confidence blossomed. The secret of my success with Henry was a combination of mutual trust, and concern.

Then, I revealed the other step he had to take and Henry's happiness, his excitement, became dread; he now had to read his essay before all the fifth-grade students, their parents, their teachers, and local dignitaries. Henry's body became stiff; his smile became a frown. Looking pale, he said, "Oh, my Lord! No, I can't. I don't read well. I'll look stupid," he said in a trembling voice. I assured him he could do it because I would help him—he was not convinced. I knew I had my work cut out for me, especially since other fifth-grade teachers questioned how a student who was not a consistent honor student could possibly be selected in the first place. But I defended Henry's honor and progress. He had beaten the odds and I would help him overcome this next obstacle.

> When the moment of truth came and Henry walked to the podium, he paused and read his essay proudly and perfectly. His family cried. I cried. And he gave me one of the most rewarding moments in my career.

Working daily for two weeks, we revised and perfected his essay. We discussed tips on making presentations and rehearsed one-on-one. Then Henry practiced before my class and our guidance counselors. When the day came for the DARE graduation and the reading of his essay, Henry's family sat proudly in the audience. Henry was shaking and so was I. When the moment of truth came and Henry walked to the podium, he paused and read his essay proudly and perfectly. His family cried. I cried. And he gave me one of the most rewarding moments in my career.

So what did this teacher learn? I learned not to have preconceived notions about students. Henry also challenged me to learn and create new ways to reach out to students who have been given roles to play. Henry came to me playing one such role—a negative one. As his teacher, though, I felt compelled to change the negativity into a positive belief in dreams. However, changing Henry was not easy because he had built a wall around himself and it was tough to tear it down, to get close, but I knew it was not impossible. Behind that wall was a delightful young man with great potential, and when I gave Henry the chance, he became the teacher. He reaffirmed that believing can make a difference in the life of a student. By taking a risk and embracing a challenge, I saw a young man's life transform. Isn't the transformation one of the fundamental reasons why we teach?

For several years Henry and his family kept in touch. I was delighted to hear that his motivation for learning and his academic performance remained high and that he still dreams of becoming a pilot. Even though Henry told me he still struggles in math, he nevertheless continues to conquer it. He believes in himself and this belief radiates externally. I will always remember his special words: "Thank you Mrs. Wooddell for all that you have done for me." I have made a difference in Henry's life, a difference that continues today. My only regret is that a previous teacher did not. As I reflect on all that has happened with Henry, I realize once again what teaching is about and why it satisfies me. Any student can achieve success if the teacher provides the opportunity and has the patience to persevere. As educators, if we can help our students to achieve this success, then we have done them a noble service. We must remain committed to discovering ways to encourage students to reflect and to tap their hidden gifts and treasures.

About Beverly Wooddell

"I see each day as a bright new beginning, a chance to focus on the positive, learn all I can, and share what I know with others, hoping to radiate a sparkle that will be contagious. If my excitement is reflected in my students, I know I have met with success."

Beverly Wooddell has been teaching in the Virginia Beach Public Schools for twenty-three years and currently teaches at Rosemont Forest Elementary where she was also selected Teacher of the Year in 1995. She serves as social studies facilitator and coordinator for all historical events and activities at Rosemont Forest. Ms. Wooddell has designed and implemented the reading incentive program, "Reading Habit for Life," that she also presented at the Virginia Beach Reading Conference. Ms. Wooddell has also been selected to serve on the Citywide Language Arts and Social Studies Curriculum Textbook Adoption Committees for four consecutive years. She has published a Native American teacher's resource manual and was selected by the Virginia Education Association to publish her innovative teaching ideas in *The Virginia Journal of Education*. Ms. Wooddell was recognized in 1996 by Superintendent Dr. Timothy Jenney when she was awarded the Total Quality Management Superintendent's Award.

The Educational Deal: A Lesson on Diversity

by Margaret Buxton

"We are caught in an inescapable network of mutuality, tied in a single garment of destiny. Whatever affects one directly, affects all indirectly."

—MARTIN LUTHER KING

expectations… here is a word educators and teachers have defined, discussed, and sometimes dismissed as a way to enhance students' academic success. What are *expectations*? How can teachers' *expectations* contribute to the behavior of students, and how do those students achieve or fail to achieve in school? Are high *expectations* for all students part of the education deal? the deal that promised so long ago an equitable and quality education for all students regardless of race, color or creed? Are all students expected to believe in themselves?

Elementary School

First grade, here I come! Happy, excited, ready to read and learn. In 1956, the expectations were clear and simple. **"Hello, students." said the teacher, "Today we will learn our ABCs and read in the Sally, Dick and Jane Reader."** I loved that reader. Spot was a good dog. Dick and Jane ran with Sally and Spot. The message was clear: all students were expected to learn and read. We did.

> Are high expectations for all students part of the education deal? The deal that promised so long ago an equitable and quality education for all students regardless of race, color or creed?

In elementary schools, in black neighborhoods, with black teachers, the expectation was clear. Black teachers encouraged, praised, and made us feel important every day. Sometimes the teachers demanded that we pay attention and complete our work or they would take us home to talk to our parents. That was a frightening thought in the fifties! Our parents wanted a better life for us and education was the answer, so I knew at a very early age I was going to college, as did my brother and sisters. And we did. Education meant a decent job, a nicer home in a better neighborhood—the American dream.

In elementary school, the teachers were strong, determined, and intent on teaching even though the books were used, the schoolhouse was old, and the materials were few. Everyone learned. I loved elementary school. All the kids were from the same neighborhood, so we were not embarrassed about our lack of nice clothes. We were close and understood what was expected. The teachers instilled in us values, confidence and self-respect. We memorized the "Pledge of Allegiance" and "My Country 'Tis of Thee," then recited both in front of the class. Though we were sheltered within our community and had little contact with other races, we were proud to be Americans. We communicated in our special language; we were comfortable in our world. Until... .The change: the education deal that would better our world. But junior high school would not hold the promise elementary school did.

> I loved elementary school. All the kids were from the same neighborhood, so we were not embarrassed about our lack of nice clothes. We were close and understood what was expected.

Junior High School

With change... expectations became cloudy. I was bombarded: the vision, black teachers, white teachers, different schools, more kids, all kinds of kids, new books, mean looks. What happened to my world in elementary school? Is college now just a dream? College? How can I think of college when the teachers expect so little of me? These teachers say I cannot learn. They say, *"Speak proper English."* They say, *"Did you really write this?"* Where is Miss Smith and Mrs. Johnson who loved teaching me so much and who encouraged me to read and write and smile every day? Mama, Mama, help me!

Too many rules. The white kids sit in front of the class all of the time, and the teachers keep telling the black boys in the back to sit still and be quiet. The black girls must act like ladies. What happened to my world? integration and civil rights, learning and achievement, Martin Luther King?

Two parents seem cool. Where is my dad? Any money for school? I haven't any money. *"Go to the end of the line. That is where we serve students with free lunch tickets,"* yells the teacher. I know I'm poor, but I can still learn. I talk funny. I look funny. I can't afford new clothes. *"Read this book. Multiply that number. Can't you write a story? Don't look at me like that. Go to the office!"* The black kids from the neighborhood band together for strength and comfort. We still have dreams. I still have dreams... .That was junior high.

High School

The Real Deal… high school. *"May I have your attention, please? All students in this high school work together; no separatism allowed. All students are expected to complete all requirements for high school graduation,"* the principal announced over the intercom. However, someone forgot to tell the teachers. I recall each Monday morning my English teacher saying, *"Good morning, Mary. How was your weekend?" "Good morning, John. Tell your mother and father hello."* Well, she doesn't really know my mom or me. Why would she ask about my weekend or tell my mom hello? But I am here. I want to fit in. I'll try a little harder. Maybe she will see we're really not all that different.

Should I try to fit in and act white? *"I'm sorry, young lady,"* the teacher replied, *"college isn't for everybody."* Why can't she see what's really inside of me? Inside of me are dreams. I dream of writing a book, becoming an astronaut, traveling to the moon. I often thought of becoming a teacher and helping students learn about other cultures. Does the color of my skin or the texture of my hair mean that I am not worthy of your friendship or of being in your school? I'm not the girl with the long blonde hair or the boy in the starched white shirt. Why can't the teacher see what's really inside of me? High school… survival.

The Lesson

I survived high school and managed to acquire a few friends. The era of "Black Power" and "Black History" provided America with a glimpse of black culture and black pride, so a heightened awareness of cultural differences emerged. However, in junior high and high school, I still kept searching for fulfillment of that educational promise, the promise that would benefit all students regardless of race or socioeconomic background. As an African American growing up in the 1950s, I suspect that my educational experiences were not so dramatically different from other African Americans. For me, integration created a heightened consciousness of what can happen to all children when that education deal falls short, especially for the African American

> **Does the color of my skin or the texture of my hair mean that I am not worthy of your friendship or of being in your school?**

child who watched her snug world of the early years slip away or watched a school of indifference thrive. African Americans watched their leaders diminish in power. We watched achievers become underachievers. Low expectations from teachers and shattered goals became a way of life.

However, a lesson is to be learned. It's not too late to improve this educational deal. Teachers have the power to make a difference in the life of a child. Take time to know your students and their families. Encourage and praise each student to help him or her see the value of an education and a belief in dreams. Learning is not about where you live or how you look; it is about self-worth and accomplishment. **"You can. You will."** Let those words echo for each student, echo from our schools, and echo from our society. Because our country is changing demographically, minority populations continue to increase. Expectations must remain high for all students of color and for all students of different socioeconomic backgrounds. It is the responsibility of all American schools not only to prepare students intellectually but to nurture them culturally—their stories, their beliefs, their pasts.

> **It is the responsibility of all American schools not only to prepare students intellectually but to nurture them culturally—their stories, their beliefs, their pasts.**

Conclusion

Reflect upon past promises and past educational deals to challenge all students to become the leaders and achievers of the next century. It is imperative educators recognize the gifts and talents of their students and that they utilize the strengths of each culture. All parents want the best education possible for their children. Help students accept responsibility for their own actions and their own learning. Provide firm discipline and encouragement. Model high expectations each day in class and encourage active parental involvement. Cultivate a climate of respect and trust, and display in your school an appreciation for all cultures, *all* year long. This would be a true educational deal, a lesson that would last forever. Look into the eyes of your students. Their eyes tell a story.

References

Barger, N. J., and L. K. Kirby. (Fall, 1993). "The Interactions of Cultural Values and Type Development: INTP Women Across Cultures." *Bulletin of Psychological Type* 16: 14-16.

About Margaret Buxton

"To teach is to touch a life, to bring meaning to our existence, to create a world of imagination that builds dreams and prepares leaders for tomorrow. Teaching and learning are constantly changing and educators of the next century must be adept in strategies that will connect with the young minds of our students. My vision is that all students can view learning as meaningful, achievement as attainable, and hold themselves in high esteem. We are learners and teachers together. We must work in peace and harmony. Our lives connect directly and indirectly. Trust, respect, and genuine love for our fellowman is surely a means to our true destiny. I believe that which affects one, affects us all. I live as I believe."

Receiving her B.S. and M.A. from Hampton University and her Ed.D. from George Washington University, Margaret Buxton has been active in a variety of different roles in the Virginia Beach City Public School System since 1972. She has served as a second- and third-grade teacher, an assistant principal, a Human Resources Specialist, and currently, she serves as a Staff Development Coordinator. Because of her expertise and educational experiences, Margaret Buxton is a frequent conference presenter and guest lecturer. She specializes in diversity awareness issues and has presented lectures on the following topics: "Creating a Culturally Sensitive Climate for Minority Students," "Increasing Achievement Through Reading," and "Dealing and Discovering Diversity." Her publications include: *The Real Choice: A Career in Early Childhood Education*, and *Teachers' Perceptions of Giftedness in Euro American and African American Third-grade Children.*

Maslow's Hierarchy of Needs and the Mentoring of the New Kid on the Block

by Tonilee Oliverio

as a result of my husband's career in the military, I have been privileged to teach in several different school divisions in various geographic locations throughout the United States and overseas. Each new teaching position meant, of course, that I would, once again, be the *new kid on the block*. It also meant that, despite several years of teaching experience, I would need to start at the beginning to prove myself and to pay my dues the first year in a new school... a familiar story.

Often I was left to fend for myself in my new school. I was reminded, in one school, to just "hang in there until December." Then, when December came and went, I was encouraged to "stick it out until June." Somehow, some way, I did make it to June. Another new teacher, however, wasn't as lucky. She was a beginning teacher, right out of college, and, unfortunately, *she* didn't make it until December. She left with the rest of us for the Thanksgiving holidays but never returned to her classroom. She resigned. The rumor was that teaching was not what she had expected and all the responsibilities had become too much for her.

> Another new teacher, however, wasn't as lucky. She was a beginning teacher, right out of college, and, unfortunately, *she* didn't make it until December..

I couldn't help but ask myself, "Would she have made it if someone had helped her or if someone had answered her questions or if someone had taken the time to tell her what to expect next?" Summer vacation came, went by quickly, and soon a new school year was ready to begin. That year new teachers were assigned mentors, a first-time effort by school administrators to help new teachers make the transition from college classrooms to classrooms of their own.

Mentoring, according to Oliva and Pawlas in their textbook, *Supervision for Today's Schools*, is a broad concept which implies "the assistance of a knowledgeable, more experienced person" (428). The authors of *Organizational Behavior: An Experiential Approach* state that mentoring should include efforts to help new employees live up to their full potential. From the *Odyssey* we learn that Mentor was an elderly advisor and faithful friend to Odysseus, the hero in the ancient Greek epic. We are told that before Odysseus went to fight in the Trojan War, he appointed Mentor as the guardian of his son, Telemachus. Mentor was to teach, advise, and protect Telemachus. Thus, the word *mentor* has come to mean "wise, faithful counselor" (World Book 411). Mentoring, in the context of the educational setting, is intended to help motivate and assist new teachers in fulfilling the hierarchy of needs as described in Abraham Maslow's *Hierarchy of Needs*.

At the very least, one of our responsibilities should be to assist in providing a safe and non-threatening environment where new teachers will feel welcomed and will be motivated to move up through Maslow's hierarchy.

Maslow, in *Toward a Psychology of Being*, described these human needs as five need systems which all individuals are thought to fulfill in a hierarchical order from the most primitive needs to the most sophisticated needs. He is recognized for his theory on the five motivational needs of: (1) physiological needs; (2) safety and security; (3) belonging and love; (4) self-esteem and status; and, (5) self-actualization. Maslow noted that these needs are interrelated rather than distinctly separated and that most people satisfy these basic needs in the order indicated in the hierarchy (Maslow 51). Throughout his research, Maslow noted a sense and order in the succession of motives that seemed to drive and motivate individuals to succeed and to accomplish goals, and that "people ascend upward toward more complex needs *only* after successfully fulfilling lower-order needs" (Wiles and Bondi 1993). Furthermore, he theorized that "when a particular need emerges, it determines the individual's behavior in terms of motivations, priorities, and actions taken" (Wiles and Bondi 1993).

In an effort to show the relationship between Maslow's *Hierarchy of Needs* and the needs of new teachers, a review of the literature and research related to mentoring must occur. A review of such research reveals one study, a doctoral dissertation entitled, "Perceived Quantities and Qualities of Supervisory Assistance," in which 240 first-year teachers were provided more supervisory assistance by peer mentor teachers than by administrators. The new teachers "valued and preferred supervisory help from peers over administrators or other supervisors" (Coleman 1986). In the November 1996 issue of the *Phi Delta Kappan*, research indicates that "new teachers should have the support from an expert mentor during the first year of teaching" (Hammond 197). This same research states that "such support improves both teacher effectiveness and teacher retention" (Hammond 197).

In addition to recent research, a review of educational literature also supports mentoring as a successful means of assistance for new teachers. The National Council for Accreditation of Teacher Education and the National Board for Professional Teaching Standards, two professional bodies which have combined efforts to set standards for teacher education and benchmarks for teacher performance, suggests that one phase of teacher preparation programs should include an expanded role of experienced teachers serving as mentors for new teachers (Hammond 197). Furthermore, other literature proposes yearlong internships in which beginning teachers are mentored extensively and evaluated continually as they move toward receiving professional licenses (Wise and Liebbrand 203). Several state accreditation agencies also support the use of mentoring with new teachers as reported by Scannell and Wain in their description of the Minnesota and Indiana Professional Standards Boards, both of which provide new teacher internship programs (212). Additional support for mentorship is evidenced by the National Board for Professional Teaching Standards in its proposal that peer intervention and mentorship would help provide quality teaching and improve the profession (Shanker 223).

The recurring theme throughout much of the literature concerns the use of mentoring as a tool to provide on-site support to new teachers. Maslow, in *Motivation and Personality*, reminds us that "individuals, in new situations, will seek equilibrium and self-preservation" (284). What can or should experienced educators do to assist new teachers as they begin to satisfy this hierarchy of needs? At the very least, one of our responsibilities should be to assist in providing a safe and nonthreatening environment where new teachers feel welcomed and motivated to move up through Maslow's hierarchy. In retrospect, I wonder how welcome, how safe, and how nonthreatened that young, new teacher was made to feel? Was that beginning teacher encouraged to pursue her professional goals or was everyone too busy, too concerned with their own classrooms and

> **Maslow's Hierarchy shows us that these new teachers, if they are to be productive individuals, must continue to move up through the all the levels of needs as they become more confident and self-assured in their teaching.**

their own students? How could she have ever fulfilled *self-actualization*, the ultimate need in Maslow's *Hierarchy of Needs*?

Even the most basic *physiological needs* of hunger, thirst, and bodily comforts might need to be addressed by beginning teachers just out of college with years of college loans and related debts to repay. The *safety needs* which involve job security and feeling safe from real or perceived threats of not performing well during probationary periods or of losing one's job might also be of concern to new teachers. Maslow's Hierarchy shows us that these new teachers, if they are to be productive individuals, must continue to move up through all the levels of needs as they become more confident and self-assured in their teaching. Ideally, these new teachers should eventually fulfill what Maslow describes as *self-actualization* or *self-realization* needs where they are able to achieve their full potential professionally. In order to implement and support mentoring initiatives, principals, too, must be reminded of the factors that motivate individuals as reflected in Maslow's *Hierarchy of Needs*.

Ultimately, a principal's responsibility should be to ensure that "all new teachers have the opportunity to observe and be observed and mentored by highly accomplished teachers" (Shanker 224). As a result of these mentoring opportunities, the new teacher should be better able to move satisfactorily up through the levels of motivational needs described in Maslow's *Hierarchy of Needs*, with the intent of reaching the ultimate level of *self-actualization*. In an effort to make these mentoring opportunities optimal, Kolb, author of *Organizational Behavior: An Experimental Approach*, suggests that the principal and mentor should:

- establish a nonthreatening positive environment characterized by effective communication and trust;

- make certain new teachers understand expectations clearly and provide positive, constructive feedback to rechannel new teacher efforts from ineffective to effective teaching practices;

- allow time during the school day for collaborative planning to occur between the new teacher and the mentor through creative scheduling;

- develop and implement mentoring programs to provide guidelines and explain the responsibilities of the mentor as well as the new teacher;

- provide staff development activities and training in-services which address the needs of new teachers;

- offer meaningful, relevant curriculum and instructional workshops to ensure the new teacher has a thorough understanding of the content to be taught;

- allow for opportunities which promote teamwork and collaboration such as placement of the new teacher on a school-wide committee with the mentoring teacher;

- provide a variety of opportunities to develop social hospitality, fellowship, and friendships in the context of achievement and accomplishment; and

- communicate frequently to new teachers upcoming deadlines and policies concerning progress reports, grading, report cards, pacing charts, and other information vital to the school division.

Of course, this is not an exhaustive nor extensive list of the responsibilities a principal should consider when supporting the mentoring of new teachers; however, it does highlight some of the more critical responsibilities. It seems apparent that the efforts of a mentor will do much to assist teachers in satisfying the basic needs as identified in Maslow's *Hierarchy of Needs* (Appendix I). Programs such as the Peer Intervention Program developed and implemented by the Toledo School System provide principals with a conceptual framework and deliberate steps for establishing mentoring programs. In this effort, a number of outstanding, experienced teachers were selected "who set standards by which novice teachers were to be trained and assessed, and they took charge of the training and assessment" (Shanker 223). In addition, these mentoring teachers offered practical assistance and administered intervention programs to help those teachers who were having difficulty (Shanker 223).

> **Perhaps we all had some responsibility to help this new teacher, *because of* or *in spite of,* our own experiences.**

When I think back to the new teacher who didn't make it until December, I can't help but wonder what happened to the enthusiasm that was so evident during her first few months of the new school year. What might have happened if she had been given a mentor to assist her? Perhaps we all had some responsibility to help this new teacher, *because of* or *in spite of,* our own experiences. Our experiences as the new kid on the block will determine how we approach other new teachers. Whether we were fresh out of college, new to a grade level or school, or new to the school division, we all have techniques and strategies which helped us make it until June. We must not forget those experiences because they will help us mentor other new teachers—to teach them, advise them, and protect them.

Appendix I

**Application of Maslow's Hierarchy of Needs
to Mentoring of New Teachers**

**SELF-
ACTUALIZA-
TION**
Being encouraged to
enroll in higher level
graduate programs; Being
encouraged to "be the best you
can be"

SELF-ESTEEM AND STATUS
Being chosen for recognition and awards such
as Teacher of the Year

BELONGING AND NEED TO BE LOVED
Being included in grade-level get-togethers and
after-school social activities; Being placed on building-level committees

SECURITY AND SAFETY NEEDS
Being free from the threat of not having contract renewed or not being granted
tenure; being free from the threat of receiving an unfair or negative evaluation from
the principal or instructional specialist

BASIC PHYSIOLOGICAL NEEDS OF HUNGER, THIRST, SHELTER, BODILY COMFORTS
Being able to get a job upon graduation or when new to the community, sign a contract,
receive a paycheck and other job-related benefits

Works Cited

Coleman, J. B. *The Perceived Quantities and Qualities of Supervisory Assistance Provided to Beginning Teachers in Florida and Georgia.* Diss. Athens, University of Georgia, 1986.

Hammond-Darling, L. (1996). "What Matters Most: A Competent Teacher for Every Child." *Phi Delta Kappan* 78(1996): 193-200.

Kolb, D., J. Osland, and I. Rubin. *Organizational Behavior: An Experiential Approach.* Englewood Cliffs, New Jersey: Prentice Hall, 1995.

Maslow, A. *Toward a Psychology of Being.* 2nd ed. New York: Van Nostrand Reinhold, 1968.

Maslow, A. *Motivation and Personality.* 2nd ed. New York: Harper and Row, Publishers, Inc., 1970.

Oliva, P., and G. Pawlas. *Supervision for Today's Schools.* 5th ed. New York: Longman, 1997.

Scannell, M., and J. Wain. "New Models for State Licensing of Professional Educators." *Phi Delta Kappan* 78(1996): 211-214.

Shanker, A. "Quality Assurance: What Must Be Done to Strengthen the Teaching Profession." *Phi Delta Kappan* 78(1006): 220-224.

Wiles, J., and J. Bondi. *Curriculum Development: A Guide to Practice.* New York: Macmillan Publishing Company, 1993.

Wise, A. E., and J. Leibbrand. "Profession-Based Accreditation." *Phi Delta Kappan* 78(1996): 202-206.

World Book Encyclopedia. Vol. 13. Chicago: World Book, Inc., 1989.

About Tonilee Oliverio

"Work done with love is work well done."

—Vincent Van Gogh

Having received her B.S. and M.A. in Special Education and Elementary Education from Slippery Rock University, Tonilee Oliverio has most recently received her Ed.S. in Administration and Supervision from George Washington University. Currently, she teaches first grade at Betty F. Williams and Glenwood Elementary where she also serves as an LD specialist. At Glenwood, she has served as the chairperson of the School Renewal Accreditation Initiative from 1991 to 1997. She has also been honored as Glenwood's Teacher of the Year in 1992 and Reading Teacher of the Year in 1993. As a member of the Association of Supervision and Curriculum Development, Tonilee was selected as keynote speaker for the Southern Association of Colleges and Schools in 1996, in Williamsburg, Virginia. In December of 1996 she was also a presenter at the National Conference for SACS in Nashville, Tennessee.

As a member of Delta Kappa Gamma, Gamma Zeta Women Educators, Tonilee completed two consecutive years as chairperson of the Ways and Means Committee and currently serves as vice-president. No matter where Ms. Oliverio teaches, she leaves her mark. During her employment with the Antilles Consolidated Schools in Puerto Rico, she received two Sustained Super Performance Incentive Awards.

Creating the Optimum Learning Environment

by Kathryn Bateman

"I hate it!" was the emphatic reply I got from the student when I prompted him to talk about school. And even though this was not the first time I've gotten such a response from a student, it still gives me quite a jolt whenever I hear those words.

This particular student had been referred to me, the school counselor, because of his disruptive behavior and lack of achievement. Further discussion with him revealed that he believed his teacher did not like him and thought he was stupid. This was his honest perception of the situation, even though he admitted that the teacher had never verbally expressed those thoughts to him. Sometimes, however, all it takes is a frown or a frustrated sign from a teacher to a student, particularly one with a poor self-concept, to generate such an interpretation. This example serves to demonstrate to educators not only the importance of being aware of our body language, but also, and more importantly, the sheer power we have over our students!

> Sometimes, however, all it takes is a frown or a frustrated sign from a teacher for a student, particularly one with a poor self-concept, to generate such an interpretation.

Helping **all** of our students to become proficient in the basic skills is our primary responsibility as educators. No matter what subjects we teach, certain conditions must be created in the classroom to maximize our students' learning and prevent students from shutting down emotionally. I call those practices the principles of the **other** 3 R's: **reach, respect**, and **reinforce**. These are not subjects we will teach, but rather principles we model on a daily basis. Then, students will learn positive behavioral attitudes that will lead them to improved social skills and a lifetime of success.

Reach refers to getting to know our students; they are all unique individuals bringing with them diverse cultural backgrounds, personal experiences, academic strengths and weaknesses, and emotional needs. Acquainting ourselves with their personal and academic histories will enable us to understand their perspectives.

We must make connections by listening to each student, stopping what we are doing, facing the student, and looking him in the eye when he speaks. Listening, really listening, means being nonjudgmental. This behavior affirms in the student's mind what he has to say is important. We need to be reminded that we may be the **only** person in our students' lives who takes the time to validate their worth. At times, a kind word or a pat on the back will be appreciated by a student who hungers to know someone cares. Humanity is the key and will help students reap immense dividends in the learning arena. As Egan (1986) points out, most individuals are aware of and sensitive to the attention or inattention of others; therefore, it is paradoxical that **we** can at times be so insensitive. We also need to know when flexibility is necessary. Should we really expect the student whose alcoholic parent was on a drunken rampage last night to have his homework the next day?

> At times, a kind word or a pat on the back will be appreciated by a student who hungers to know someone cares.

Respect, the second of the three R's, is what we all need and deserve. We should all strive to stamp out what I call the "Lucy Syndrome," excessive negativity, the need to be overly critical in pointing out another's faults (as Charles Schulz's Lucy does regularly to Charlie Brown). Many of our students have a number of Lucys in their lives already; they **don't** need any more. Maslow (1970) writes that individuals have basic needs that must be fulfilled in order for us to reach our potential. What does his research mean for our students? Lower-level needs such as those related to survival and security must be met first, followed by the need to belong and the need to acquire a positive self-concept. The satisfaction of basic needs, according to Maslow, contributes dramatically to the acquisition of knowledge.

Respect is a two-way street, and we usually get back what we give out. Some students go to any length to annoy teachers, yet these same students are usually the ones most in need of positive attention. Educators need to make a concerted effort to try to "catch them at being good," by reinforcing the behaviors we do want students to repeat. Power struggles are consistently a no-win situation. Oakes and Lipton (1990) point out that students' confidence is put on the line daily in the classroom. They "receive a steady barrage of messages about what others think about their prospects for success. As time goes on, children's views of themselves will correspond more and more to their classmates' and teachers' opinions and responses… (they) find it nearly impossible to sustain confidence, hard work, and persistence if everyone expects them to fail… eventually, negative judgments lead many children to give up."

Take a moment to imagine how you might feel and react if your supervisor reprimanded you in front of everyone at a faculty meeting? Would you feel like being cooperative or more like retaliating? How would you feel if that same supervisor read your evaluation form aloud to your colleagues? If either of these practices would make you squirm, then you know how students feel when their grades are announced or their behavior is chastised in front of their classmates.

It is amazing to watch the transformation students can undergo when they change classrooms from one year to the next or even during the same day! A move into a more supportive, encouraging classroom climate can change a withdrawn, unmotivated student into one who eagerly participates in class activities. A student who is a "discipline problem" in an earlier class can become a model of cooperation in the next, like the chameleon who changes colors in response to environment.

Reinforce, the third of the three R's, refers to the practice of acknowledging the smallest amount of progress or success. Educators need to consistently focus on the positive to reinforce effort rather than dramatize mistakes. For example, instead of marking up students' papers with red ink to point out errors, try using a bright highlighter to mark good choices. Dinkmeyer and Losoncy (1980) address the differences between "encouragers" and "discouragers" and describe how an encouraging teacher can help a student overcome a fear of failure and believe himself to be more capable, thus raising his expectations and also his achievement. All of our students are not likely to achieve honor roll status; some of them may never make an "A," but if they apply themselves and do their best, they deserve positive recognition just as much as the high achievers. This recognition and validation will build their confidence and encourage them to persevere through any academic or social circumstance.

As educators, we must guide students to see their successes and help them realize that making mistakes is part of the learning process; it doesn't diminish them in any way. This mindset reduces the likelihood of students becoming unmotivated underachievers or anxiety-ridden perfectionists, neither of which is a healthy, productive state. To achieve this positive, confident attitude in our students requires that we model appropriate responses to our mistakes when they occur, neither overreacting nor refusing to acknowledge them. Modeling appropriate behavior also involves modeling levels of expectation.

Oakes and Lipton (1990) remind us of the importance of teacher expectations in relation to the self-fulfilling prophecy phenomenon. Extensive research has

> Take a moment to imagine how you might feel and react if your supervisor reprimanded you in front of everyone at a faculty meeting?

supported the concept that a teacher's expectations significantly affect how well students will perform. The teacher's attitudes and actions impact students' levels of motivation, effort, achievement, and aspirations. Gardner (1989) writes that "students have always learned as much or more from the **ways** teachers present themselves—their attitudes; their beliefs; their moral codes; their daily modes of thinking, acting, and above all, **being**—than from a curriculum" (306). A widespread movement is underway to adopt character education programs in schools so that we may teach our students how to be responsible, respectful, diligent, and caring. However, these concepts are not taught so easily, especially with the societal pressures placed on today's students. Character education cannot be learned overnight or through the use of worksheets. Instead, students must continually be exposed to the modeling of appropriate, positive behaviors by their teachers and other role models. Damon (1995) states that "as a moral matter, teachers have a responsibility to embody good values in their interactions with their students. If teachers shirk this responsibility, they harm their students by leading them in the wrong direction" (217).

> Just as we are more motivated to do our best in a positive working environment, so too are our students.

Educators need to take advantage of teachable moments in the classroom, moments where we encourage good citizenship; this practice makes the sometimes abstract concepts of respect, trust, and honesty more concrete for students, and may help them apply these social skills to real life situations. Just as we are more motivated to do our best in a positive working environment, so too are our students. Practice the other 3 R's: **reach**, **respect**, and **reinforce**. It is our charge to do no less!

References

Damon, William. *Greater Expectations*. New York: The Free Press, 1995.

Dinkmeyer, Don, and Lewis E. Losoncy. *The Encouragement Book*. New York: Prentice Hall Press, 1980.

Egan, Gerard. *The Skilled Helper*. 3rd ed. Monterey, Calif: Brooks/Cole Publishing Co., 1986.

Gardner, Howard. *To Open Minds*. New York: Basic Books, Inc., 1989.

Maslow, Abraham. *Motivation and Personality*. 2nd ed. New York: Harper & Row, 1970.

Oakes, Jeannie, and Martin Lipton. *Making the Best of Schools*. New Haven: Yale University Press, 1990.

About Kathryn Bateman

"We must always remember that we are teaching the whole child, not just his brain, but his heart and soul; nurture him and he will learn."

Having received a B.S. in Elementary Education, an M.S. in Guidance and Counseling, and a C.A.S. in Education Administration from Old Dominion University, Ms. Bateman has been teaching in the Virginia Beach City Public School System for twelve years and has been serving as a guidance counselor since 1988. Maintaining active involvement in her school, Arrowhead Elementary, Kathryn Bateman offers her expertise as a presenter for parents and colleagues, is an active member of the School Planning Council and a member of the C.A.P. S. committee that has developed a character education program recently incorporated into the Virginia Beach curriculum. In addition to her active school involvement, Ms. Bateman is also a frequent presenter at the Virginia Beach PTA Guidance conference, the Planning Council EXPO, and the VAESP conference. Being an active member of Phi Delta Kappa, her commitment to educational reform is commendable. She participated in the production of the ASCD video: "Building Support for Public Schools," and has published articles in the journal, *Principal*. She is the recipient of the Distinguished Service Award from the Virginia PTA and was named Arrowhead's 1996 Teacher of the Year.

No More Chalk Dust: Using Multimedia Presentations in the Classroom

by Lee Mitchell

"Y ou need to use more visuals in your lessons," said the mentoring teacher to the new student teacher. That student teacher was I in 1991; I was forty-seven years old. After almost twenty years in the construction industry, a series of business reversals led me to consider a major career change—into teaching. Why teaching? I felt that I had the ability to explain things to people in simple terms they could understand. I had recently developed and presented two successful seminars on new home construction to real estate agents. It was that experience that led me to believe that I could be a good teacher. But, what did I know about visuals? Nothing. I thought all you had to do to teach was to get up in front of a class and lecture for fifty minutes. After all, wouldn't my students find business law just as exciting as I did? How wrong I was. After seeing many glazed eyes and faces hitting the desks, I quickly learned that a straight lecture was at the bottom of the well when it came to teaching strategies.

> After seeing many glazed eyes and faces hitting the desks, I quickly learned that a straight lecture was at the bottom of the well when it came to teaching strategies.

A Look Back

I thought the tried and true blackboard would solve my problem. I soon realized there are three major disadvantages to using a blackboard: (1) the students couldn't read my writing; (2) valuable class time was lost while I wrote on the board; and (3) chalk dust got all over me every time I erased the board. The discovery of colored chalk helped me organize the material in a more visually pleasing layout, but it didn't solve the time and chalk dust problem.

After I became a full-fledged teacher at Princess Anne High School in the fall of 1993, white boards were installed in place of the old-fashioned blackboards. With plenty of various colored markers in hand, I really had something to work with. These big and bold markers were "state-of-the-art." However, this system did not solve the legibility and time problems either. So, I set out in search of new ways to use "visuals."

One day I discovered how to make transparencies and use an overhead projector. Now I know how Mr. Edison felt when he discovered the light bulb. I was ecstatic. Soon I had all my lessons and notes neatly typed on transparencies; in fact, I had an entire notebook filled with them. Now my students could see exactly what I was saying and take accurate notes from the material on the screen. All I had to do as I delivered my lecture was slide a piece of paper down the transparency, uncovering only what I wanted the students to see. Of course, I recognized a slight problem as I got about two-thirds down the page. If I let go of the paper, the fan from the projector would blow it off, revealing the great mystery at the bottom before I was ready for students to see it. This little inconvenience had the effect of trapping me at the projector, with one hand on top as if stuck in glue. Magnetic signs did not work either. Even though the pieces could be moved around the board in any layout, after a particularly long lesson the board reminded me of my refrigerator. So the search continued. Then, I heard about multimedia presentations and decided to investigate.

I also noticed how attentive the class was to each presentation. I was hooked.

A "New Media"

What is a multimedia presentation? A medium is any physical means by which people communicate; therefore, multimedia is a presentation that incorporates more than one medium. Today, we think of multimedia as incorporating text, graphics, animation, pictures, sound, and video. This is nothing new. Film strips or 35mm slides with accompanying audio cassettes could incorporate most of those elements and were, in fact, early multimedia presentations. One difference between those early presentations and the ones that I am referring to is that today's presentations are created on a computer, using software that is easily learned.

I saw the potential for using multimedia in the classroom while taking a Master's level course at the University of Virginia during the summer of 1996. All the students in the class were full-time teachers. We had to develop, either alone or in pairs, a multimedia project in our subject area and present it to the class. Two advantages became obvious. We agreed that the presenter's subject knowledge increased as a result of the preparation that goes into each slide. I also noticed how attentive the class was to each presentation. I was hooked. Now, I was eager to create my own lessons, but I needed to overcome two hurdles before using multimedia presentations in the classroom: (1) getting access to the proper equipment to present the lesson, and (2) learning to use the software to create a presentation. A little ingenuity solved the problem.

Equipment and Software Needed

A TV/VCR on a cart had been assigned to me the previous year. I put one of the Compaq computers and monitors from my keyboarding lab on the cart with the TV/VCR, and installed a scan converter from the PC to the TV. This device converts the computer signal to a TV signal. Then, I plugged all cords into a power bar on the cart, leaving only one cord from the cart to be plugged into the wall. The advantages of this setup are several. They include: (1) lower cost—$100 to $200 for the converter vs. a LCD panel costing several thousand dollars; (2) a setup that is portable and easy to use in any room; (3) a classroom that does not have to be darkened; and (4) a presentation that may be copied to videotape and shown in any classroom equipped with a TV/VCR. This setup was so well received that Princess Anne High School purchased 13 PC/TV/VCR portable workstations for use by all departments. The next question was which software package to use. After sampling several, I chose Powerpoint from the Microsoft Office 97 suite. This is an easy-to-use program that can be learned from the "Help" menu by anyone with word processing experience.

Across the Curriculum

Now I was ready to share my discovery with other teachers. I demonstrated the equipment, gave a sample presentation, and a start-up lesson to forty teachers during a staff development day. Many of them got excited about the possibilities and are now busy creating their own multimedia presentations. One science teacher told me that this was the best idea he learned from a staff development activity in the last three years. Pictures of lab experiments (using a digital camera), material lists, and instructions can be incorporated in a science presentation. A picture and sound of an explosion may be added to emphasize what could go wrong if the directions are not followed.

With a little creativity, the possibilities for using multimedia presentations are endless. Math concepts can be demonstrated visually by animating geometrical shapes and graphs. English teachers can use a multimedia presentation for dramatizing poetry readings or teaching revision techniques. History lessons can be linked to videos on encyclopedia CD's or to the Internet. "Electronic flash cards" can be created in a presentation to be used for math, foreign language, or vocabulary drills. A presentation pat-

> One science teacher told me that this was the best idea he learned from a staff development activity in the last three years.

terned after the quiz show "Jeopardy" can be effectively used across the curriculum at any grade level.

Elements of Design

Once the software is mastered, learning some elements of design can create a more effective presentation. The trick is not to make the presentation so high-tech that students lose the purpose of the lesson. There are so many features to choose from that there is a temptation to become too cute. Definitely "less is better than more." For example, fonts should be sans-serif such as Arial because they are easier to read. Limit the font selections to two or three and make them as large as possible. Many designers say you should use nothing less than a size of 18 point (Microsoft); others say, use a minimum of 24 point (Treuhaft).

Keep in mind the underlying concept of an effective multimedia presentation is to make major points, not to rewrite the textbook. Therefore, Microsoft recommends following the "6 x 6 rule": no more than 6 lines per slide and 6 words per line. They recommend using short words such as "aim" for "objective." I find that this challenge increases my editing skills and subject knowledge as I revise lengthy textbook definitions. Also, be consistent. Change fonts, colors, transitions, and backgrounds from lesson to lesson rather than from slide to slide within a lesson. That way, each lesson will be unique and memorable in its own right.

Incorporate a graphic or picture to illustrate major concepts being taught; this visual aid breaks up the text and holds the students' attention by associating the concept with the graphic. Sometimes, I animate the slide by bringing in the graphic as an illustration *after* I have explained the concept using text. Reversing that process is also effective. Show the graphic, discuss with the class what they think it represents, and then bring in the text. This variation within the presentation allows different learning styles to be addressed simultaneously.

> There are so many features to choose from that there is a temptation to become too cute. Definitely "less is better than more."

Sound adds variety and a sense of mystery to the lesson. Again, resist the temptation to overdo it. Avoid using several sound effects with every slide. Instead, I try to use sounds that enhance the graphic I am using. For example, in a slide on the topic of drunk driving, I used a graphic of a crowd of people and then animated a car coming at them from the right. The added sounds of a scream, screeching tires, and broken glass were definitely a wake up call for the students.

Controlling the Presentation

Presentations may be either linear or random where links to various topics in the presentation are used, similar to the links on a web page. If linear, transitions between slides should be controlled manually rather than automatically, so that the teacher can control the pace. I have used automatic transitions in a slide show with music and "looped" (set to run continuously) slides to provide directions and clarify objectives to the students as they enter the class between bells. A random presentation gives the teacher added flexibility when discussing several concepts in a unit because the teacher always has the ability to back up for reinforcement. The random presentation also can be used as a computer-aided instructional program where students review an entire unit without the teacher's assistance.

> They recommend using short words such as "aim" for "objective." I find that this challenge increases my editing skills and subject knowledge as I revise lengthy textbook definitions.

Test the Water—Make the Leap

Teachers may get frustrated if they try to make these presentations perfect the first time around. Because it's possible to spend hours on just one slide, I suggest completing a basic presentation of mostly content; then going back and trying to improve the presentation with graphics, color, transitions, and sound. A "work-in-progress" may always be revised and improved.

Creating multimedia presentations is definitely work, but it can be extremely rewarding. I have discovered creative talents within myself that I never knew I had. It's exciting to find new ways of using multimedia presentations in lessons. For example, I am now using an "inquiry" method where I am able to draw the students into the presentation by posing questions about each slide rather than merely disseminating information. If students are drawn into the presentation and become participants rather than observers, real learning happens.

Does it Pay Off?

The use of multimedia presentations in the classroom is just one of many "lesson delivery methods." Since it is relatively new, confirming an increase in student achievement by employing this method of instruction is limited. Perhaps that will be a subject for a future article. So, is it effective? It has been for me. To confirm the success of this strategy, I took an informal survey of students in my business law class to determine if they thought multimedia presentations were beneficial to their learning. Eighteen of nineteen replies were positive. One student wrote, "The presentations benefit me as well as others who want to learn, so you should continue to do what you do." And another student commented, "The multimedia lesson is creative, and it makes learning a lot easier. It seems like it saves time, too."

Student achievement cannot always be measured by the number of correct answers. The payoff for me came when a pair of students created a multimedia presentation for the oral portion of their semester project. If more students wish to do the same, they will have to learn how to use computer technology. That skill by itself is an achievement, one that leads to further personal and professional growth. I plan on encouraging my students to create multimedia presentations as part of the learning experience in my business law classroom in the future.

> **Creating multimedia presentations is definitely work, but it can be extremely rewarding. I have discovered creative talents within myself that I never knew I had.**

I mentioned earlier that writing on a blackboard wasted precious time that could be used for instruction. Now, I'm finding that multimedia presentations allow me to present a lesson faster which allows for other enrichment activities. This helps improve student attitude and discipline. The use of multimedia presentations will pay off in the long run because it appeals to all learning styles, holds the attention of students and helps motivate them to learn. That is half the battle. And... I have no more chalk dust!

References

Microsoft Corporation. "How to Prepare and Deliver Effective Presentations." 4 Mar. 1996. <http://www.microsoft.com/powerpoint/productinfo/experttools/present.HTM>.

Treuhaft, Jack. January, 1995. "Multimedia Design Considerations." Algonquin College of Applied Arts and Technology. <http://www.algonquinc.on.ca/edtech/mmdesign>.

UCLA Faculty New Media Center. "What's a New Media?" UCLA Office of Instructional Development. <http://www.oid.ucla.edu/FNMC/whatnm.htm>.

About Lee Mitchell

" 'A teacher is someone who can take something complicated and explain it so it seems simple.' That's what I try to do. If a student doesn't understand something that I've said (or shown him), I take it as a challenge and look for a simpler way to explain it."

Prior to moving to Virginia Beach in 1971, Lee Mitchell worked in New York City as a media buyer and stockbroker. Also prior to 1971, Mr. Mitchell became a partner in a construction firm for twenty years—he accomplished all this before becoming a teacher. After earning his teaching certification in Business Education from Norfolk State University in 1991 and his M.A. from the University of Virginia in 1997, Lee Mitchell began his teaching career at Princess Anne High School where he currently serves as Faculty Council Chairperson. Continually recognized for his work with technology, Mr. Mitchell received a Tandy Technology Scholar "Outstanding Teacher Award" in 1997 from the Office of Technical and Career Education in Virginia Beach and was also named a "1998 Champion of the Exceptional Child" for his work with special education students. Currently Chairperson of Princess Anne High School's Technology Action Team and "webmaster" for the school's internet site, Mr. Mitchell remains an avid videographer, noted for the numerous videos he produces for Princess Anne High School.

Drama Exposed

by Eva Roupas

I magine students who take ownership of their class. They discipline themselves to achieve. They have equal input as to the direction each class project takes—the choices, decisions, perspectives, success in the class are student-centered. This is a drama class. Nowhere are any symptoms of a classroom that is unfocused, dreamy, chaotic, undisciplined, lackadaisical. This class has developed performers with drive and purpose, goals and desires, professionalism and maturity. This class is Drama Exposed.

"Sometimes nothing is the best thing to have." And sometimes "nothing" is the sole impetus that forces all of us out of our overused, overrated, overdone, out-dated lesson plans and reminds us to implement the ideals and creativity that have remained dormant too long. This happened to me.

> Nowhere are any symptoms of a classroom that is unfocused, dreamy, chaotic, undisciplined, lackadaisical. This class has developed performers with drive and purpose, goals and desires, professionalism and maturity. This class is Drama Exposed.

Time: June, 1991

Where: Salem High School, Virginia Beach, VA

Situation: Desperate

Salem High School was barely two years old, and having been hired as the drama teacher when the school opened, I quickly discovered money and support were not anywhere to be found. Here was an instructional program really beginning to flourish, a plethora of talent, an enthusiastic teacher, a bare stage, and a budget of pennies.

"Creativity (and desperation) is/are the mother(s) of invention." I was becoming a crazy person, asking what am I going to do with these kids thirsty to perform? Around the time I was in full panic-mode, the administration was noticing a major shortage of classrooms due to the overcrowded school population. As a result, since I taught a performance-based course, my classroom was assigned to the "schola," a lecture hall with a stage that seated 112 audience members. When faced with challenges of the fall school semester, I remembered the successes of the summer.

"I'd rather be lucky than smart." Luckily, a windfall came my way during the summer of 1991. In July, I was selected to participate in a program for theater teachers at Virginia Commonwealth University. While there, I heard a teacher state that her drama class performed for other English teachers and accommodated their bell schedules to do so. My thought was, "Why can't students perform for the entire faculty regardless of the subject matter?" With the schola as my classroom and the curriculum as my performance source, I began devising my plan.

"Be careful what you wish for; you just might get it." As Drama III/IV students strolled into class that fall, none of us realized that this was the last "free" day we would have for the next 180 days; implementation of the program began. The students created their title, "Drama Exposed," and one student was elected to design the logo and have it printed on black t-shirts. They decided to wear this shirt with matching black pants for all performances — cutting out the cost for the use of costumes. For a mere $5.20 per student, this acting troupe was entirely equipped to perform anything for anyone. Our first two projects were to perform the epic poem *Beowulf*, for twelfth-grade English, and to create a 1920s variety show for Virginia U.S. History classes.

> **Here was an instructional program really beginning to flourish, a plethora of talent, an enthusiastic teacher, a bare stage, and a budget of pennies.**

"Don't sweat the small stuff." These first two projects were hits. As a result of the visibility, other teachers bit into the idea; other students watched what a theater class could do with an English and social studies class, and the program continued to flourish.

Within eight months, Drama Exposed performed between fifteen to twenty individual productions at a minimum of two performances apiece. Maintaining above average grades and near perfect attendance are musts when auditioning to get into Drama Exposed, so students become incredibly conscientious about grades and absenteeism. Peer pressure also serves as an incentive for each class member to maintain above average standards, because if one falters, they all do. In order to deal with the inconsistencies that may occur, we developed an understudy system implemented early in the rehearsal stage and began rehearsing with the understudy so he or she felt comfortable in the role for the bell in which he or she would be performing.

"Give them the chance to be brilliant, they are; expect them to produce, they will." The pride my performers took in the projects they manufactured that first year, and the subsequent six years, was (and still is) incredible. What this pro-

gram has done for students' discipline, self-esteem, education, insights, maturity, and responsibility has been nothing shy of amazing. The ownership they feel when a project has been created, written, directed, produced, and performed by them FOR THEIR PEERS is awesome. The excitement within the class is palpable. And it reaffirms my faith in the fact that education is still a vital, living, tangible thing. Performing fifteen to twenty projects a year, with no more than two to four weeks to get a performance up and running, forces these artists to focus and meet deadlines. In order to do so, they are forced to work after school at additional rehearsals as well as at 6:00 a.m. dress rehearsals the day of every performance — they never allow the "show to go on" without one. According to Kevin Piper, currently a senior, "Sometimes we learn more from the rehearsal process itself than the actual performance." Coupled with the pride students feel is the commitment to their work. As a result, the entire class feels, collectively and individually, each person's input counts and is vital to the success we all enjoy. The creative (playwrighting, directing), artistic (drawing, dancing, singing, guitar playing), and technological (computers, lighting, set design) gifts the students bring to the class make the performances diverse, eclectic, and relevant to all audience levels. My student Nichole Evola sums it up best by stating,

> We don't just learn about "drama," we learn to understand it. We don't just learn it; we are taught to teach each other what we all learn. We put our ideas into each and every performance. What I've done in this class I will take with me forever in my future endeavors.

"Is not life a hundred times too short for us to bore ourselves?" The pertinent social twists created by Drama Exposed soon became their signature on every production as is true of the addition of three levels of scripts. The first level involves scripts that are literal scenes from existing plays (i.e. *The Crucible, Man of La Mancha, The Importance of Being Earnest*). The second level becomes an adaptation from existing, nonplay material such as the epic poem, *Beowulf, The Adventures of Huckleberry Finn*, and *1984*. The third level of the project requires the most work: these scripts are developed from scratch. For example, sample performances utilizing this unique effort may involve a fifteen- to twenty-minute parody of the entire play *Macbeth* — complete with encore and music, or 1920s, 1930s, 1940s, 1950s, 1960s, 1970s variety shows emphasizing major events and personalities of these decades, or a Cinderella-like fable centering around Algebra II's conic sections featuring parabolas, or a Mickey Spillane mystery illustrating the concept of inertia to physics classes.

The creation of Drama Exposed scripts, especially those based on broad ideas proposed by the teacher, involves extensive research. And the students probably enjoy these projects most because their personal signatures are all over them. Initially, the class depends on students who either know the material by having previously had the class or on those who are currently enrolled. These individuals briefly teach the class any pertinent information and then help to generate possible topics for further research. We also enlist the help of the requesting teacher, who provides supplemental materials that the textbook or library may not have available.

The group collectively brainstorms genres, styles, formats, and characterizations and through a trial and error process, the outline of the performance is determined. Smaller groups then fine-tune separate portions of the outline. This dramatizes the eclectic brilliance of the class. In the variety shows, for instance, the dancers, singers, instrumentalists contribute music of the era (e.g. 1940s), and we find ourselves swinging to the big band excitement the entire show. And if students aren't singing and dancing, then background music is provided during scene changes or during the profiles of World War II, reenactments of *Tom and Jerry*, or parodies of *Arsenic and Old Lace*. After the outline is completed, one or two members of the class volunteer to organize all the information into a script. The class' knowledge of pop culture and their rapport with one another allows them to address subjects in a way that sells to even the most unmotivated audience: *Macbeth* performed as a soap opera, *Beowulf* as a rapper, Hitler speaking with a Yiddish accent, *1984* sung to the tune of "Old MacDonald Had a Farm."

Because this course is so dramatically student-centered, my limitations as a teacher due to age, race, and background force me to defer to these teenage experts and my horizons continue to expand. As the years progress, the inventory of exclusive quality scripts continues to mushroom and subsequent classes not only pen their own originalities, but can fall back on the previous class' legacies. My current class rehearses these now-staple scripts that are regular fare on the performance agenda.

> **...*Macbeth* performed as a soap opera, *Beowulf* as a rapper, Hitler speaking with a Yiddish accent, *1984* sung to the tune of "Old MacDonald Had a Farm."**

"Sometimes the road less traveled is less traveled for a reason." I would hate for you to think I have cruised through an effortless seven years with this project. Ahh... the lessons we learn. Trial and error have been immense, and I would have second-guessed my sanity in taking on this idea had I known the hurdles facing me,

especially that first year.

The work and organization at times seemed insurmountable. In addition to the four or five classes I taught and the after-school plays in production, I now had eighteen other performance projects to get off the ground, most of which hadn't been written yet. Periodically, the pressure became paralyzing, but fortunately my worst days were the students' best because my students never forget this class is a privilege, not a right.

"We are starting to realize using drama to help others learn in other subject areas is quite effective and Drama Exposed was on the ground floor with some of that."

"Let no man imagine that he has no influence." The impact these students have had on the Salem High School community has been tremendous. Consistently over the last seven years the results have been a resounding success. Due to the high visibility of students involved in the program, the student body has a great appreciation of individual talents. Currently we perform for various departments including social studies, English, foreign languages, math, marketing, physical education, and health and human services. Each year one more department has been added to the itinerary and wants to "play."

Also, this program is one of those rare vehicles where students learn and enjoy themselves simultaneously. Drama Exposed has transcended time periods extending from Anglo-Saxon to the present; covered a plethora of genres; reenacted a multitude of characters and, in some cases, animals as in *Animal Farm*. They have also addressed social issues such as violence, stress, and racism among their peers. According to sophomore, Maura Meuser,

> I think the beauty of this class' purpose is when a fellow student remembers something from a performance like a dramatization showing how food travels through the digestive system. Students constantly approach us and say, 'Hey, you guys were awesome!' Just that makes the strife worthwhile!

The class has learned to appreciate the cultural variances of a variety of eras; they have been taught to dance the lindy, the jitterbug, the tango, and the cha-cha, instructed by community members, as well as to coordinate fashion and dialectical patterns. Educational Theater Association spokeswoman, Toni Brotons, recognizes Drama Exposed's importance to the curriculum: "We are starting to realize using drama to help others learn in other subject areas is quite effective and Drama Exposed was on the ground floor with some of that."

Lastly, the general feedback has been unbelievable. We have been interviewed and filmed by the media and toured several of our performances to elementary and middle schools. As a result of the successful interdisciplinary approach, Drama Exposed continues to create a widening vehicle for young people to be "exposed"; the program has received an Excellence in Education Award from Virginia Tech in 1992, and the Innovative Theater Arts Award from the Educational Theater Association in 1994.

Senior classmates Matt Beard and Bobby Poole reflect clearly the sentiments I have heard over the seven years Drama Exposed has been in existence:

> Experience is the best teacher in all things. Drama Exposed gives something that any other drama class could never experience. I have learned so much about performing, audiences, and life in general from this class. The opportunity to perform has allowed me to not only just be on stage, but it has given me a better understanding of audiences and how to present myself to all I come in contact with, says Matt.

And according to Bobby, "This class works because we love what we're doing. The teacher loves teaching, and we love learning and being on stage. We all want to be here."

About Eva Roupas

"Find a job you love and you'll never work a day in your life."

Eva Roupas, a native of Elm Grove, WI, has recently completed her eighteenth year in the classroom. After spending time in three states and five schools, she "landed" in Virginia Beach eleven years ago. Currently, she teaches drama at Salem High School in Virginia Beach. In the time she has been in Virginia Beach, her drama program has received the Excellence in Education Award from the Virginia Polytechnical Institute in 1992, and the Innovative Theater Arts Award from the Educational Theater Association in 1994. Also in 1994, Ms. Roupas published an article in *Teaching Theater* and conducted a workshop on Drama Exposed at the ETA National Convention. In 1998, Eva Roupas was selected as Virginia Beach Citywide Teacher of the Year, a school system that employs over 6,000 educators.

Michelle Tillander

Cosmic House, 1997

Computer-generated
image

"*From ancient dwellings to modern buildings, the house design form creates spiritual roots that reflect the heart and mind of man. In this image Cosmic House, I am exploring the dwelling structure as a metaphor that speaks to us about sheltering humanity.*"

Michelle Tillander

Biographical Information

Michelle Tillander received her M.A. in Fine Arts from Old Dominion University and is currently Visual Arts Chairperson for the Governor's School for the Arts. Previously, she taught six years at Old Donation Center for the Gifted and Talented, Virginia Beach City Public Schools. Michelle Tillander has published numerous articles in the journals, School Arts and Arts and Activities. Her photography is represented in the permanent collections at the Chrysler Museum, the Children's Hospital of the King's Daughters, and the Medical College of Richmond. Ms. Tillander is the 1997 recipient of the Virginia Elementary Art Educator Award and she serves on the Virginia Beach Art Scope and Sequence committee, and the Teacher Advisory Committee for ARTSEDGE, at the Kennedy Center.

Art Education Statement

"Assignments which challenge students' minds creatively and develop a balance between form and content provide an in-depth comprehension of the artistic medium. Even though part of my teaching philosophy includes setting some definite parameters for my students, I also give them freedom of choice. This delicate balance in the classroom enables students to experience the greatest personal satisfaction in their exploration of what art is and should be. Because I believe that knowledge and insight about art are critical for effective teaching, my active commitment to my own work and development as an artist enable me to be a more effective educator."

Chapter 2
Collaborative Teaching: Shared Visions

"The growth of any craft depends on shared practice and honest dialogue among the people who do it. We grow by private trial and error, to be sure—but our willingness to try, and fail, as individuals is severely limited when we are not supported by a community that encourages risks. When any function is privatized, the most likely outcome is that people will perform it conservatively, refusing to stray far from the silent consensus of what "works"—even when it clearly does not."

—PARKER PALMER, THE COURAGE TO TEACH

i *think we can all remember teachers who affected our lives, mentors who encouraged us, who decided we were destined to teach. Our mentors listened to our ideas, our pressing educational issues, our visions. Our "mentors evoked us"; we collaborated about classroom ideas and theory. We realized that "mentors and apprentices are partners in an ancient dance, and one of teachings's great rewards is the daily chance it gives us to get back on the dance floor. It is the dance of spiraling generations, in which the old empower the young with their experience and the young empower the old with new life, reweaving the fabric of the human community as they touch and turn" (Palmer 25).*

It remains a sobering thought to think about where I would be today were it not for my mentors. And today, they remain great teachers, never appearing too busy for yet another question, always encouraging me when confronted with a challenge, helping me see that I can make a difference in this calling of education. And each time I return to my classroom with strands of their wisdom, I am reminded once again of the powerful impact collaboration can have on the lives of students and teachers.

A recent scenario from my classroom in November: "I can't wait until Thursday," Sara said. She was a blast of energy as she busily prepared her court case with her legal partner, Crystal. My classes were trying main characters from the play Hamlet for first and second degree murder. During class, in group planning sessions, I overheard the efforts of the defense team: "We can do this, Shawnta," Erin said. "They might be stronger public speakers, but you know the text much better than Crystal or Sara. I heard you quoting direct lines from memory!"

I stopped for a moment. My students were memorizing lines, critically analyzing key passages and I hadn't even assigned it? My students delved into the play with more energy and enthusiasm than I had seen all year. All students were engaged, even students, who up to this point, appeared withdrawn and shy. Now, because of this collaborative activity, students were actively preparing and discussing with their classmates, counting down the days of preparation before they would present and perform their court cases. One of the many objectives underneath this assignment was to encourage leadership, and to my great satisfaction, I noticed not only one leader emerging in each group, but several. Students shared responsibilities, discussed their work schedules, and how they would organize all the duties within the group to meet project deadlines—all the significant problem-solving, communication, life skills I wanted them to take to college and out into the world as graduating seniors.

Throughout the course of two weeks, my students became a team of thinkers, writers, and critical readers; they were research partners. While I held them individually accountable for their written preparation, they also worked together sharing textual references and splicing together the strongest parts of opening and closing arguments. As the days neared for student cases to be heard, I noticed their discussions became much more literary—they needed as much knowledge of Shakespeare as possible. They discovered that using criticism from the library would strengthen their cases and asked me if it were possible to call expert witnesses, (students disguised as literary critics), to the stand. I listened intently to groups discussing debate strategies for winning the case. My students not only supported their basic character generalizations with relevant textual evidence, but were also challenged to search the text for evidence that would relate to the guilt or innocence of their clients. They devised questions that fused textual references to pose to each of the witnesses (characters) they would call to the stand. They analyzed the psychological impact on the jury when and if they were to call certain characters to the stand. During the two weeks of preparation, students stayed after school to debate further because they wanted to.

The next day, during the change of classes, I overheard one of my students talking to an underclassman: "Wait until you get to be a senior and you prepare for the Hamlet trials!" She brushed past me in her suit with her briefcase and her Hamlet text marked with neon post-it notes. "Guess what, Ms. Self," she said, I've been waiting for this day since ninth grade." When I evaluated my students' learning progress from this culminating activity and watched their excitement on video tape, I contemplated other areas of the curriculum where I could incorporate the same strategies that would challenge and inspire my students.

And yet, since I have been reshaping this lesson over the past four years— changing the way I focus my students, creating different prewriting, reading, and thinking activities, I have only shared this approach with three other colleagues, and, because of time constraints and scheduling difficulties, I have collaborated with only one of the three. And since my colleague and I have been planning together and reworking the way we present various lessons, she, too, has enjoyed the same benefits I have experienced with my students.

And I continue to rationalize. Have I not shared these techniques because I didn't have the time, or, better yet, didn't make the time? Did I feel I would be intruding on another colleague's planning time? Did I feel that sharing my classroom successes would be perceived as boasting? Surely, I'm not the only teacher to experience this nagging guilt.

Yet what would happen, could happen, if as a group of educators we were to move past the success of an individual idea or private moment in the classroom, to discover as a community of educators the underlying reasons why an idea motivates students and challenges them—if we listened to another educator discussing similar struggles and celebrations, attended conferences where, as colleagues, we debated educational issues, shared results from pilot programs, and then returned to our own school districts to imagine the possibilities? What a difference we could make if we informed, enlightened, encouraged, and revised our thinking regularly? if we felt more compelled to share pieces of ourselves and our classrooms with others? if we published regularly?

The underlying premise of the "Collaborative Teaching: Shared Visions" chapter and of the creation of A Tapestry of Knowledge is the notion that through collaboration, teamwork, and active reflection, entire schools and communities would be strengthened so that every discipline and every grade level would affect the largest number of students dramatically and positively. What parent, what administrator, would not want to see two teachers, twenty teachers so excited about the art of teaching that they question, struggle, and reexamine what they do in the classroom and why? Not until we really listen, coach, and critique one another and our classroom practices will we experience the freedom of shared decision making and realize the significance of being empowered through change.

The teachers featured in "Collaborative Teaching" are consistently making a positive impact on individual schools and on the educational system of Virginia Beach. They reinforce excellence and dramatize the power of shared goals. These educators discuss integration, the success of multidisciplinary projects and the impact these student-centered projects have on academic achievement and community awareness. They offer a reflective glimpse at what they have learned by working closely with colleagues to make an idea become a reality. Another collaborative team uses integration and problem-solving in conjunction with the fourth-grade curriculum. Students investigate the names for the planets in the solar system by reading Greek myths and poetry; they discover the diameter of a new planet by changing fractions to decimal equations and metric measurement; they offer presentations to a panel of experts from NASA. Two high school educators write about the successful implementation of The Firm, a program that individualizes instruction and prepares students to compete successfully in the business community. These educators reveal what can happen to student lives when a program truly reaches beyond classroom walls. The fourth article in this chapter involves two educators willing to risk as they share personal reflections and classroom scenarios of the positive results of looping, a practice which allows single-grade teachers to remain with the same class for a period of two or more years. These teams closely examine how the act of collaborating in various ways leads to a more effective means of assessing the efficacy of teaching practices and the results on student learning.

These teachers remind us all that even though self-renewal demands continual thoughtfulness, part of that thoughtfulness must involve a wide perspective and that any one vision will become skewed if that vision is rooted in only one perspective. The ongoing ruminations of the mind involves examining combined philosophies, various strategies, and positive and negative outcomes of specific programs. To test our reactions and interpretations against those of our colleagues is crucial so that we may reexamine our own. As educators, we have a vision of what we want our students to become. What is our vision of the kind of teachers we want to become—daily?

—LEANNE SELF

Integration Mania:
A Student's Chance to Shine

by Jenny Flannagan and Susan Puckett

Alice: *"Would you tell me, please, which way I ought to go from here?"*

Cheshire Cat: *"That depends a good deal on where you want to get to."*

— Lewis Carroll, Alice's Adventures in Wonderland

Jerry was a gifted child for whom socializing with his friends was more important than academics. He had a trusting smile that helped him charm his way into your heart, but his lack of task commitment could drive the most tenacious teacher to drink. "I'm not good at math" was his constant refrain. "Why are we learning this? This is just another project. You said this year would be different." What would it take to mold Jerry into a productive, eager, gifted student, one who would want to use his talent and abilities to accomplish a goal? The answer was simple: four teachers who worked well as a team, a team with a plan that would simply "knock Jerry's socks off." We had a vision of taking the regular curricula, molding it, working magic with it, and making it become a breathing application of real life. We wanted Jerry and our other students to be proud of the products they would be creating. How would we do this? Our answer: a personal and intellectual immersion in a real-world task, one that incorporated four core disciplines: math, science, history and language arts.

> We had a vision of taking the regular curricula, molding it, working magic with it, and making it become a breathing application of real life.

Our teaching team, a mixture of young and old, experienced and inexperienced, was new to Kemps Landing Magnet School. What did we have in common? A desire to make our various disciplines relevant to our students, to make students realize social studies was connected to language arts, and science and math to humanities because, too often, students see no relevance in what they do. Ernest Boyer, author of *The Basic School*, explains: "I am convinced that the problems of our schools are inextricably tied to this larger problem — the feeling on the part of many of our youth that they are isolated, unconnected to the larger world outside their classrooms" (Boyer 99). They see "little, if any, connection between what they are doing and learning in school and the communities in which they live" (Boyer 99). We wanted to help our students make that connection.

Our project was simple, really. The theme for the nine weeks was "Exploring the Past: Been There, Done That, What's Next?" We wanted a real-life application of the curriculum content and wanted to apply it to something students saw every day: Kemps Landing Magnet School. Our research expedition began in social studies where students explored the history of Kempsville, our community, and our school that only three years before had become a magnet school for gifted children grades six through eight. Our social studies teacher and English teacher began by taking the students on a walking tour of the school. After all, the school dates back to 1942 and has a history. We looked at different types of brickwork on the exterior, speculating when the new addition had been built, where the coal chute had been placed, and whether our two classrooms had been part of the original structure. Then, for the next two weeks, students researched the history of the area, looking at old yearbooks, reading books by local authors, interviewing librarians, and consulting maps of the area from different time periods. Working in groups, students wrote articles about their discoveries and created and published newspapers. Our personal favorite was one about the Turkey Bowl, a dance held in the gymnasium in honor of Thanksgiving which our students found in one of the yearbooks. Once the research was complete, fifty eighth-graders signed up for various tasks.

What did we have in common? A desire to make our various disciplines relevant to our students, to make students realize social studies was connected to language arts, and science and math to humanities.

Students began applying what they learned to a real-life project. We found that Kemps Landing Magnet School did not have a school song, so we needed someone to write music and lyrics. Neither did we have a school seal, so we needed a group to attack that problem. Students wrote brochures for the school that could be distributed to prospective students. We also planned a scrapbook to be kept on permanent display in the office for potential students to enjoy. The scrapbook contained poetry, short stories, illustrations, political cartoons, and essays, each a result of research the students conducted. Students designed time lines, some of which depicted the history they learned, and one which traced the history of the gifted program in Virginia Beach. These would be displayed in the main hallway. Our students decided that as a finale we really needed an evening to discuss and celebrate what we had accomplished. The play, which we teachers originally envisioned as a skit, turned into a mammoth affair with six or seven acts encompassing the history students discovered through their research. The play began with the arrival of Captain John Smith and Captain Newport at the mouth of the Chesapeake Bay in Virginia Beach, moved to the dunking of Grace Sherwood, witch of Pungo, and on to the battle of Kempsville. A talented student director proved to be a masterful organizer and encouraged even the most recalcitrant students to listen and obey. This hour event, complete with student emcees and speakers, taught and entertained an audience full of excited parents. Teachers and students performed the song, "Here We Are," as a way to conclude the hour performance.

Finding an interdisciplinary connection with math and science was easy, but as our students would remind us, the integration of math and science with humanities was not. Yet, the answer was all around us. As we explained to our students, though they had learned a great deal about the school's history, they needed a physical image to communicate those facts. Without a concrete representation, the essence of the project would be lost. With this added image, student stories would take on an added dimension. Students began a three-dimensional model of the school to be displayed with the scrapbook. It revealed to visitors the floor plan and building to scale, illustrating not only the present-day building but the historical building as well. Again the students, and most especially Jerry, reminded us that we had to make the integration connection real: "How is building a model science?" "We have to use dimensional analysis in order to convert these units. Remember we learned this at the beginning of the year!" Alan answered. The answer to the question was provided not by teachers but by students themselves. We procured the original blueprints to allow students to create the walls and the outside structure out of foam board. One of the major problems that the students encountered was how to design the structure. Certainly, they could do the math and convert units from the English system to the metric system, but how did that relate to the larger picture of creating this model? Luckily we were able to enlist the help of a parent/architect who came in and instructed the students on cutting techniques and the process of fitting the model parts together.

> The final design called for a removal of the roof to reveal classrooms and halls below. Suddenly, students exclaimed, "Science is not what I expected!"

The final design called for a removal of the roof to reveal classrooms and halls below. Suddenly, students exclaimed, "Science is not what I expected!" After creating the model, students voiced some concerns about how confusing our school really was! The school had undergone alterations over the years and finding one's way around could be tricky to a visitor. Again our students' voices were nagging us to solve another problem: how could we develop a directional system for the school? Soon, students began work on signposts which would be suspended from the ceiling to guide visitors to the main office, to guidance, to the gym, and to other essential classrooms. Using the map-making skills they learned in science, students created a map of the existing floor plan and labeled the strategic places where the directional sign posts would be placed. This map also included accurate mathematical measurements in order to calculate distances from signpost to signpost. Made from carpet tubes and painted bright colors, the signposts were a first for our school which, until this project, had no directional elements.

Was the project successful? Yes, highly so, we all thought. Our students delved into the project with far more enthusiasm than ever before. They took complete ownership, and leaders surfaced quickly. Woe to any student whose work was not up to par, for classmates either forced him to redo it or took it upon themselves to complete the work. The scrapbook became a visual work of art and included not only the literature and pictures about the past, but letters and pictures from our principal, assistant principal, and team teachers. The skit — now a play — involved props, costumes, spotlights, strobe lights, and curtain closings. Our project, "*Celebrating Kemps Landing Magnet School: Past and Future*," had its own letterhead.

> Was the project successful? Yes, highly so, we all thought. Our students delved into the project with far more enthusiasm than ever before.

Students spent two teacher in-service days in school, either practicing the play or the song or working on the 3-D model. Students were sent to the computer lab for a ninety-minute block of time to compose and create invitations to the play for their parents as well as for the principal, assistant principal, and teachers.

Would we do this again? Certainly! Students took a passionate ownership of this project, knowing their work would be preserved and used. This was no essay that went into a portfolio never again to see the light of day. Everything our students created was displayed, copied, and distributed. This real-life project was an investment and created a tremendous sense of pride for our team, the "Trailblazers." Most importantly, this project solidified our belief as teachers that a multidisciplinary curriculum will meet and even surpass curriculum objectives in gifted and regular classrooms. Many teachers resist using integration because they are afraid they will lose time or not cover all of their material. However, we found that integration not only satisfied curriculum requirements, but dramatically enhanced them.

For instance, in English, students wrote in a variety of modes, read articles, stories, and nonfiction as they conducted research. Students scrutinized sentences for grammatical structure and wrote and delivered speeches. In science, students applied dimensional analysis as they converted English units into metric units, created a three-dimensional model to scale, and applied what they learned about map-making skills to their product in math. As Joseph Renzulli, noted leader in gifted education points out, teachers need to "allow their students to explore authentic knowledge as first-hand inquirers" (58).

As students pointed out, a driving force in the project was their active collaboration with one another. Each student was part of a group and assigned to a specific task whether it was to build the classrooms for the three-dimensional model, research the jail, or organize the scrapbook. This cooperative situation enhanced teamwork, critical thinking skills, and creativity. It facilitated both the depth and the breadth of student learning. This "careful integration of process and content promotes creation of true learning community" (Secules 58). Learning to collaborate was definitely one of our students' greatest achievements.

> **Would we do this again? Certainly! Students took a passionate ownership of this project, knowing their work would be preserved and used. This was no essay that went into a portfolio never again to see the light of day.**

As teachers, one of our greatest achievements was leaving the traditional classroom behind, giving up that comfortable teacher-centered environment for a fluid, dynamic environment where our students took the lead. We found that integration requires a total commitment to taking risks and a reliance on one's colleagues for encouragement and support. Luckily, working as a team allowed us to make the transition fairly easily.

One aspect we enjoyed most about this project was the complete transformation in classroom environment, a classroom environment Krystal Goree highly advocates:

> Normally, we think of the ideal learner as one who comes to class everyday, sits quietly at his or her desk without asking too many questions, turns in his or her work in a neat and timely fashion, makes good grades, and causes few problems for the teacher. This type of student is considered by many to be a joy to teach and may be one of the most creative minds in the group, but the class-

room environment may not allow the child to explore creatively as well as intellectually. Furthermore, if we are truly trying to teach our students to become communicators and problem solvers with effective interpersonal skills, the above mentioned classroom setting may not be the one that is conducive to students' needs (Goree 36).

Jerry obviously responded well to the loosely structured classroom environment that empowered students to take charge of their own learning. He saw the relevance of what he was learning and selected his own mode of expression. Curriculum was no longer just math, science, English, and social studies to Jerry, but an integrated entity that worked toward a common goal. For Jerry, his triumph over the ever poignant refrain, "But that's just another project," was the creation of *The Spirit of the Phoenix."* His story was the hit of the evening production as Jerry recounted a fantasy whose protagonist was our principal, Dr. Jessee, as she became Hazel, Defender of the Earth. Jerry's wry humor, his eye for detail, and his quick wit brought down the house.

> As teachers, one of our greatest achievements was leaving the traditional classroom behind, giving up that comfortable teacher-centered environment for a fluid, dynamic environment where our students took the lead.

What Jerry and our other students learned was what Alice learned in Wonderland: One learns by doing, by discovering. Our students can now answer Alice's question, "Would you tell me, please, which way I ought to go from here?" because they've experienced getting there for themselves.

Work Cited

Boyer, E.L. "Service: Linking School to Life." In *Combining Service and Learning*. Ed. J.C. Kendall & Associates. 1978: 99.

Boyer, E.L. *The Basic School*. New Jersey: The Carnegie Foundation for the Advancement of Teaching, 1995.

Goree, Krystal. "Creativity in the Classroom...Do We Really Want It?" *Gifted Child Today* July/August 1996: 36-37.

Renzulli, Joseph. "The Multiple Menu Model: A Successful Marriage for Integrating Content and Process." *NASSP Bulletin* March (1997): 51-58.

Secules, Teresa, et. al. "Creating Schools for Thought." *Educational Leadership* March (1997): 56-60.

About Jenny Flannagan

"In my classroom I am a guide and a facilitator of knowledge, traveling on a fantastic journey along with my students in the great expedition of exploring the earth. Throughout the year, I challenge my students to take on different scientific roles and become geologists, paleontologists, astronomers, oceanographers, and meteorologists in order to unlock the secrets and mysteries of the earth. As their personal guide, I try to expose them to the power, beauty, and wonders our planet holds for those who choose to explore her many layers. I strive to instill in my students the insight to recognize the impact they have, not only on the earth, but on our school and classroom. Our journey together opens new horizons for not only me as their facilitator, but for them as learners."

Jenny Sue Flannagan received her B.A. in Biology from Longwood College and is presently pursuing her M.A. in Curriculum and Instruction from the University of Virginia. She has been teaching in the Virginia Beach Public Schools since 1992. In her first year teaching, Jenny was recognized nationally and named the 1993 recipient of the Sally Mae First Year Teacher Award. Ms. Flannagan is consistently active as chairman and team leader of various committees and planning councils. A frequent presenter on the local and state level, Ms. Flannagan received third place in Cox Cable's Educator of the Year program, and received Honorable Mention in the Rufus W. Beamer Excellence Awards Program for "Girls and the Elizabeth River." This same project earned her a Technical Career Educational Grant. An active advocate for gifted education, Ms. Flannagan teaches summer magnet programs in elementary marine biology as well as advanced sixth- and seventh-grade Earth Science at Kemps Landing Magnet School in Virginia Beach.

About Susan Puckett

"After thirty years of being in the classroom, one thing I am convinced of is that students and teachers need not exist on opposite sides of the desk. I enjoy watching my students use their imaginations, indulge their dreams, and challenge themselves as they explore the heights and depths of their own knowledge as well as mine. I try to provide my students with compassion and a belief in their uniqueness."

Having received her B.A. and M.A. from State University of New York, Susan Puckett has been teaching in the classroom for thirty years. Her teaching experiences range from teaching grades five through twelve, from Gifted Resource to Assistant Professor of Education. Ms. Puckett has consistently remained active in numerous planning councils, and advisory boards and is currently the co-coordinator supervising the conceptual framework for the new gifted elementary school. An advocate for gifted education, Susan has co-authored a course on ethical and moral reasoning entitled "Think Tank for Superthinkers" which is now part of the gifted academy.

She has been published in *The English Journal, Gifted Child Today, The Virginia English Bulletin,* and *The Writing Project Magazine.* A frequent presenter on the local, state, and national levels, Susan Puckett has received an Excellence in Education Award for A Habitat Housewarming: A community Service Project for Special Education and The First Educator's Award for Excellence in Holocaust Education. In 1987, she was named Cox High School Teacher of the Year and also received the Virginia Association of Teachers of English Service Award in 1988. Currently, Ms. Puckett teaches sixth and eighth grades at Kemps Landing Magnet School in Virginia Beach.

Integrating the Fourth-Grade Curriculum with Problem-Based Learning

by Bobbye Bartels, Ph.D. and Michele Johnson-Deneau

One parent discusses the differences problem-based learning made in her daughter's life saying, "Our daughter hated school and getting her out the door most mornings was an ordeal for all concerned. She had been tested for learning disabilities but none were found. She was simply not being reached by her teachers and the school curriculum. Now she is excited about school and can't wait to leave each morning. The best thing is her big change in attitude. She has a positive outlook on her future and increased self-esteem." Another parent comments, "My son has been stimulated to learn and perform in an exemplary manner. Prior to coming into this class, he did not want to do homework or study. Now he comes straight home to do his homework, and he also studies before quizzes and tests. Wow! Problem-based learning. What a program!"

> They were highly motivated to learn new material, such as changing fractions to decimals, decimal equations, and metric measurement.

Despite the current emphasis on interdisciplinary teaching, it can still be difficult to integrate disciplines, especially at the elementary level. Through participation in a NASA-Langley Research Center Teacher Enhancement Institute, I learned about problem-based learning (PBL), a highly effective inquiry-rich method of instruction. The following presents my successful experience implementing problem-based learning in a fourth-grade, non-gifted class.

Problem-Based Learning

Originally, problem-based learning was developed for use in medical schools and, subsequently, has been applied successfully in social science classes (Aspy, Aspy, and Quinby 1993) and in gifted education. Proponents of problem-based learning, however, now hope to see it used in elementary, middle, and high schools and in a variety of subjects.

In a problem-based learning lesson, students are presented a motivating, global problem, a problem for which the solution requires more than students' prerequisite knowledge (Stepien and Gallagher, 1993). For example, some students may investigate problems such as how an airplane flies, the cost effectiveness of repairing a satellite, or sending a hot air balloon to the moon instead of a space shuttle. In order to obtain information that students need to solve the problem, they research aspects of the question based on information given within the problem.

> One student wrote, "I never even thought about flying before. Now I want to be an astronaut. I know I have to be really good in math and science."

Once the teacher presents the problem to the class, students discuss possible solutions through the use of a KWL chart; for example, they ask questions such as, what do we **know** already, what do we **want** to know, and what have we **learned**? Students use resources such as the library, the Internet, local public officials, engineers, scientists, and community businesses. As they revisit the problem, students experiment, work in cooperative groups, pose questions, and suggest possible solutions. Then they share research information with the class. At the end of the problem-based learning unit (PBL), the students present a project or a report on their findings to the class.

Implementation of Problem-Based Learning

One of the PBL problems I used in my fourth-grade class was a unit on the planets, which covered a nine-week grading period. Every morning, the class devoted two and one-half hours to the PBL unit. Every day the students revisited the KWL chart and modified it to reflect what they had learned. Sometimes the class revisited the KWL chart at the end of each day's research as well. A major advantage of PBL units is that they offer a great deal of flexibility with scheduling. Other configurations include meeting once a week for one to two hours, every day for two to three weeks, or after school with science clubs.

The problem that prompted the planet unit and that my class worked on for nine weeks was the following: "NASA's Hubble telescope has discovered a new planet beyond Pluto. It is the same distance beyond Pluto as the distance between Venus and Mars. It has the same number of satellites as Neptune and one-half the orbital velocity of Pluto. A year is three times that of the Uranian year and a day is four times a Saturnian day. The diameter of the planet is the same as that of Mercury and its earth-mass is ten times that of Mars. Its atmosphere is similar to that of Jupiter. Describe this planet in detail, illustrate the planet, and tell whether NASA can expect to find life there as we know it on Earth." Although the problem is very mathematical, the unit also addressed science and language arts curricular objectives.

Mathematics

The students found the problem intriguing, and because they needed to know mathematics to describe the new planet, they "bought into the problem." They were highly motivated to learn new material, such as changing fractions to decimals, decimal equations, and metric measurement. As an added benefit, the students grasped new concepts earlier in the year than they ordinarily would have simply by using the sequential movement of the traditional curriculum. Most importantly, they learned the new material well. From my observations, my students in the PBL class scored 42 percent higher than a similar, but non-PBL, fourth-grade class in the same school on the Math subtest of the Iowa Test of Basic Skills.

Science

Before students could describe the new planet, they needed to know information about the planets in the solar system, including earth. The general and specific concepts learned in the unit included rotation, evolution, measurement of time and seasons, and relationship of sun and planets in the solar system. Students also learned about the layers of the earth, causes of earthquakes and volcanic eruptions, weather, gravity, erosion, natural resources, and ecology.

Using the electronic sources in the library, students, working collaboratively, discovered additional information regarding the planets. They pursued hands-on activities that demonstrated the concepts of rotation and revolution, volcanoes, earthquakes, erosion, and gravity. In addition, a scientist from NASA helped students investigate gravity and weightlessness. Because the air and atmosphere had been studied in a previous unit, students used information they already knew in describing the new planet. Then they constructed models of the layers of the earth, the earth's core, and diagramed the solar system drawing comparisons among planet sizes.

> Perhaps the most exciting aspect of the method is that the teacher's role changes from being the definitive source of knowledge to that of a facilitator, guiding students toward constructing their own knowledge.

Language Arts

To incorporate language arts, students investigated the names of the planets in the solar system by reading Greek myths and poetry. A creative writing activity was planned around constellations. Students kept journals and wrote comparison and contrast paragraphs about the planets, which reinforced skills of correct spelling, grammar, punctuation, capitalization, and handwriting. Students also wrote business letters to NASA scientists explaining how much they had learned through problem-based learning. One student wrote, "I never even thought about flying before. Now I want to be an astronaut. I know I have to be really good in math and science."

For the culminating activity in language arts, the groups made presentations to their peers. A panel of experts including school administrators, school district curriculum specialists, NASA employees, college professors, the librarian, and other teachers evaluated the presentations using student-determined criteria that were based on observations and critiques of the speakers they heard during the unit. When presenting their information, many students used multimedia. They communicated their knowledge accurately and effectively to their classmates and the experts so that all research findings were clear. Thus, these presentations increased students' critical thinking, communication, and public speaking skills. In addition, the composite results from the Iowa Test of Basic Skills revealed a dramatic increase from 48 percent to 72 percent when compared with the previous year. This analysis also represented an 11 percent increase over a similar fourth-grade class using a more traditional teaching approach and curriculum.

> Virtually all students participated. There was an intellectual vitality about the classroom environment that I did not expect.

The Teacher's Role

Perhaps the most exciting aspect of the method is that the teacher's role changes from being the definitive source of knowledge to that of a facilitator, guiding students toward constructing their own knowledge. As facilitator, the teacher develops the problems that guide the unit, designs or identifies assignments that help the students get the information they need to solve their problems, conducts research to find appropriate activities that support the unit, organizes and sets up activities and speakers, keeps supplies available for team projects and activities, continually monitors students as they conduct their research, and reflects daily and weekly on the students' progress in moving toward solutions to the assigned problem.

Results of Implementation

Students realized many gains by using PBL units in the classroom. Not only were there increases in student learning, but there were fewer classroom management problems. However, the changes in student learning attested to by the significantly higher quantity and quality of the content covered during the unit were most astounding. Because students needed to understand complex operations, they learned higher level mathematics. They were motivated to learn because the problem was important and because they needed the content to solve the problem.

Because problem-based learning encourages interdisciplinary teaching, planning became easier because connections could be made among various disciplines, and the identified problem gave each discipline a purpose. Almost every discipline was covered in the unit, and the mandated curriculum not covered could be taught during the afternoon; therefore, not only did I have sufficient time to cover all objectives, but I could oftentimes surpass those objectives with my students.

For all students, and especially those identified as being at-risk, the quality of work improved as well and was reflected in an increased ability to think critically and creatively. When working in the problem-based learning unit, at-risk students were indistinguishable from the other students in the classroom. This is particularly noteworthy in this fourth-grade class because so many of my students were identified as being at risk. One at-risk student was the first to invent a correct algorithm for adding like fractions and was able to explain it to other students. Another student developed an understanding of algebra by using variables to explain relationships in mathematics.

Speakers who made presentations to the class were amazed at the quantity and quality of the questions the students posed. The speakers asked me if the class was a "gifted class" and were very surprised when they found otherwise. One Old Dominion University professor, a resource for information on rocks and minerals, wrote a letter to the school principal stating, "The students' questions were thoughtful and incisive. These students asked questions about how rocks originate, about when the first minerals and rocks were 'discovered,' and whether the physical properties of minerals could change. Virtually all students participated. There was an intellectual vitality about the classroom environment that I did not expect."

> **All students experienced an increase in self-esteem because all students participated in classroom activities, demonstrating their strengths and improving their weaknesses through group instruction.**

Another positive outcome of this unit involved attendance. Compared with previous years, daily attendance was much higher because students took ownership and did not want to miss class. Student motivation was so high that discipline referrals to the main office decreased significantly. One Tourettes Syndrome child's tics decreased during problem-based learning because of the freedom of movement, cooperative learning strategies, and stimulating curriculum. All students experienced an increase in self-esteem because all students participated in classroom activities, demonstrating their strengths and improving their weaknesses through group instruction.

Parental support also increased. When I surveyed parents through a final evaluation, I received a phenomenal 100 percent response to the survey, with all positive responses. Furthermore, 75 percent of the parents participated in classroom activities during the year, compared with only 10 percent the previous year. Parents caught the PBL excitement from their children.

One teacher who participated in the project commented,

> I have never worked so hard yet felt so rewarded by the level of learning that took place in my classroom. It was not easy to become a coach and mentor after being 'the sage on the stage' for so many years. Personally I found it difficult to change teaching styles after so many years because I was too comfortable. I knew what to expect from day to day. I could copy lesson plans from year to year with minor modifications. So initially, PBL was difficult.

Because the program is student-driven, teachers need to be ready to travel with students, deciding the turns along the way. Student discovery requires teachers to be fearless and comfortable saying, "I don't know. Let's find out!" For many teachers, during the first year of teaching when you're fresh out of college, the classroom comes alive. Yet, as the years pass, many teachers find a comfort zone. Through the use of problem-solving units, teachers and students must consistently step out of that comfort zone. Learning and teaching then stays fresh, exciting, and alive.

As revealed through this fourth-grade classroom, problem-based learning can be an effective method for integrating curricula and can be implemented not only in middle school and high school, but in elementary school. Although the development of the PBL unit was time consuming, the learning experience was rewarding and positive for the students and the teacher. If we, as teachers, are to motivate and teach by example, excitement for education must be a part of our everyday teaching. Excitement is infectious. Enthusiasm is contagious. How can a teacher not be excited about teaching when students are learning so much, so well, and when they love coming to school?

References

Aspy, D., C. Aspy, and P. Quinby. "What Doctors Can Teach Teachers about Problem-Based Learning." *Educational Leadership* 50 (1993): 22-24.

Stepien, William, and Shelagh Gallagher. "Problem-Based Learning: As Authentic as It Gets." *Educational Leadership* 50: 25-28.

About Bobbye Bartels, Ph.D.

"To do what you do and feel that it matters—how can anything be more fun?"

— KATHERINE GRAHAM

Bobbye Hoffman Bartels is a former middle school mathematics teacher who decided to pursue a Ph.D. and now teaches mathematics education courses at Christopher Newport University. She worked as a mathematics consultant to middle schools in Illinois, taught summer gifted classes, and for two years was the lead teacher for the Teacher Enhancement Institute at NASA Langley Research Center where she became interested in problem-based learning. Her research interests encompass various strategies dealing with effective mathematics teaching.

About Michele Johnson-Deneau

"Teaching and learning are reciprocal processes which begin at birth and don't end until death. My goal is to teach my students life-long learning skills, as well as the three "R's," while continuing my own education, usually through them."

Michele Johnson-Deneau received her B.S. in Elementary Education from George Mason University and currently teaches fourth grade at White Oaks Elementary School in Virginia Beach. Her affiliations include NEA, ASCD, NCTM, NSTA, and the Virginia State Reading Association. A frequent presenter, Michele Deneau has shared her expertise regarding innovative teaching techniques at the Virginia State Reading Conference, the Virginia Education Association Instructional Conference, and has published a paper entitled, "Teaching the Gifted Student" at Norfolk State University in Norfolk, Virginia. She has been named to the Educational Product Advisory Board for NASA and the Hampton Roads Institute for the Advancement of Teaching. She also serves as part of the clinical faculty at Norfolk State University. In 1996, Michele was named runner-up in the A. Scott Crossfield Aerospace Education Teacher of the Year competition and was also selected as one of five finalists for the Virginia Beach Citywide Teacher of the Year. Most recently, Michele was selected as the Tidewater Science Teacher of the Year in 1997 and named 1998 YWCA's Outstanding Woman in the field of education.

More than Pink Crayons: Two Educators Reveal the Offerings of The Firm

by Nancy Dowding and Kathleen Malone

Shantele was a beautiful, energetic, intelligent five-year-old ready to enter kindergarten. Being a proud parent, her mother knew Shantele would be at the top of her kindergarten class because she was so advanced in her reading and writing skills. On the first day of school, Mom dressed Shantele in her cutest outfit, fixed her hair with matching ribbons, and took her to meet her kindergarten teacher, Mrs. Baker.

When they arrived, Mrs. Baker welcomed Shantele and her mom and asked Mom to sit by the door while she showed Shantele her classroom. "Shantele," Mrs. Baker explained, "it is so much fun to come to school. You will learn how to do so many new things each day. Shantele is such a beautiful name. Would you please pick your favorite color crayon from this new box and write your name on this paper for me?" asked Ms. Baker.

Mom sat in the corner and beamed. Her daughter could not only write her own name but could also write the names of all family members. Her mother knew Shantele would pass the "test" with flying colors and really impress her teacher. Shantele looked at the crayons, then at the paper, and then at her teacher. Her teacher encouragingly repeated, "Shantele, would you please pick

> Her mother was perplexed because she knew Shantele could write her name. Why was she trying to hide her knowledge from her teacher?

your favorite crayon and write your name on this piece of paper for me?" Again, Shantele stared at her teacher but did not move. Her mother could say nothing. Not wanting Shantele to be nervous about coming to school, Mrs. Baker put her arm around Shantele and said, "That is all right, Shantele. You will learn to write your name soon. I'll see you in two days when class begins. Thanks for coming to meet me and see our room."

Her mother was perplexed because she knew Shantele could write her name. Why was she trying to hide her knowledge from her teacher? On the drive home, Mother calmly asked, "Shantele, sweetheart, why didn't you write your name when your teacher asked you?" Almost in tears, Shantele looked into her mother's eyes and exclaimed, "Mom, she didn't have a pink crayon!"

Though an amusing anecdote, Shantele's story may be more true than many realize, especially for educators. What happens to our students when we limit their choices? How often has the traditional education system hindered student learning because the system did not provide that "pink crayon," did not meet individual needs? What changes must be made to empower students to make the necessary social and academic transitions from elementary, to middle, to high school? How can we, as educators, encourage students like Shantele to take responsibility for their own learning and their lives so that as students grow and mature, they acquire the necessary competencies to insure academic success?

One change that is highly successful on the high school level is the brain-child of Renee Pay, a teacher of twenty-six years in the Jordan School District of Sandy, Utah. She created The Firm, an Advanced Computer Applica-tions/Management Training Program. The underlying philosophy of this program is the expectation that all students will be successful no matter what their educa-tional record or what their personal challenges may be. Developing this program, Pay relied on the expertise of local businesses to determine the necessary skills and qualities employees would require for an employee to be successful in the corporate world. She discovered that beginning employees must possess essential skills, among them time management, punctuality, teamwork, organizational skills, goal setting, problem-solving, and task prioritizing. In addition, "The Commission on Skills of the American Workforce" (1990), a commission concerned with preparing today's youth to enter the job market, found that more than 80 percent of employers dis-covered workers needed to possess a good work ethic and appropriate social behav-ior. Since The Firm has been an integral part of Virginia Beach City Public Schools' business training program, local Virginia Beach and Norfolk businesses have been extremely pleased, not only with the expertise of students completing the program, but with their tremendous work ethic as well.

One Norfolk employer, JoAnn J. Frazier of London & Norfolk, Ltd., who is reaping the benefits of working with students in the program, says, "The Firm pro-gram has afforded us the opportunity to take advantage of the resources available through the educational system. The Firm program matches the student's unique talents and skills to the business environment."

Thus, The Firm program is a success support system where learning is per-sonalized so that a student competes only with himself/herself. The situation for Tracey is a good illustration of personalizing curriculum. With only one semester of keyboarding, she entered the program and through her hard work and dedication will complete the program with certificates in communications and data processing: "I am completing the program with more than enough knowledge to take on an office career and participate fully and effectively," Tracey said. "I feel I have learned two years of computer classes in one year. I enjoyed being given the responsibility of selecting my own course of study and the opportunity to set goals and achieve them at my own pace with guidance from my instructor/CEO."

Kristi, on the other hand, entered The Firm with knowledge and skills in both keyboarding and computer information systems. She remarks,

> The Firm is the best class to take during your senior year; it brushes you up for the future and paints your way to the world. It teaches you things that you will have to know later in life like management skills, strong presentation skills, deadlines and how to overcome the battle of meeting them, and most importantly, motivational skills—how to be successful and happy at the same time. My computer skills were enhanced and broadened. I was in charge of the guidance scholarship booklet, which gave me a sense of ownership and responsibility in getting a job completed. The course is unique and interesting, and I would definitely take it all over again!

The underlying philosophy of this program is the expectation that all students will be successful no matter what their educational record or what their personal challenges may be.

Students set their own pace in The Firm. They do not wait to learn. Classes are heterogeneous with students of varying ability levels and physical competencies. In The Firm all students can be successful and achieve. Here, they all find their favorite color crayon!

Students' participation in The Firm requires a paradigm shift for both teachers and students. Because students are "employees" in a professional "company," they have a choice in what they learn, thereby giving them total responsibility and accountability for their learning. According to Dobyns and Crawford, authors of *Quality or Else*, this program helps top management ask itself the right quality questions: Are its leaders really focusing on quality? Are they really understanding quality? Are they really managing in a quality way? Are they really getting the best from their people? Are they really finding out what barriers there are to people being able to do a good job? (178). Teachers are "directors of learning," helping every "employee" reach success. In contrast to "the coercive care of boss management," persuasion and problem solving are central to the philosophy of lead-management, or teacher as "director of learning" (Glasser, *The Quality School*, 31). Employees contract to receive training in their chosen area of interest by completing modules of learning offered in five areas of competencies (Appendix I).

This contract approach helps students take active ownership. The whole point is to help students move from the "mindset that school is covering ground to the new mindset of quality schoolwork," and that "the competition is with oneself as each student works to improve what he or she does" (Glasser, *The Quality School Teacher*, 79). A major part of the program is that students receive more than 200 hours of hands-on computer training using authentic business hardware and software. Students hold management positions in The Firm, learning management concepts as they use them. Each company writes its own textbook after research of current journals and periodicals. In addition, each employee submits a goal contract each week that lists modules/goals they hope to achieve, and that organizational plan commits them to being accountable for their own learning. Thus, teachers meet students at their levels of competency and help them achieve as much as possible in all five areas of study.

In the process, students learn principles of time management, organization, prioritization, and goal setting. They learn to use their company time effectively each day so that they can complete their weekly goal contracts. Total emphasis is placed on "teaching students how they can use information, like the parts of a cell, in their lives either now or later" (66). Individual planners and company calendars are kept by each employee so he/she knows when company meetings will be held and how much work he/she can expect to accomplish each day. In addition, students learn management principles taught in concept units; however, unless they actually apply the knowledge learned, chances are they will retain little. Therefore, each week one employee is the office manager, responsible for maintaining company functions effectively. Another position is testing manager. For that week, the student schedules test times and administers, times, corrects, and verifies tests. Other management positions include vice president of resources, production manager, and administrative assistant. All management positions help students learn how to supervise a team, how to handle pressure and responsibilities, how to delegate, and how to meet deadlines. Because The Firm simulates the business world, it instills in students the confidence necessary to succeed in the real corporate world. As one student, Pamela, states:

> The Firm is very different from all the other classes I have
> taken here at Green Run. It has taught me responsibility, how to

In The Firm all students can be successful and achieve. Here, they all can find their favorite color crayon!

manage my time wisely, and how to sharpen my communication and business skills. Since the "CEO" was not giving a day-to-day outline of what exactly to do each day, I had to learn how to prioritize my assignments and decide what I wanted to work on for that week. I was so used to procrastinating, but since the teacher left us with the responsibility of getting the work done on our own and working at our own pace, I had to learn how to be organized and responsible. If I did not, then I would be the one suffering with a bad grade. So, we had no choice but to work hard to get the work done. This is the first class that I have taken that I could apply 100 percent to work. Everything I worked on in The Firm, I applied at a real job, whether it was telephone techniques, machine transcription, or filing. The Firm really helped me to secure the job that I have now.

(Appendices II & III for letters received from former students).

Even though individualizing instruction and simulating the business world requires an immense amount of effort and commitment, teaching is a million times more rewarding. The classroom teacher must create the individual learning modules that match student competencies, introduce the material creatively, and teach organizational skills to maintain the students' continuous learning process. As educators, we must validate learning for each student. We must empower students rather than just disseminate information to them. William Glasser, author of *Control Theory in the Classroom*, explains his educational theory:

> The control theory explanation of behavior is that we always choose to do what is most satisfying to us at the time. If what we choose is consistently satisfying, we will choose it with less and less deliberation, but even if it is as quick as a flash, it is an action, not an automatic reaction. With this knowledge we should be able to restructure our classes so that many more students will choose to work and learn because they find it satisfying to do so (19).

We must never forget about students like Shantele who, in elementary school, became apprehensive about writing her name with the wrong color crayon even though she knew how. Giving Shantele that pink crayon and meeting her individual needs as a student is analogous to the underlying premise of The Firm—that once students become empowered and excited about learning—that once they realize the benefits of acquiring the wealth of marketable skills which will change their lives, they will all feel like winners. The Firm program truly "reaches beyond classroom walls."

Appendix I

MAJOR CAREER OPPORTUNITIES AND AREAS OF STUDY
AVAILABLE IN THE FIRM

Word Processing Specialists	Communication Specialists	Data Processing Specialists	Management	Accounting Specialists
❑ Basic and Advanced WordPerfect	❑ Basic and Advanced WordPerfect Applications	❑ Basic WordPerfect Applications	❑ Basic WordPerfect Applications	❑ Basic WordPerfect Applications
❑ Desktop Publishing with WordPerfect	❑ Desktop Publishing with WordPerfect	❑ Basic and Advanced Spreadsheet Applications with Quattro Pro	❑ Basic Spreadsheet Applications with Quattro Pro	❑ Basic and Advanced Spreadsheet Applications with Quattro Pro
❑ Basic Spreadsheet Applications with Quattro Pro	❑ Basic and Advanced Applications with WordPerfect Presentations	❑ Graphing Data	❑ Basic Applications with dBASE IV	❑ Basic Applications with WordPerfect Presentations
❑ Transcription	❑ Scanner Operations	❑ Alphabetic Filing	❑ Basic Applications with WordPerfect Presentations	❑ Business Ethics
❑ Alphabetic Filing	❑ Alphabetic Filing	❑ 10-key Calculator		❑ Advanced Accounting Concepts, Techniques, and Procedures
❑ 10-key calculator	❑ 10-key Calculator	❑ Basic and Advanced Applications with dBASE IV	❑ Alphabetic Filing	
❑ Basic data base Applications with dBASE IV	❑ Time Management and Organizational Skills	❑ Time Management and Organizational Skills	❑ 10-key Calculator	❑ Payroll
❑ Basic Applications with WordPerfect Presentations	❑ Psychology of Achievement	❑ Psychology of Achievement	❑ Dictation	❑ Bank Reconciliation
❑ Time Management and Organizational Skills	❑ Telephone Techniques	❑ Telephone Techniques	❑ Supervisor, Leadership Styles	❑ Time Management and Organizational Skills
❑ Psychology of Achievement	❑ Professional Business Dress	❑ Professional Business Dress	❑ Group Dynamics	❑ Psychology of Achievement
❑ Telephone Techniques	❑ Oral and Written Presentation Skills	❑ Oral and Written Presentation Skills	❑ Time Management and Organizational Skills	❑ Telephone Techniques
❑ Professional Business Dress			❑ Psychology of Achievement	❑ Professional Business Dress
❑ Oral and Written Presentation Skills			❑ Telephone Techniques	❑ Oral and Written Presentation Skills
			❑ Professional Business Dress	
			❑ Oral and Written Presentation Skills	

Appendix II

June 11, 1997

Mrs. Kathleen Malone
Ocean Lakes High School
885 Schumann Drive
Virginia Beach, VA 23454

Dear Mrs. Malone:

The Business Supervision and Management (The Firm) program is an amazing course. It is a remarkable experience to get into this class. The opportunities the course offers you as a student are how to run an office, computer training in various programs from WordPerfect for DOS/Windows, PageMaker, WordPerfect Presentations, Master Clips, or Microsoft Publisher, and personal commitments to get your job done.

For me, this program has made me manage my time. Datelines, projects, and presentations also help me stay organized and on time. I found myself working really hard to meet a dateline. A lot of times I thought that I wouldn't be able to finish or make the grade, but in the end I always did. I adjusted to a place (the office) that I had never known anything about. No classes I ever took were like The Firm. During the class I was required to write goals, long-term and short-term, every week and keep together all my grades and projects. I had my own desk and THAT provided privacy and concentration. We weren't just students, but employees. I worked at MY own pace instead of having homework assignments like in normal classes. The time just flew by each day.

Not only did The Firm teach me computer skills, but also team work by working in small groups to carry out tasks of different projects together, and it taught me to be more confident in my personal presentations and oral speeches. You, my CEO, were my strongest motivator throughout the year. You helped teach us commitment to each other and positive self-esteem; these were our greatest lessons in this class.

This program was fun and exciting. It was the best learning experience I could ever have had. I really don't think I will forget The Firm or my teacher. This is where it all started.

Sincerely,

Stacey L. Zielinski

Appendix III

June 11, 1997

Mrs. Kathleen Malone, CEO
Ocean Lakes High School
885 Schumann Drive
Virginia Beach, VA 23454

Dear Mrs. Kathleen Malone, CEO:
Wow! What an exciting year I had in this business. I really enjoyed it very much. I have learned a lot of things this year. I have learned to become responsible and take care of my own actions. I am so glad that I was able to have you as a teacher and to have the opportunity to take this class.

The Firm has shown me lots of things this year for my co-workers and even for myself. I have learned to manage my time throughout the year. I have learned to set goals every week for myself. Setting goals is very meaningful throughout life. It makes you productive and meets your deadlines. I have learned so much this year even though I missed two months of school. During those months of school, I was working two jobs and not going to school. During that time, I realized that I was making the worst mistake of my life. I knew that I had to come back to school and finish my education. I didn't work hard for thirteen years so that I could throw it down the drain. I was really grateful that my school, classes, teachers, friends, and, most importantly, my family accepted me back into their lives.

The Firm has given me the opportunity to start over and do the best that I can. I have been grateful for everything that I have learned this year. This program was something that I really enjoyed doing in high school. I would put things aside till the last minute, but I would get it done. Mrs. Malone, I just want to thank you for all of your help and motivation. You have been a great teacher to me this year and the last three years that I have known you. Thank you again. I hope to see you later in my future.

Sincerely,

Amy Munet

References

Anderson-Yates, Marcia A. "WorkPlace Readiness Skills." Ed. Heidi R. Perreault, *Classroom Strategies: The Methodology of Business Education.* 34 (1996): 136-147.

Pay, Rene. "Catching the Vision: An Effective Way to Manage Student Learning that Works." Company Training. Visual presentation. Green Run High School, Virginia Beach, Virginia. August, 1997.

Pay, Rene. The Second National Company Conference. Gardnerville, WV. June, 1997.

Pay, Rene. Three-Day Training Workshop for The Firm. Green Run High School, Virginia Beach, Virginia. August, 1997.

Pay, Rene. Telephone Interview. November, 1997/May, 1997.

Pay, Rene. "Jordan District Technical Center Home Page." May, 1998.
<http://www.surweb.org/company/jdtc.html.>.

Works Cited

Dobyns, Lloyd, and Clare Crawford-Mason. *Quality or Else.* New York: Houghton Mifflin Company, 1991.

Glasser, William. *Control Theory in the Classroom.* New York: Harper & Row Publishers, 1986.

- - -. *The Quality School.* New York: Harper & Row Publishers, 1990.

- - -. *The Quality School Teacher.* New York: Harper Perennial, 1993.

About Nancy Dowding

"My goal as the coordinator of The Firm is to increase students' self-esteem by helping them perform to their highest potential by implementing the newest technology and state-of-the-art equipment. This is accomplished by providing additional help when needed and by setting goals that are attainable and realistic to the world of work."

Nancy Dowding teaches business at Green Run High School in Virginia Beach and also serves as the Firm Coordinator within the business department. She has taught at the Adult Learning Center and at Tidewater Community College. Nancy received her B.S. in Business Education from Longwood College and her M.S. in Administration and Supervision from George Washington University. A frequent presenter at local, state, and national conferences, Ms. Dowding has also served as Norfolk State Regional Advisor for the Future Business Leaders of America and on the FBLA State Advisory Board. Currently, Nancy Dowding is a 1998 mini-grant recipient and uses her knowledge of and expertise in the Firm's concept of business education to instruct educators throughout the region.

About Kathleen Malone

"I want to teach my students how—To live this life on earth—To face its struggles and its strife—And to improve their worth—Not just the lesson in a book—Or how the rivers flow—But how to choose the proper path—Wherever they may go—To understand eternal truth—And know the right from wrong—And gather all the beauty of—A flower and a song—For if I help the world to grow—In wisdom and in grace—Then I shall feel that I

have won—And I have filled my place…"

—JAMES J. METCALF

Having received her B.S. in Business Education from Norfolk State University and an M.Ed. from Virginia State University, Kathleen Malone decided to continue her education by earning her Ed.S in Administration from George Washington University in 1991. She has been teaching in the Virginia Beach City Public Schools since 1971 and currently serves as Business Department Chairperson and Firm Coordinator at Ocean Lakes High School, Virginia Beach. She is active in a variety of professional organizations and attends and presents seminars dealing with curriculum and instructional strategies in the area of business and administration. Throughout her teaching experience, Kathleen Malone has revealed her commitment and dedication by becoming actively involved with her school. She has served on numerous school planning councils while, at the same time, maintaining her involvement with students by sponsoring clubs and enrichment activities. Twice, Kathleen Malone has been named Teacher of the Year—the first time in 1982 at the Virginia Beach Technical and Career Education Center and then at Green Run High School in 1993 in Virginia Beach.

Looping - An Old Idea for Today's Children

by Beverly Berman and Windsor Shewbridge

the temperature was only 95° with 100 percent humidity; the sweat was pouring down my cheeks. As I balanced on the counter putting up my back-to-school bulletin boards, I heard a faint knock at the door. I saw Mrs. Smith and her son, Joe. What a *great* first impression, I thought. I jumped down, wiping my hands on my tee shirt and introduced myself. Mrs. Smith introduced me to Joe whose head hung to the floor. She shyly explained that they had just moved into our school zone. "Joe attended kindergarten at Shore Road Elementary," she said. "He is very shy and had a difficult time with the kindergarten curriculum." I tried to strike up a conversation with Joe, but had no luck. I knew I had my work cut out for me.

Joe's mother understated Joe's difficulties. He was dramatically behind, academically and socially, which would explain his grades of N (Needs Improvement) in most areas of the kindergarten curriculum. However, his academic progress was not my main concern initially. Joe was more than shy—he was non-communicative. Not only would he refuse to answer my questions, he rarely spoke to his peers. When purchasing his lunch in the cafeteria line, he would freeze. When asked what he wanted for his lunch choice, Joe would stand rigid, not answering or gesturing a choice. This hesitancy caused the cafeteria line to back up frequently and frustrated the workers and the other children. I rescued Joe daily.

> However, his academic progress was not my main concern initially. Joe was more than shy—he was non-communicative.

That was Joe in September before he began working with the speech therapist. By December, Joe made a major breakthrough and was able to ask in a rapid whisper, "May I go to the bathroom?" But I was still not certain whether Joe's silence was due to severe shyness or something more serious. His mother remained unable or unwilling to give me any answers.

Nothing I tried was working. Feeling discouraged, I decided to attend a professional conference in February. It was at this conference that I heard about the success of looping. I learned that "looping is a practice which allows single-grade teachers to remain with the same class for a period of two or more years. It requires a partnership of two teachers in contiguous grades. A first-grade teacher progresses with her students while her second-grade teaching partner moves to first grade and begins a new two-year cycle" (Grant et. al 12). Because Joe was making such slow progress in first grade, I wondered if this program would help him. Joe was the catalyst that urged me to experiment with this teaching technique. There comes a time when one simply must rely on that little voice inside and take risks for the sake of the children.

> There comes a time when one simply must rely on that little voice inside and take risks for the sake of the children.

Before going to my principal to discuss the possibility of incorporating the looping approach with Joe and his classmates, I began posing questions. Who would instruct Joe, empathize with him? He had worked so hard, achieved so much, but still had miles to go. Who would encourage Joe so that all the reading and math objectives would be mastered by third grade? Would Joe respond to a new teacher? What would happen if Joe remained in my classroom another year? Then ,would he be ready? I reflected on the challenges ahead—learning a new curriculum, leaving the security of my grade-level team, and traveling into uncharted territory. With a growing conviction to risk, I presented the idea of looping to my principal who warmly responded to the challenges of looping because, as a student, he experienced the educational and emotional benefits of looping in another division. He also realized that implementation of the program would be feasible. Excited to begin learning the second-grade curriculum, I eagerly drafted a letter to parents explaining the benefits of a looping program with an "opt out" for those who did not want their child included. (In three years only one parent opted out of the program.)

The end-of-the-year party was different because we knew our class family was not ending. Plans were made for summer get-togethers to continue the social interaction the children had enjoyed during the school year. Writing journals were passed out and used to record the students' personal reflections about summer activities and their questions about summer learning experiences. We planned to share all journal entries in the fall.

We started second grade as a "welcome back," not a new class, and we were excited to share our "summer journals" which we used to begin editing and publishing books during Writer's Workshop. Although we met over the summer, I was amazed at how much students matured in such a short time. We added four new students to our class that fall from different schools; these four quickly joined our family, and I was able to concentrate on their needs because I already knew the strengths and weaknesses of the rest of my students. Although many hours were spent in learning a new curriculum, I had the luxury of not having to learn a new set of students and parents. It was a great trade off! We were a community of learners sharing in one another's triumphs, joys, sorrows, and losses. It was a good feeling, like "being home."

The great fortune continued and I discovered one of my former first-grade team members was especially interested in collaborating with me to become part of the looping program. As a student, she too experienced looping and knew about its educational benefits. She was also interested in working with me because her class had many challenging, at-risk students. We became a collaborative team and began working with at-risk students, many like Joe and Sue. On the first day of school, Sue, one of our students, shared with us that her mother moved out of their home and into John's house down the street. Mornings she would see her mother from the school bus and would pound on the window to tell her she loved and missed her. Her mother never noticed. Obviously, it was difficult for her to concentrate on her school work, and she was unable to meet grade level objectives. Her mother never noticed. Because of her dysfunctional family, we were concerned about Sue's progress—but Sue was merely one of many students who came to school each day, products of dysfunctional families. As educators, we knew we could do nothing to change the family, but we could and would promote the looping concept which enables at-risk students like Joe and Sue to become comfortable with two consecutive years in a consistent, nurturing learning environment.

As educators, we also firmly believed that the foundation and stability we were able to give Sue, Joe, and our other first and second graders was well worth our learning a new curriculum! Joe, although a weak student, was more prepared for third grade. He began interacting with the other classmates and would willingly converse with me. He still, however, had difficulty with other adults. Even though Joe moved the summer after second grade, I think of him often and know that we gave him the "benefit of the doubt" and the additional academic and emotional support he needed to succeed. Sue's third-grade teacher continues to confirm that looping was the key to Sue's successful educational and emotional progress; and even though Sue's family situation has not improved, her ability to concentrate on her schoolwork has. And she has been able to achieve honor roll status two consecutive grading periods!

> We were a community of learners sharing in one another's triumphs, joys, sorrows, and losses. It was a good feeling, like "being home."

The dramatic changes we have witnessed in student performance have been confirmed by the research from *Looping Q & A 72 Practical Answers to Your Most Pressing Questions* (Forsten 31). As a result of our experiences in this looping program, we have noticed a 43 percent decrease in retention rates. We attribute this decrease to the developmental approach of looping, giving educators like us the time and resources to rethink first-grade lessons and make appropriate adjustments to reflect on the objectives to be assessed in second grade. Take mathematics, for example: for students who are not yet developmentally ready, we concentrate less on mastery and more on reinforcing and refining specific skills before introducing addition and subtraction strategies. In first grade, number concepts can be taught using the Hundreds Board manipulative; this strategy aids students in developing a clearer awareness of number concepts, including place value, money, and mathematical operations. Placing more emphasis on this number strategy in the first grade makes a significant impact on *how* students grasp the more complicated second-grade learning objectives. In Language Arts, instruction of the more difficult vowel patterns may be delayed until the child is ready to learn them, so rather than including these skills as part of a "prescribed" Language Arts Program, the looping approach encourages mastery of these phonetic skills first. As a result, the child becomes empowered through his own learning progress, and reading and writing mastery is enhanced.

> ...this strong bond between teacher and student, and student and student, has given those weaker students an extra edge to continue to compete with their more able peers and to realize their own potential.

Looping causes students and teachers to continually reflect. As a collaborative team, we consistently begin lessons with "remember last year when we?" Even though our students are now in the fourth grade, we still maintain contact with them and continue to watch them grow from a distance. Parents from both our classes have been overwhelmingly positive and confirm that their children are more confident students and better prepared to take on the challenges of third grade; this strong bond between teacher and student, and student and student, has given those weaker students an extra edge to continue to compete with their more able peers and to realize their own potential. According to Grant, author of *The Looping Handbook*, "looping is accepted primarily because it is based on one of the most basic human needs: the need to form strong, enduring relationships with others," (Grant 15) and in a world of constant change, social pressure, and family instability, we need to give parents hope and our students hope.

As each year progresses, we continue to experience the positive effects of looping. Often, our former students return to read their favorite books, some of the very same books we first shared together, to our new first graders. Therefore, based on our classroom research thus far, the concept of looping continues to be represented in a positive light, as long as the teacher, administration, and parents are in agreement on issues of pacing, student mastery, and learning strategies. We have discovered that school districts in Antioch, Illinois; Raisin City, and West Port, California; Attleboro, Massachusetts; and Hilton Head, South Carolina, are practicing looping successfully. In "How Looping Works," leading advocate, Char Forsten continues to validate what we have realized and continue to experience— that it is our mission to provide students with the successes necessary to becoming life-long learners, that we must foster the feelings of acceptance, security, and trust among our students to create future risk takers and reflective problem solvers.

During our first three looping cycles, sixteen children were candidates for retention, yet fourteen children have made a positive transition to third grade instead of being retained in first grade. In addition, "suspected" learning disabilities have lessened in the second year because students were given the necessary time to mature appropriately and master the curriculum.

For all the questions about looping that we have answered, we still continue to pose new ones: How can we strengthen our communication with parents whose children can not meet the second-grade challenge? How do we maintain the integrity of our program with others who do not see its value? What other learning strategies do we need to incorporate in order to enhance the emotional and academic success of our students? Even though the looping approach dates back to 1913, isn't it amazing how such a simple concept, a concept with such positive benefits for teachers, students, and parents, has not taken a stronger hold in our educational system?

I will always remember going to lunch one early fall day, feeling a pair of arms wrapping around me, and looking down, to see Sue with a big smile. She received a 100 percent on her spelling test. So is looping worth it? We both say YES! without any hesitation. As long as our students continue to benefit, we will continue to loop.

> I will always remember going to lunch one early fall day, feeling a pair of arms wrapping around me, and looking down, to see Sue with a big smile. She received a 100 percent on her spelling test.

Works Cited

Forsten, Char, et al. *Looping Q & A 72 Practical Answers to Your Most Pressing Questions.* Peterborough, N.H. Crystal Springs Books, 1997.

Grant, Jim, Bob Johnson, and Irv Richardson. *The Looping Handbook.* Ed. Aldene Fredenburg. Peterborough, N.H.: Crystal Springs Books, 1996.

About Beverly Berman and Windsor Shewbridge

"Successful teaching is meeting the needs of all students by individualizing instruction. Providing every child with challenges they can master and successes they can take pride in will enable them to become life-long learners. We believe that all students, given guidance, time, and a nurturing environment, will embrace the skills they need to succeed and contribute to our society."

Having received a B.S. in Education from York College of Pennsylvania, Beverly Berman has been teaching at Princess Anne Elementary in Virginia Beach since 1977. Currently, she teaches first and second grades and also serves as first-grade level Chairperson and first-grade cluster teacher for the academically advanced. Beverly Berman is active in her role as Co-Chair of the School Renewal Committee and the Language Arts Curriculum Committee. She was named Princess Anne Elementary Reading Teacher of the Year in 1994, and, most recently, was named to the 1998 "Showcase of Success" by the Virginia School Board Association.

A graduate of Virginia Commonwealth University with a B.S. in History Education, Windsor Shewbridge has been teaching in Virginia Beach Public Schools since 1992. Windsor Shewbridge currently teaches first and second grade at Princess Anne Elementary where she is also the cluster teacher of the second grade academically gifted. In 1996, Ms. Shewbridge was named as Princess Anne Elementary Reading Teacher of the Year, and, most recently, was named to the 1998 "Showcase of Success" by the Virginia School Board Association.

As a collaborative teaching team, Windsor Shewbridge and Beverly Berman are presently examining guided reading techniques; their research continues to concentrate on discovering accurately a child's developmental reading level. Princess Anne Elementary, where both Ms. Shewbridge and Ms. Berman teach, is one of the few schools in Virginia Beach to incorporate and facilitate the transition from one grade level to the next through the process of looping.

Nancy Prichard

Growth Cycle, 1997

Electrostatic
transparency and
holographic paper

"Many of my paper collages represent rhythms of life: night and day, the seasons, tides, cycles of the moon, growth cycles. I describe these forces as Eco-Logic. In the last few years, I have been adding high tech processes to my work, including computer generated imagery, electrostatic transparencies, and holographic paper. I also enjoy the juxtaposition of old and new images to create a different context."

Nancy Prichard

Biographical Information

Nancy Prichard, an elementary art teacher in the Virginia Beach Public Schools for twenty-one years, has taught elementary, secondary, and postsecondary students. She has been involved in curriculum development through the years, served on school and district curriculum committees, and has made numerous presentations at local, state, and national conferences. In addition, she has received grants from the Virginia Commission for the Arts and the Virginia City Public Schools. Currently, Mrs. Prichard is the Art Specialist at the Old Donation Center.

Mrs. Prichard's collages have been exhibited regionally and nationally in invitational and juried shows. Her work with handmade paper and lessons related to the fiber arts has been published in several books and magazines, including Fiber Arts Design Book III, *Edited by Kate Pulleyn;* Fiber Arts Design V, *Edited by Anne Batchelder;* Fiberarts, Felt and Paper: A Portfolio, *Kate Mathews-Pulleyn, and, most recently,* Molas *from Lark Publications.*

Art Education Statement

"I love giving students a creative problem and seeing the wide variety of responses and interpretations. Art is such a dynamic, exciting discipline, where strands of all areas of learning connect and interweave. The possibilities are limitless! I want my students to experience the joy, wonder, and excitement that is possible through the worlds of ideas and images, whether personal or universal."

Chapter 3
Assessment: Looking In and Beyond

Through most of this century, our society has been in the grip of narrow conceptions of intellectual development and academic achievement; we operate with inadequate, even damaging notions of what it means to be excellent. For all the hope we place in what school will do for our children—and we have always placed great hope in the benefits of education—we have a tendency to diminish the day-to-day practice of schooling, the richness and mystery of the challenges and achievements of the school day. Few discussions of schooling in policy papers, in legislation, in the endless flow of books by nonteachers telling us how to make it right, few of these discussions take us close to teaching and learning. They tend to work at a high level of generality and opinion, thereby relying more easily on one-dimensional portrayals of the classroom.

—MIKE ROSE, POSSIBLE LIVES: THE PROMISE OF PUBLIC EDUCATION

*t*hrough multidimensional portrayals of classrooms and teachers at work in them, the educators featured in the "Assessment" chapter communicate how they actively vary the kinds of assessment they employ in the classroom. They discuss thinking and explore their conclusions about how students learn and how they are assessed. They reveal how they encourage reflection, collect data, and incorporate a variety of assessment tools to formulate conclusions and reexamine strategies that will shape future lessons.

Assessment has always been a compelling and somewhat troubling concern for educators...to assess...to evaluate...to judge...to contemplate whether a student is ready for the next grade level...ready for an exam...ready to attend college...so...

Late at night, listening to Mozart's Jupiter Symphony, I worry about thinking...

I worry because our society is changing rapidly and our student populations are changing as rapidly.

I worry about our new enthusiasms for measuring thinking, our search for easy-to-mark, forced-choice, pencil-and-paper tests yielding single, numerical scores that "tell all."

Yet these measurements never tell all. We would like to believe they would —that assessment is a simple matter that addresses the intricacies of our students' intellectual growth and subject mastery. Therefore, instead of students reading from textbooks, multiple choice tests, one answer is the only answer, the teacher poses all the questions, and grades are the only landmark, the educators in this chapter place more emphasis on application and synthesis rather than merely covering material.

The teacher becomes an active, reflective facilitator; students generate questions, write with their teachers, and witness their teachers struggling to learn with them. Multiple answers become possible. Final tests become portfolios. Visualizing history takes the place of notes on a chalkboard. These educators use personal stories and learning experiences as building blocks to make learning more meaningful for students; they analyze research involving learning windows to pose questions relating to a student's readiness to learn certain information. In sum, these educators communicate an awareness of understanding that how students learn directly relates to how they must be assessed and evaluated. They emphasize that students must assume leadership roles within the classroom and participate daily in collaborative learning situations.

These teachers honestly reveal to the reader their own learning processes and the questions they pose in order to discover assessment techniques that impact student learning. In addition, these educators offer us before and after glimpses of their students so that we will fully understand the difficulties and then the successes of employing a specific strategy. These educators show us how they encourage their students to become active critics capable of assessing their own learning—which is never an easy task—even with the most cooperative students. As I ponder their words and capture images of their students, I continue to learn about educators who never view what does not work as a failure, and instead, turn the negative into a positive, a failure into another challenge. The classroom is crowded with something, and that something in this chapter involves questions and creative, well-thought-out solutions, solutions that require continual reflection and exploration and examination.

In the lonely, peaceful moments in my classroom when students have left for the day, I oftentimes worry...

that, in the measures we choose, we might trivialize our most wonderful human capability by measuring simply one process and judging all students by that single standard

...a single standard that may ignore the emotional and intellectual needs of many of our students. While this awareness is a real concern, the teachers in this chapter, after watching too many students fall through the cracks, develop intervention strategies for assessing and identifying the at-risk.

Another writer, experiencing both the isolation as a special education teacher and witnessing the isolation her students were experiencing, suggests that by reducing the cognitive demands in a regular education classroom and making the material personally relevant to students, all isolation vanishes and students progress both academically and personally.

The reader entering these classrooms through the vivid articles presented will feel a kinship with the voices as educators discuss the struggles of addressing assessment each day, each year, in the classroom. It is the very struggle I address during the first week of school. Each year I begin by asking my students questions—process questions about how they read, engage with a text, apply certain revision skills to reshape a piece of writing—all in an effort to assess where my students are so that I will know where to take them. Each year I watch them on those opening days of school, sitting in silence with frozen stares not really knowing how to answer my questions.

What does she mean, how do I read? I open the book and I...And what about writing? I pick up my pen and write what I'm thinking...Reshape...Reshape what? If I reshape my draft, it destroys the spontaneity of the piece. Something tells me this won't fly with this lady. I need to see my guidance counselor about a schedule change. I like it the old way. You give me a yes or no question; I answer it in one or two sentences like...

When you read, do you pose questions?

Now what is she asking? Why can't I be lucky and have the old tried and true, the teacher's answer is the only answer. With these questions she's asking us, I'll bet she will turn the responses into more questions. I can feel it and then we will be "inside" a discussion, as she puts it, and then I'll have to think...and I'm a senior and this is supposed to be my easiest year.

And teaching reflection as it relates to assessment is never easy. So whether the types of assessment discussed in this chapter involve Reading Recovery techniques that unequivocally reveal an increase in reading fluency and accuracy or the degree to which rapid identification of learning styles enhances student ownership and academic success— these educators understand their students and that classrooms are sacred, soulful places where together, teachers and students rub minds—because minds matter. So does exploring outside, looking back, looking in, and beyond.

—LEANNE SELF

Mining for Diamonds in the Rough...
Students at Risk: Identification and Intervention

by Laynee Timlin

"Human potential, though not always apparent, is always there — waiting to be discovered and invited forth."

—WILLIAM W. PURKEY

as a special educator for nineteen years, I've discovered that teaching is analogous to mining. Perhaps the analogy occurred to me because of my Western Pennsylvania roots and the experiences shared with me by my grandfather, who was a miner (of coal, not diamonds!). Some students arrive at school with their potential readily apparent, already shining and brilliant; the potential of others needs to be mined by caring, competent educators. My caseloads over the years have been filled with the latter; after all, special education was intended to assist in the discovery of potential not readily apparent.

> **As I listened to the discussion, it occurred to me that we should simply ask the teachers.**

"At risk" has been an extremely popular term in education for many years. The term has become synonymous with students in danger of school failure and, ultimately, of dropping out of school. Like many other schools, the school where I served as the Child Study Team Coordinator had identified a specific school improvement goal to focus on the identification of and appropriate educational interventions for our "at risk" student population.

At one of our committee meetings, the "at-risk team" was brainstorming ways to identify our students deemed to be at risk. We considered administering a test, analyzing available test data, grades, and school history as well as conducting observations. As I listened to the discussion, it occurred to me that we should simply ask the teachers. After all, they easily pointed students out to me as candidates for remediation. I suggested that, for our purposes, teacher perception might be a powerful tool in identifying our at-risk population.

Locating the hidden diamonds...

The procedure for identifying students resulted in our creation of an At-Risk Inventory (Appendix I). The inventory included the following specifics:

1. Request that teachers bring class rosters and grade books to a faculty meeting. Ask that they list the names of the students considered to be "at risk" for success in their classrooms. Collect the names.
2. Place these names across the top of the At-Risk Inventory (Appendix I). Return the inventory to the teachers and ask why. Request that the educators identify factors contributing to each student's at-risk status.
3. Analyze data collected from each At-Risk Inventory.
   • Determine the number and percentage of students perceived to be at-risk out of the total school population. (This number would serve as a baseline for tracking any increase or decrease resulting from strategies employed.)
   • Data may be disaggregated by gender, ethnicity, or grade level.
   • Primary reasons for students' at-risk status may be useful for planning future staff development activities.
   • Identify factors that staff can influence and develop a plan of action.
4. Implement strategies for addressing needs of at-risk students.
5. Evaluate the effectiveness of the plan.
6. Data collected from this teacher perception inventory may be utilized to
   • support the school's strategic plan,
   • plan for further staff development,
   • assist in implementing a remedial education plan,
   • offer support for an inclusion/collaboration program, and
   • identify additional strategies needed for enhancing curriculum and designing more effective instruction.

Following our model, this process for the identification of at-risk students was implemented at four elementary schools in our district. According to teacher perception, the top four factors which contributed to students' at-risk status at each of these schools, in varying order, were:
   • inattentiveness,
   • lack of organizational skills,
   • poor ability to decode words, and
   • lack of motivation.

Other factors identified, in order of their frequency of occurrence on the survey, were inappropriate behavior, limited intellectual ability, poor attitude, emotional concerns, limited language skills, and a lack of parental support.

The mining begins…

So, what can educators do to increase a student's attention or organizational skills? What can educators do when "traditional" methods are unsuccessful? How can we help students become more motivated? The following philosophies have assisted me in the quest to uncover diamonds in the rough.

Adhere to developmentally appropriate practices. According to The Society for Developmental Education, "childhood should be a journey, not a race." We must teach children where they are and not where the curriculum says they should be. Teaching them "where they should be," when that's not where they are developmentally is a sure-fire way to guarantee their disinterest and inattention. Are we teaching children or a curriculum?

A Scenario:

Mrs. Johnson, a kindergarten teacher, anxiously awaits my arrival in her classroom for a language lesson. She can't wait to show me Sara's homework. "Just look at this!" she says, "Sara was supposed to write her name five times in the lines for homework." What I saw was Sara's name printed neatly five times on the page. "She didn't do this herself," Mrs. Johnson continued, "she can't even make the S correctly… she cheated and got her second-grade sister to do it for her!"

My amazement was not that Sara had industriously enlisted the assistance of her sister to do the work, but that the teacher would assign homework that she knew was beyond the child's developmental capabilities! Instead of just practicing the "S," first dotting it to trace on unlined paper, Sara practiced nothing, turning the work over to her capable sister, thus affirming that she was incapable. Careful observation and attention to individual abilities allow perceptive educators to determine a student's developmental level—that level at which skills are beginning to emerge. By using task analysis, breaking learning into incremental steps, and experimenting to discover what the student is able to do successfully and independently, we can gradually increase the complexity of the task until the desired outcome is achieved. Such was the case with Sara. When we issue assignments that are far too challenging, we force students to seek another means for the assignment's completion. Therefore, the challenge of writing her whole name on lined paper, without a model, was overwhelming to Sara.

In the words of former National Teacher of the Year, Guy Doud, "Every adult needs a child to teach… that's the way adults learn" (Doud 107). Our students will show us how to teach them. If we will only watch for their cues, we will

> Careful observation and attention to individual abilities allow perceptive educators to determine a student's developmental level—that level at which skills are beginning to emerge.

become adept at assigning practice that is appropriate. Students will complete the work independently and be challenged sufficiently enough to improve their skills. Though it may be easier and more efficient to assign one task for all students, it is naive to think that all students are performing on the same level. With practice, effective educators can develop adaptations to the central task which more effectively meet the needs of all learners. The system should be flexible enough to adapt to the needs of the child. The child should not have to "fit" the system. I believe we teach children through the use of the curriculum. Yet, teaching curriculum with blinders on does not serve the best interest of the student, the sole reason our profession exists.

> **Our students will show us how to teach them. If we will only watch for their cues, we will become adept at assigning practice that is appropriate.**

Teach to learning styles. The motto for the Learning Disabilities Association is, "If a child can't learn the way we teach him, we'd better teach him the way he learns." Mr. Evans, a fifth-grade teacher, once expressed his frustration with Shelly, a student considered to be at risk. Mr. Evans remarked, "I taught it, but she didn't get it!" It has always been my contention that the goal was for the Shellys in our classrooms to comprehend, but if they don't, then we aren't finished yet. By offering instruction which incorporates many learning modalities, teachers engage a greater number of students.

Howard Gardner, in formulating his "Theory of Multiple Intelligences," based his belief on not just one form of cognition which cuts across all human thinking; instead, his theory proposes that there are multiple intelligences with autonomous intelligence capacities (Lazear 5). Often, I found myself wondering about the number of students who have been placed in special education because we did not "mine" for their "way of learning." When educators plan to accommodate all styles, attention, motivation, and learning are likely to increase. An ideal lesson, at the very least, encompasses talking and listening (auditory information), many illustrations and images (visual information), and hands-on practical application, as well as physical movement (kinesthetic information).

During a sixty-minute all-auditory lecture, I'm reminded of the inattentiveness and resulting boredom of Ramone, a student with significant auditory processing difficulties. His general education instructor said often that he "was consistently in another world." When we began planning together, including visual representations of the auditory information in each lesson, his interest and attention increased. Ramone needed visual images to make language connections because drawing the "Redcoats" advancing toward Breeds Hill during the Battle of Bunker Hill conveyed much more meaning to him than the spoken word alone. Soon, he learned to pair auditory information with visual symbols to create meaning. This knowledge about his learning style was life-changing and positively affected his future school success.

I recall a social studies unit I co-taught with a fourth-grade teacher on the states and capitals. Students were arranged in cooperative learning groups which offered the opportunity for them to learn by style. Several preferred to sing the states and capitals, associating their names with music (musical/rhythmic intelligence), some learned best by standing on a floor map and moving from state to state (body/kinesthetic intelligence) as they said the names out loud (verbal/linguistic intelligence), while others drew their own maps and labeled them (visual/spatial intelligence). Students were given the option to work in pairs, with a group (interpersonal intelligence), or individually (intrapersonal intelligence). The diverse instructional format allowed for great variability, and because the class devoted time at the beginning of the school year assessing their learning preferences and discovering through experimentation what strategies worked best for them, student participation and achievement increased. As educators, we set the direction for what is to be learned, but we need to allow the students to take more responsibility for *how* to learn. By offering a variety of options and careful guidance, we become facilitators of learning, and students become empowered to "own" the learning experience. Psychologist Jean Piaget says, "Every time we teach a child something, we keep him from inventing it himself." By its very nature, teaching homogenizes. On the other hand, learning liberates (Bennis 26).

No Involvement, No Commitment. Empowering students to learn more about how they learn engages them directly in the process. I have frequently observed students who view their educational experiences from the back seat, as passive observers. Many of our educational practices actually encourage this stance. At parent-teacher conferences, for example, where is the child? A more effective method of communicating may be a parent-teacher-student conference where the student explains his perceptions of what he is learning and has input into the continual improvement of his learning process. Plans of action generated during a conference are likely to be more successful if the student is involved in creating and implementing the plan. In *Education is Not a Spectator Sport*, Daggett

> I often found myself wondering about the numbers of students who have been placed in special education because we did not "mine" for their "way of learning."

explains, "Learning is an active process. Unfortunately, in many classrooms children are placed in a passive role. They come to school to watch their teachers work" (Daggett 4). From the first day of school, it is vital that we, as educators, ensure that students have ownership and involvement in their own education. Education is not something that we do *to* them, but that they do *for* themselves. Teachers who develop the philosophy that it's you and I working together to master the curriculum are much more successful than educators who adopt the stance that it's the curriculum and I against you, the student.

> Psychologist Jean Piaget says, "Every time we teach a child something, we keep him from inventing it himself." By its very nature, teaching homogenizes. On the other hand, learning liberates (Bennis 26).

Learning the curriculum and mastering the Virginia Standards of Learning are mandatory, but how that occurs may be very flexible. Students who are involved in deciding how they learn often feel an integral part of the learning team. Just as there is a major shift going on in the workplace, classrooms are also being transformed from a superior-subordinate system to one of teamwork. The challenge for educators then is to "mine" continually for ways to involve students and tap into their inherent energy.

Value learning, not grades. In a society that demands grades and test scores and delights in publishing them and in making comparisons, it is difficult not to get caught up in the emphasis on grades and test scores. But is education about earning good grades or is it about learning? Has the student who makes "straight A's" learned the most? I can remember coming home from school, proudly rushing in to show my parents my "A" test grade, only to have my father reply, "Great! Now tell me what you've learned? What do you know now that you didn't know before?" He always claimed that the grade didn't matter—that he'd rather have us make C's and learn something, than A's and not have learned anything new. Back then, I wished he had been like other fathers and just paid me for the A's. Now, I appreciate him for the progressive educator that he was... one who focused on learning.

To illustrate the learning versus grades issue, I'm reminded of a fourth-grade science unit that I co-taught with a regular education teacher. Seven students with significant language delays were "included" in her classroom. At the beginning of the unit, a pretest was given. Bobby, a student with language learning disabilities knew 10 percent of the information on rocks. Michelle, a student considered to have average ability scored 40 percent on the pretest, and Carl, a student with above average ability, knew 80 percent of the subject matter on the pretest. At the completion of the science unit, the posttest was administered and graded. Bobby scored a 64 and earned a grade of E; Michelle scored 82 and a grade of C; and Carl scored 100, with a grade of A (Table 1). Who learned the most? Who earned the best grade? Though Bobby's knowledge gain was the greatest, he still received a failing grade. The question is obvious. How long do students like Bobby keep trying their best, when their best earns them a failing grade? If Bobby had done nothing during the study of this unit, he would have earned a failing grade. Rewards must be given for improvement and learning because, often, grades alone don't fit the bill.

Table 1

Student	Pretest Score	Posttest Score	Gain	Grade
Bobby	10%	64%	54%	E
Michelle	50%	82%	32%	C
Carl	80%	100%	20%	A

Instead of focusing on the test score, the percentage, the rank, why don't we focus on the content and quality of a student's work and on individual growth? Portfolio assessment, where students have the opportunity to gather examples of their work and give evidence of their progress, is an effective method of demonstrating what and how the student is learning in a meaningful presentation. Portfolios put the emphasis where it belongs, on the content of learning.

Success Motivates. How often do we hear parents and teachers say, "If he just tried harder, he'd do better?" Actually the reverse may be true... if he just did better, he'd try harder (Lavoie 9). Success is motivating. How many of us work hard at the things we are not good at? Wouldn't we rather spend our time improving what we don't do well? For all students, especially those with learning difficulties, we must continually strive to enable them to be successful and then build on that success. First grader Sean, after mastering the concept of opposites, exclaims, "This is fun. Let's do more!"

Search for prescriptive teaching techniques. If a student is unsuccessful in learning a new skill after it is first taught by traditional methods, we need to pursue alternative methods of instruction. Reading Recovery (Clay) provides an excellent example of a program that "roams around the known" or begins with what a child knows well and uses that knowledge as a springboard, as a firm foundation on which the teacher can build. At this point in Reading Recovery, it is important for the educator to become a researcher and carefully observe and record the actual reading behavior of the student. The program addresses confusions students have about print with effective strategies for correcting them. A teacher directs a student to "look at the picture and get your mouth ready to say the sound." And students are encouraged to self-correct and develop accountability for their own reading skill. Educators need to discover effective methods, like Reading Recovery, to help children acquire efficient patterns of learning.

Fairness doesn't mean treating everyone the same. Fairness means giving everyone what he or she needs. This definition of fairness is articulated by Richard Lavoie who points out that we often operate under a child's definition of fairness... everyone gets the same. He contends that "there is nothing so unequal as the equal treatment of unequals" (Lavoie 24).

> Back then, I wished he had been like other fathers and just paid me for the A's. Now, I appreciate him for the progressive educator that he was... one who focused on learning.

During a fourth-grade social studies test, one of the students, Nate, raises his hand for assistance. How fair is it that Nate comes to school with low intellectual ability, limited parental support, a minimal background of experiences, and numerous adverse medical conditions, while his classmate Jessica enters the same room each morning blessed with an intellectual capacity of 130 IQ; well-educated, supportive, involved parents; many rich life experiences; and exceptional health. Fairness means giving each student what he or she needs, not treating them the same. I'd give Jessica assistance if she needed it. It's only fair for me to assist Nate. Comprehension of what the question is asking is difficult for him, so I break down the vocabulary to simpler terms and rephrase the question for him. Do I tell him the answer? No. I help him by restating the question in language he can understand. That's only fair.

Collaboration among professionals improves instruction. Teaching can be an extremely isolated profession if we allow it to be so. I hope the days when teachers enter their classrooms and shut the door, isolating themselves and their students from the outside world, are over. We gain so much—and so do our students—when we share ideas, strategies, and confront challenges together. Incredible teaching and learning occur when the curricular knowledge of general educators is combined with the instructional strategies of special educators. Collaborative teaching promotes communication and improves instruction to benefit all students. More and more school professionals are concluding that what is required for them to be successful in their work is a commitment to a higher degree of professional sharing, a sharing of educational tools, professional skills, and, most importantly, a sharing of responsibility for all students. Collaboration among school professionals is an effective unifying work relationship enabling them to achieve this sharing (Bauwens and Harcade 6).

Encourage rather than criticize. "Encouragement is like a seed: a little encouragement planted in the right place can cause something wonderful to grow!" With these words, Connie Podesta, in her book *Self-Esteem and the Six-Second Secret*, reveals a key to better self-esteem. She illustrates how we tend to criticize, rant and rave for about sixty seconds when we notice a mistake, and we tend to praise for approximately six seconds when we are pleased. If we make a conscious effort to reverse that tendency, express our displeasure for six seconds and praise for sixty seconds, we will be on the right track toward motivating others to make improvements. The Final Report of the California Task Force to Promote Self-Esteem contains the following definition for self-esteem: "appreciating my own worth and importance and having the character to be accountable for myself and to act responsibly toward others" (Podesta 4).

Podesta also suggests a strategy for motivating students who continually say, "I can't!" She recommends that we not argue but agree with them and respond, "I know you can't, but if you could, how would you do it?" This question encourages the student to begin task analysis, to break down the task into steps. I tested this technique with Mark, a kindergarten student who continually said, "I can't." The task was the identification of initial consonant sounds, and students were instructed to record the letter which represented the sound. When Mark said, "I can't make a B," I replied, "I know you can't, but if you could, how would you do it?" He resisted by repeatedly saying "I can't," and I persistently responded with the same statement. After a while, he said, "Well, I guess I could look at the B on the wall, and I could make a straight line down." I said, "Good. What would you do next?" "Make a big belly on the top and one on the bottom," said Mark. "Look what you've done! You made a B," I said. "Can I make another one?" asked Mark.

> I hope the days when teachers enter their classrooms and shut the door, isolating themselves and their students from the outside world, are over.

Reward perseverance. In his essay "The Common Denominator of Success," E. M. Gray writes, "The successful person has the habit of doing the things failures don't like to do. They don't like doing them either necessarily. But their disliking is subordinated to the strength of their purpose" (Covey 149). In much of the literature about successful people, the common trait in their success is not necessarily intelligence, socioeconomic status, or luck, but rather the ability to "stick with it" even if not successful after the first, second, or third attempt. Oftentimes, failure provides valuable learning experiences. For educators, rewarding a student's attempts and encouraging him to try again in a different way provide such valuable learning experiences.

Polishing diamonds...

In our continual search for the key to providing the shine to our precisely mined diamonds, we must adopt that same perseverance as we search for answers to success for all students. The following poem appeared in a special education publication and has been on my wall for as long as I can remember.

Some people see a closed door
    and turn away.
        Others see a closed door,
            try the knob,
                if it doesn't open...
                    they turn away.
Still others see a closed door,
    try the knob,
        if it doesn't open,
            they find a key.
                if the key doesn't fit...
                    they turn away.
A rare few see a closed door,
    try the knob,
        if it doesn't open,
            they find a key,
                if the key doesn't fit...
                    they make one.

Effective educators are "key makers"—those rare few who continue to "mine" for ways to ensure all students are successful. We can never give up the search for uncovered potential and the will to invite it forth. We must model the perseverance we wish to see in our students. After all, parents and families create the diamonds; educators polish them.

Appendix I

At-Risk Inventory

Teacher_____

Check below all that apply	TOTALS	STUDENT	STUDENT
Poor Motivation			
Limited Intellectual Ability			
Second Language Background			
Poor Organizational Skills			
Inappropriate Behavior			
Poor Attitude			
Lack of Parental/Home Support			
Inattentiveness			
Limited Language Skills			
Poor Attendance			
Frequent Transfers			
Medical Concerns			
Emotional Concerns			
Poor Decoding Skills			
Single Parent Family			
Other (Add Reasons)			

What factors contribute to the student's at-risk status?

References

Bauwens, Jeanne, and Jack J. Hourcade. *Cooperative Teaching: Rebuilding the Schoolhouse for All Students*. Austin: Pro-Ed, 1995.

Bennis, Warren. *On Becoming a Leader*. Illinois: Nightengale Press, 1989.

Covey, Stephen R. *Principle Centered Leadership*. New York: Fireside, 1990.

Daggett, Willard R., and Benedict Kruse. *Education is NOT a Spectator Sport*. New York: Leadership Press, 1997.

Doud, Guy Rice. *Molder of Dreams*. Pomona: Focus on the Family Publishing, 1990.

Lavoie, Richard D. *Integrating Learning Disabled Students*. East Moline: LinguiSystems, Inc., 1992.

Lazear, David. *Seven Ways of Teaching*. Palatine: IRI/Skylight Publishing, Inc., 1991.

Podesta, Connie. *Self-Esteem and the Six-Second Secret*. Newbury Park: Corwin Press, Inc., 1990.

Works Cited

Clay, Marie M. *Reading Recovery*. Portsmouth: Heinemann, 1993.

Covey, Stephen R. *The 7 Habits of Highly Effective People*. New York: Fireside, 1989.

Gibran, Kahlil. *The Prophet*. New York: Alfred A. Knopf, 1973.

Harris, Hazel Wiggins, and Judy Brown Lehr. *At-risk Low-achieving Students in the Classroom*. Washington: National Education Association, 1988.

Lehr, Judy B., and Craig Martin. *We're All At Risk: Inviting Learning for Everyone*. Minneapolis: Educational Media Corporation, 1992.

McClanahan, Elaine, and Carolyn Wicks. *Future Force*. Glendale: Griffin Publishing, 1994.

Peters, Tom. *Embracing Chaos*. Illinois: Nightengale Press.

Purkey, William W., and John M. Novak. *Inviting School Success*. New York: Wadsworth Publishing Company, 1996.

Reavis, George H. *The Animal School*. Rosemont: Programs for Education, 1988.

About Laynee Timlin

"Education, like mining, is a business of discovering gems; only in education, our gems are much more valuable... they come in the form of human potential."

Laynee Timlin currently serves as the Partnership Coordinator for the Virginia Beach City Public Schools, supporting the development of mutually beneficial partnerships between the schools and the community. She is the vice-president of the Virginia Association of Partners in Education.

Following graduation from California University of Pennsylvania with a Master's degree, she began her career with the Virginia Beach City Public Schools in 1976 as a speech/language pathologist. Her nineteen years as a special educator were devoted to serving the special learning needs of students in regular education classroom settings, in collaboration with general educators. Being a parent of three children enrolled in the Virginia Beach City Public Schools and having served as the Adopt-a-School Coordinator, Student Activities Sponsor, and Chairperson of the Child Study Team, Special Education Department, and School Climate Committee have expanded her opportunities to view a child's education from varying perspectives.

As Holland Elementary Teacher of the Year in 1985 and Tallwood Elementary Teacher of the Year in 1990, Laynee is also the 1997 recipient of the Superintendent's Quality Award. Receiving certification as a TQM facilitator, Laynee is a 1997 graduate of the Hampton Roads Education Leadership Academy and currently serves as a motivational speaker and facilitator/instructor of adult education.

A World of Difference in My Class

by Shary Schlain

I t was 2:30 on a hot Wednesday afternoon in May. The sun was shining brightly outside, but inside the class, gloom prevailed. The teacher announced that the class would be taking turns reading out of the textbook and to please pay attention since everyone would have to answer questions on page 304. Twenty-five bodies were present in the classroom. Minds were elsewhere.

"I could do better if she would just let me build a model castle."

"My true intellectual ability is demonstrated when I'm working on my music."

"If she would only just allow us to work in groups."

"Her multiple-choice tests do not reveal my creativity."

"I need to experiment to learn this material."

"Just let me do it by myself."

"I wish she'd let me draw or paint my impressions of this lesson."

If these students were able to share these thoughts with their teachers beginning in kindergarten—classrooms would look differently than they currently do. Do students share with teachers their learning styles? Of course not. Then, how will we know how to teach them?

Many researchers have thoroughly discussed the inherent differences in learning styles. We have a host of measures to indicate how different we all can be. A significant difference exists between those individuals who are right-brained and those who are left-brained. Educational theorists have been asking teachers to provide accommodations for those students who are visual or auditory, tactile or kinesthetic learners. Researchers like David Kolb divide us into accommodators, divergers, convergers, and assimilators; while Priscilla Vail asks us to determine which students learn best with three-dimensional or two-dimensional materials, or if they are simultaneous or sequential processors. Howard Gardner has identified at least eight intelligences (linguistic, logical-mathematical, spatial, musical,

> **Do students share with teachers their learning styles? Of course not. Then, how will we know how to teach them?**

bodily-kinesthetic, interpersonal, intrapersonal, and the naturalist-environmental); and Myers and Briggs have further divided us into sixteen types, depending on introversion-extroversion and sensing and intuitive types. Finally, Dunn and Dunn have found twenty-one individual elements that they divide into environmental, emotional, sociological, physical and psychological stimuli.

So, when looking at individual differences, do we look at them two ways, three ways, four ways, six ways, eight ways, sixteen ways, twenty-one ways, or do we look at all of them together, which would be sixty-four ways? Are you crazy yet? Why did you ever go into teaching in the first place? Are all sixty-four "types" in your classroom now?

Even though we all have our own "best" learning styles, this does not mean we cannot learn by other methods; however, often we must stretch to do so. We must first discover our own special styles and talents by taking inventories, doing research, and, most importantly, by participating in active reflection regarding the stages of our individual learning process. For example, I know I am a right-brained, visual learner, who learns from "hands-on" experiences. I know also that I am fairly linguistic, that I need bright light, flexibility, background noise, activity, group work, and soft pillows to lean on.

Chances are, my classroom environment will reflect my particular learning preferences and styles, and because we are more comfortable with our own learning styles, we tend to teach that way most of the time. Unfortunately, if this is the *only* way we teach, students with other learning styles will be left out all of the time.

> **Though students may believe that only certain types of educators are qualified at this learning game, they need to understand teachers differ just as they do.**

So, what can we do? The answer is obvious: Identify strengths and weaknesses of our own learning styles and admit that we are more comfortable with some methods than others.

Then, share your learning styles with your students. Let them see that teachers are learners who also have strengths and weaknesses, and that stretching can be positive. Their teachers next bell — or next year — may have very different styles of learning and teaching. Though students may believe that only certain types of educators are qualified at this learning game, they need to understand teachers differ just as they do. When I have shared Kolb's learning styles inventory with teachers, I've found representation in each of the four quadrants he specifies.

Next, review the research. Learn the different characteristics of auditory, visual, and kinesthetic learners. Learn about multiple intelligences and identify ways to encourage these in your students. Be mindful of the stimuli preferences noted in the work of Dunn and Dunn. Identify ways to bring about the learning of both left- and right-brain students.

Take a look around your class. Who is having difficulty this year? Who seems to be breezing through? Who is sick every time you decide to divide the class into cooperative groups? Who loves to listen to stories on tape, and who drifts off into space when manipulatives are not included in the lesson? These will be the students you target for change.

Students are learners for a lifetime and will be much more successful if they understand what their particular needs are in the educational setting.

Show students who are having the most difficulty how to become advocates for themselves. Teach them to identify strategies that are helpful for learning new material, and then help them reflect about why these seem to work for them. Students are learners for a lifetime and will be much more successful if they understand what their particular needs are in the educational setting. Many inventories and checklists are available to help determine the learning preferences of students at-risk to help them achieve academic and behavioral success.

Finally, reflect carefully on your lesson plans. Do they incorporate a variety of learning styles and student preferences? If not, experiment with a new style for one activity each day. Teachers cannot possibly provide activities that match every student's preference in every lesson. However, within each unit of study throughout the week, it is possible to select a variety of activities with learning styles in mind. Look to others on your grade level and share plans for lessons with other colleagues. No matter what the grade level or subject area, all students, from the intellectually gifted to the learning disabled to the emotionally disturbed, will benefit from experiencing a variety of instructional strategies. Examples of these strategies include the following:

- Use graphic organizers whenever lecturing.
- Have the students learn a part of the lesson and then teach it to others.
- Incorporate the making of music into activities.
- Provide small and large group activities as well as individual ones.
- Assist students in using logic and problem-solving techniques.
- Provide activities where movement is essential.

- Create or have students create visuals for the unit.
- Provide linear structure and then open-ended activities.
- Encourage students to identify personal relevance with the material.
- Enable students to locate source materials to learn what the experts think.
- Provide activities that answer the questions how, what, why, and what if.
- Balance hands-on activities with philosophical ones.
- Utilize both deductive and inductive reasoning.
- Allow reflection time for new concepts.

Provide choices and alternatives for classroom and homework assignments. For every assignment where a choice is possible, offer a list of suggested activities. Ask your students how they would like to demonstrate mastery of material. They will come up with many great ideas that will not only stimulate the class, but also enhance the learning experience for everyone. Ironically, students will ultimately choose activities that most effectively match their learning style preferences. They will actively engage in the work, no longer be discipline problems, and learn the information they need to experience success within a specific unit of study.

> **Ask your students how they would like to demonstrate mastery of material. They will come up with many great ideas that will not only stimulate the class, but also enhance the learning experience for everyone.**

Retain your sense of humor. Students need to see teachers laugh at themselves, especially if aspects of a lesson fail. Enjoy the moment and try again tomorrow. Attempt new strategies even if administrators are observing because, remember, when a lesson fails miserably, it is our fault, not the student's fault. As educators, we have an obligation to meet the intellectual and emotional needs of students in innovative ways.

When I was a teacher in elementary school, I will never forget one of my students with a learning disability. We battled for over a year before I realized this student could not understand new concepts when I incorporated visual and auditory input simultaneously. However, he could understand new material when I presented it either orally or visually. Finally, I figured out David's learning style; it was by accident. His learning soared after that.

Let's go back to that high school classroom. It is 2:30 on a hot Wednesday afternoon in May. The sun is shining brightly outside, but no one is interested in that. Social studies class is underway with the teacher dividing the chapter into five sections and dividing the class into five groups. Two students are working independently. Class members are teaching one another the important information contained in their sections. The teacher provides a checklist of significant objectives for the lesson, but the students are free to add to this list or change it in any way if they have sufficient cause. Students make choices within groups and participate in lively debates. One group dramatizes their section of the chapter, while other students are busy discussing costumes and set design. Another group writes a news report, complete with a news anchor, feature journalist, and a weatherman for a simulated TV broadcast. A graphic organizer is developed by yet another group. Students actively utilize the overhead projector and provide handouts for each student during their class discussion. One student, who decides to work alone, composes a musical rap using the information in his section to rewrite the section as if he were present. Another group creates a diorama for their assignment. And yet a final group creates a cost analysis of events presented in their section, including the battles, travel, employee costs, food for the troops and animals, clothing, and even the telegraphs that are sent.

> **Retain your sense of humor. Students need to see teachers laugh at themselves, especially if aspects of a lesson fail.**

Now, tell me. Which classroom would you like to be in?

References

Dunn, R., and K. Dunn. *Teaching Students Through Their Individual Learning Styles: A Practical Approach.* Reston, VA: Reston Publishing Company, 1978.

Gardner, Howard. *Multiple Intelligences: The Theory in Practice.* New York: New York Basic Books, 1993.

Kolb, David A. *Learning-Style Inventory.* Boston: McBer and Company Training Resources Group, 1981.

Myers, Peter, and Katharine Myers. *Myers - Briggs Type Indicator.* Palo Alto: Consulting Psychologists Press, Inc., 1987.

Vail, Priscilla L. *Learning Styles.* Rosemont, NJ: Modern Learning Press, 1992.

About Shary Schlain

"If it weren't for students impeding our progress in our race to the end of the term, we could certainly be sure of covering the material. The question, however, is not whether we as teachers can get to the end of the text, but whether our students are with us on that journey."

— PAT CROSS

Shary Schlain has taught nineteen years in the classroom and has served for the past six years as a Special Education Coordinator for Virginia Beach City Public Schools. Ms. Schlain received a B.A. in Psychology from Wisconsin State University, an M.A. in Behavior Disorders from George Peabody College for Teachers, and an Ed.S in Human Development from George Washington University. Her research interests include behavioral management techniques, learning styles, and collaborative teaching inclusion strategies. Receiving the Jenny Brewer Award for excellence in teaching from the Council for Exceptional Children, Ms. Schlain is a frequent presenter at various state and national conferences. She is an active member of the Virginia Beach Council for Exceptional Children, and the Virginia Council for Administrators of Special Education. A strong leader in her field, Shary Schlain is past president of both the Virginia Beach Council for Exceptional Children and the Virginia Federation Council for Exceptional Children.

The Talking Alphabet, A Dynamic Approach for Active Learning

by Jean Palmieri, Ed.D.

"Learning through visual, animated story presentations, mnemonics (memory clues) and kinesthetic (tracing)—these are some of the potent ingredients that produce effective, efficient learners."

a little first grader with blonde, shoulder-length curls, guessed for the fourth time as she attempted to read a short sentence in her reading book. The truth was that Kimberly had not yet mastered the alphabet, even after two years of kindergarten. She had been waived on to first grade and now was faced with threatening words in sentences. Even with small group instruction, additional reading resource instruction, and very supportive parents, Kimberly was floundering, grasping any way possible for correct responses. She wanted so much to succeed, but failure, frustration, and performance anxiety predominated. My particular interest in and extensive experience with educating students like Kimberly lead me to believe that the successful teaching of alphabetic symbols is one of the greatest accomplishments a teacher ever realizes.

The learning of alphabetic symbols taps into an appreciation, recognition, and recall of visual, auditory, and written characters. For a student like Kimberly, who experiences visual and auditorial difficulty in perceiving and remembering abstract symbols, proficiency in finally grasping and employing these tools for communication is a vital breakthrough academically. Therefore, classroom practice must reflect what we know of learning theory research.

What we do know is that theories of learning emphasize the importance of more than one learning modality. Anna Gillingham and Bessie Stillman, researchers who focus on the perceptual inefficiencies of processing symbols in reading and writing, stress the use of three channels—auditory, visual and kinesthetic (344). Others, such as Allen Paivio, who specializes in research dealing with memory

> A little first grader with blonde, shoulder-length curls, guessed for the fourth time as she attempted to read a short sentence in her reading book. The truth was that Kimberly had not yet mastered the alphabet...

experiments, present imagery or mental visualization as the main focus of their memory theories and experimentations (29: 263-291). Though these theorists may seem outdated, as pioneers they are very relevant to my work. The knowledge of these theories and my interest in special education for learning-disabled students have enabled educators to develop and utilize a creative teaching tool for alphabetic symbols, what I call the "The Talking Alphabet."

"The Talking Alphabet" is composed of twenty-six letter cards and a storybook. Each card contains both a bold, colorful capital letter and a lower case small letter. The letters are somewhat disguised as story characters with props. For instance, the ⟨U⟩ is "you", and "you" hold an umbrella; large "G" or Mother ⟨G⟩ has a gift, and little ⟨g⟩ says, "Gee, give me a gift". Some letters which resemble objects or animals have the figures drawn into the letters. Ester Snake is an ⟨S⟩ s-s , and she says "s-s-s"; Art Lion is an ⟨A⟩ , and he roars, "r-r-r". Each letter has limbs and a face. These manuscript letters are outlined to accent the shapes. More importantly, and for kinesthetic value, each capital letter is made of sandpaper or sponge.

> Many Kimberlys have learned from the "Talking Alphabet." They have gained confidence and self-esteem as they learn.

Because A. Gillingham and B. Stillman emphasize the need for a three-modality, controlled and systematic approach, the "Talking Alphabet" ensures the simultaneous use of visual, auditory, and kinesthetic channels with a set procedure for seeing the character letter while tracing the letter with index finger and saying the letter name or sound. Just as Paivio demonstrated that memorization of descriptive, associated word pairs is more efficient and effective than learning abstract, unrelated, nondescript pairs, the "Talking Alphabet" has positively demonstrated efficacy in alphabet mastery.

From the story book section of "The Talking Alphabet," children hear rhyming verses which weave brief tales with cues to assist the student's memory for abstract letter names, shapes, and sounds. Here is one excerpt:

> Oh, look what letter comes next.
> What do you see? A cat in a boat.
> What is he doing?
> Captain Cat went to sea
> Sailing on the letter C.
> See the cat on the letter C.
> He waves from his boat to A and B.

Just as Paivio and others find that imagery rather than abstraction is more effective in learning, the "Talking Alphabet" personifies each letter with props and a social quality. The friendly letter pictures are presented as the story is narrated, and the student repeats the letter names and sounds. While giving the sound, the child simultaneously traces the sandpaper or sponge letter with his finger. One of my main contentions is that the alphabet is difficult for students to learn because the visual shapes, the sounds, and names are meaningless. Besides the imagery of a picture drawing in each letter, this program employs additional mnemonic devices. Auditory cues such as the "C" is the "sea" for a boat C. "C" provides a meaningful association for a meaningless letter name.

Tracing each textured letter is another significant technique which reinforces learning by supplying a third modality. Tracing the letter while simultaneously saying its sound holds a child's attention and because many students have weaknesses in the auditory and/or visual channels, the kinesthetic mode compensates, supports, and enhances learning. Many Kimberlys have learned from the "Talking Alphabet." They have gained confidence and self-esteem as they learn.

For the purpose of this study, letter cards were used individually in tutorials and speech therapy sessions. Fifth-grade peer tutors were paired with kindergarteners as part of a six-week program. Under the guidance of a teacher and school psychologist, tutoring pocket folders containing specific talking alphabet cards were created and used during three twenty-minute weekly sessions. Tutors gained responsibility, and pupils received frequent letter reinforcement. Both groups benefited from the positive interrelationships. Peer tutors and adults grasped easily all techniques involved when using the kinesthetic alphabet; they also relied on the letter cards and stories to guide the learning. Sequence of letter presentation depended on specific letters students acquired most easily. In Kimberly's situation, the "Talking Alphabet"

> **Kimberly's bright eyes and smile reveal a developing competence and increased self-esteem.**

was introduced after she already knew some letters, and this knowledge base determined her starting point for letter presentation. Kimberly's progress was positively affected by speech therapy that focused on articulation in combination with sound-letter association.

While "The Taking Alphabet" was initially used with individual students, small group instruction for students having difficulty with traditional alphabet approaches also proved a successful learning tool.

As a learning theory specialist, I encourage teachers in the regular classroom to try the "Talking Alphabet" technique. Extend this dynamic approach to kindergarten classes for teaching letters and sounds, or to first grade for short vowel sounds.

Assign each pupil a "Talking Alphabet" card to dramatize part of the story and encourage him to trace the letter while simultaneously saying the name or sound. Adapt the peer tutoring "Talking Alphabet" folder and pair an able student with a student who needs additional reinforcement with certain letters.

The use of mnemonics or memory clues programmed on flashcards may be applied to any subject. For instance, an English teacher might creatively develop a set of seven flashcards with the parts of speech on one side and a humorous, catchy sentence application with picture to aid memory on the card's flip side. I urge other grade teachers to consider whether learning cards created with memory clues, word associations, and animation can enhance their students' learning.

Kimberly has now progressed beyond the letter/name recognition stage and has forged ahead by mastering letter sounds and articulating correctly. Kimberly's bright eyes and smile reveal a developing competence and increased self-esteem. With the "Talking Alphabet" cues she now associates letters with meaningful sound blends. And, yes, Kimberly is reading!

Works Cited

Gillingham, Anna, and Bessie W. Stillman. *Remedial Training and Children with Specific Disability in Reading and Penmanship.* Massachusetts: Educators Publishing Service, Inc., 1960. 344.

Paivio, Allen. "Neomentalism." *Canadian Journal of Psychology* 29 (1975): 263-291.

About Jean Palmieri, Ed.D.

"Like the 'Talking Alphabet' which spells lasting memories, dynamic teachers build steadfast students."

Throughout her career Jean Palmieri has served as an Academic Therapist, a Psycho-educational Coordinator, a Child Psychologist, and Director of Special Education. Currently, she serves as the School Psychologist for Salem Elementary and Salem Middle Schools in Virginia Beach. She received her B.S. from Southern Connecticut State University and her M.Ed. and Ed.D. from Boston University. She is certified in New Hampshire and Virginia for school psychology and special education and is a member of the National Association for School Psychologists. Ms. Palmieri's publications include: "A Protective Study with Multicultural Students," Thesis; "Adolescent Self-Esteem," Doctoral Dissertation; as well as "Open Concept Classroom with Learning Problem Children," *Academic Therapy;* and "Pupil Tutoring," *Slow Learner Workshop.* Jean Palmieri has also co-authored "Preschool Assessment" in conjunction with the Virginia Association of School Psychologists.

Reading Rescue: Is It a Lifeline for a Sinking Student?

by Janet Hunt

a t present, it is difficult for classroom teachers to provide consistent one-on-one tutoring for any single child in a class of twenty-five to thirty students. With so many demands on teacher time, the task seems insurmountable. But what if schedules could be rearranged to make time for each teacher, resource person, or administrator to devote one or two hours weekly to tutoring one student with reading problems? If our goal as educators is to provide literacy programs for the young, we must prioritize our daily tasks and realize that the progress of a single student in need of remedial reading help is not less important than lesson planning, meetings, grading papers, or administrative work.

As an example of this philosophy, please meet David. Except for his problems with reading, David is an average boy, who regularly attends school, participates in sports, is friendly and well-liked by his peers, and lives in a stable middle-class home environment. In spite of earlier surgery to correct eye muscle control, he has no apparent vision problems. Diagnosed in the second grade with having attention deficit disorder (ADD), David does, however, have great difficulty staying on task and completing his school work. Since second grade, David has been pulled out of his regular classroom three days a week to receive small-group remedial instruction in reading. David worked very hard in fourth grade and with his parents' and teachers' support, he passed with average grades. However, in fifth grade David began to struggle with increased independent reading and writing assignments in an academically-oriented program.

We know that the middle grades are crucial in the life of a child, especially a child like David because children undergo cognitive, physical, social, emotional, and moral changes that have direct effects on learning. It is during these years that interest in learning diminishes, and social problems arise (Wood and Muth 84).

And so it was for David when midyear he became anxious, suffered from frequent headaches, was unable to sleep, and began to express irrational fears. A child psychiatrist recommended counseling and antidepressant drugs. Although counseling helped David overcome his emotional problems, the new medication made him less able than ever to concentrate on school work.

Because David used phonics as his main approach to reading, he devoted more attention to identifying words and less attention to comprehending what he read. Describing students like David, Conley, author of *Content Reading: Instruction,*

A Communication, states: "Because they have not learned to make sense of what they read, their attitudes about print are generally poor. In addition, because of their inability to process information and their poor attitudes, they view the content of what they read as inaccessible and uninteresting" (Conley 84).

Because David could not yet read proficiently, he was developing a negative, self-defeating attitude about school work. To compound this, teachers in the middle grades have high expectations of the level at which their students must read and write in order to succeed. Dependence on textbooks increases. Yet, regardless of ability level, all students receive the same textbooks and the same assignments.

Unfortunately, all too often textbooks are too difficult for students like David to read independently, and reading at the instructional level meant David had to decode with 95 percent accuracy and at least 75 percent comprehension (Woods and Moe 21).

By middle school, David needed a broader vocabulary and wider schemata of experiences, as well as a repertoire of reading strategies and skills to apply in the right place and time across the curriculum. In addition, the successful middle school reader must have a positive attitude and believe that he or she is capable of using reading as a tool for understanding school subjects.

Although counseling helped David overcome his emotional problems, the new medication made him less able than ever to concentrate on school work.

Historically, traditional remedial programs have pulled students out of their regular classrooms. According to Allington (1994), the emphasis in these programs is almost always on learning-to-read skills such as phonics and basic comprehension. The instructional groups contain two to eight students, taught by teachers who usually have graduate training in special education or hold a teaching license as a reading specialist. Individualized instruction tends to be fragmented, consisting of workbooks, and skill-builder work sheets (McGill-Franzen and Allington, 1990). Very little time is spent reading longer books or writing. Therefore, students like David become cynical about this type of instruction because these experiences fail to prepare them for the rigors of their content area classes. Students who read at different levels are often placed in the same reading class. According to Morris, Ervin, and Conrad (1996), "It is next to impossible to conduct an effective forty-minute reading lesson with four students from two different grades who read at three different reading levels. And a year's worth of ineffective lessons adds up to minimal reading growth" (376).

During the middle school years the gap between poor readers and good readers widens rapidly. Allington (1983) maintains that good readers have more opportunity to learn than poor readers because they are more often engaged in reading of whole texts. Low-ability readers tend to avoid reading because they are frequently assigned to read beyond their independent or instructional reading level.

What can be done to help these middle grade students who have fallen so far behind in reading? One program that offers hope is Reading Recovery®, a successful early intervention program developed by child psychologist Marie M. Clay (1985) to reduce first-grade reading failure. The program serves the lowest achieving twenty percent of first-grade students. Students selected for Reading Recovery® experience thirty minutes of one-on-one tutoring each day for fifteen weeks. The goal is that these students will progress in reading achievement faster than the students in their regular classroom, so that they will catch up to the average readers in their class. Educators are examining the instructional principles of the Reading Recovery® Program to find out why students seem to be making more progress than in traditional remedial programs. Spiegel (1995) suggests the following features of Reading Recovery® as guidelines for success for all remedial instruction:

- early intervention;
- reading stories from connected text;
- more time spent reading;
- reading materials at the child's instructional level;
- one-on-one instruction;
- direct instruction on use of reading strategies and ways to use strategies in new situations;
- emphasis on writing;
- direct instruction in phonemic awareness and details of print;
- congruence with the classroom reading program;
- individualized lessons based on strengths rather than deficits;
- careful monitoring of comprehension;
- expectations of accelerated progress; and
- rigorous teacher training.

Would such an intensive one-on-one approach help a middle school student like David, who has failed to learn to read proficiently in traditional programs? In 1993, Lee and Neal designed a lesson framework for middle schoolers directly based on the Reading Recovery® model. They used this teaching approach, which they called Reading Rescue, to help an eighth-grade student who was behind in reading.

Spiegel's study (1995) attempted to replicate Lee and Neal's (1993) Reading Rescue model. A second purpose of the study was to determine if a tutor, who had not received the year-long training required for Reading Recovery® teachers, could successfully implement the program. Positive results from this study would mean that the model might be used by teachers and adult volunteers to attempt to rescue middle school students not reading on grade level.

David's scores on a nationally-normed standardized test placed him in the fifteenth percentile for reading comprehension and thirty-seventh percentile for knowledge of vocabulary. David's cognitive ability scores placed him at low average in quantitative and spatial reasoning and below average in verbal ability. However, David was an active participant in class discussions and could express his ideas orally. His listening comprehension, measured by an informal reading inventory, was about three grade levels higher than his instructional reading level. Thus, David had potential to improve in his reading ability after proper instruction.

Design

This study was a single-subject pretest/posttest to determine if a significant positive difference in reading scores could be achieved by a low ability fifth-grader after thirty hours of one-on-one instruction using Lee and Neal's (1993) Reading Rescue lesson sequence. This design incorporated procedures for single-subject experimental research (McCormick, 1995).

Procedure

Prior to the intervention, the tutor administered Form B of the *Analytical Reading Inventory* (Woods and Moe 1989) to determine David's independent and instructional reading levels. The teacher then gave the Woodcock Reading Mastery Tests, Revised-H (1987) to test word identification and word comprehension skills. Finally, the Diagnostic Survey (Clay, 1991) was used to assess accuracy and reliance on meaning and structural and visual cues to gain meaning from the text.

Instructional Model

The following components of the Reading Rescue instructional model as prescribed by Lee and Neal (1993) were used in this study:

1. **Reading familiar material**. Familiar text was reread for the purpose of building confidence and fluency. David chose a favorite episode from a familiar book or his own stories from the language portion of previous lessons.

2. **Reading aloud to the student**. The teacher read aloud to help maintain David's interest in the story, since his own reading was so labored, and to develop his appreciation of reading as a pleasurable activity. The teacher's reading served as

a model of appropriate expression and adherence to punctuation.

3. **Taking a running record**. In this procedure, David read a passage aloud while the teacher noted discrepancies between print and pronunciation. Correctly pronounced words were marked with a check. Mispronounced words were indicated by writing the student's word above the printed word. Self-corrections were also noted. The purpose of a running record was to establish the instructional focus for the next component of the lesson, working with words and letters. Changes in decoding strategies for each session were closely monitored and recorded.

4. **Working with words and letters**. The activities were based on the data obtained in the running record. David's individual needs were carefully assessed by accurate observation. Some activities which occurred were identifying word parts, developing phonemic awareness, looking at word families, finding semantic, structural, and sound patterns in words, and developing flexible strategies for pronouncing unfamiliar words. Lee and Neal (1993) suggest the use of a magnetic board and plastic letters so that the student can manipulate spelling and construct and rearrange words into short sentences.

> In addition, the successful middle school reader must have a positive attitude and believe that he or she is capable of using reading as a tool for understanding school subjects.

5. **Writing through language experience**. David used the Apple IIe computer and Learning Company's *Children's Writing and Publishing* (1989) software to write a story. He either dictated to the teacher, thus using his oral language development to create text he was capable of reading, or he typed his own story. Lee and Neal (1993) refer to this part of the lesson as the language experience segment of the instructional framework. They list the benefits of using word processing software as follows: "Text editing can be done easily, thereby encouraging more risk taking; written text appears immediately on the screen to reinforce reading/writing connections; and immediate accessibility to what has been written promotes better story development and longer stories prolonging time spent in writing" (Lee and Neal 279). David printed his story each day so that he could decide on changes or additions he wanted to make during the next lesson. The following is an example of his story about pirates:

> This is a story made into a poem. This story is about two women pirates. The pirates' names were Mary and Anne. They both got in a fight with the Albion, a war ship that was to stop the pirates. The captain of the Albion was Barnet. Anne and Mary

and the crew were captured by the Albion. The pirate ship, the Vanity, was blown up. The crew was hanged but Mary and Anne were not hanged because they were each having children. Anne had two children. Mary and Anne became grandmothers. I don't think it was fair to the men that the women were not hanged. The men and the women should have been put in jail. The children should have been put in foster homes till their mothers were released from jail.

When the story was finished, a final printout became a part of a collection of stories he could choose to reread at the beginning of each session.

6. **Reading new material**. For the last part of the lesson, David read from an instructional-level, high-interest chapter book. As new material was introduced, the story passage was previewed for new words and unfamiliar concepts. After the teacher read a portion of the new material, David read the same portion aloud. Paired unison reading was used as necessary to give him a sense of fluency and mastery. This "new" rehearsed material was used to make a running record during the next session.

Data Collection

Data was collected prior to, during, and after the sessions. After establishing a baseline, the teacher administered Test 3 of the Woodcock Reading Mastery Tests-Revised H (1987) semiweekly for five weeks to measure David's progress in word identification. During the third through the sixth weeks of treatment, the teacher tested and recorded his ability to remember and recognize new words from text by having him read a word list generated from miscues in the running records. Audiotapes and a descriptive journal which included lesson plans, running records, and writing samples assured the accuracy of the data. After thirty hours of instruction, the teacher administered the Woodcock Reading Mastery Tests-Revised G, the Analytical Reading Inventory, Form C, and the Diagnostic Survey to measure David's progress in reading achievement.

> Low-ability readers tend to avoid reading because they are frequently assigned to read beyond their independent or instructional reading level.

Analysis of Results

Preliminary testing placed David at grade level 4.2, corresponding to a raw score of 66, on the Woodcock Reading Mastery Word Identification Test. This test was administered during each of the first four sessions to ensure establishment of stable baseline data. The same test was subsequently administered twice weekly for five weeks. David's average score was 72. The highest score after five weeks was 76, showing an increase of 10 correct responses over his lowest score. The Analytical Reading Inventory placed David at fourth grade instructional level prior to treatment. After six weeks of daily one-on-one instruction, David tested one grade higher in comprehension and accuracy.

David was more willing to talk and write about the stories he read. He related story events to his own feelings and world view. He was now more experienced and confident in writing and editing with the help of computer software.

David's pretest and posttest scores on the Woodcock Word Attack Test remained constant at grade level 3.7, showing no gains in ability to use phonics. However, the scores on Word Identification and Word Knowledge tests both showed a gain of 1.5 grade levels, and Passage Comprehension tests showed a gain of .6 grade levels. The Diagnostic Survey also showed a gain in reading accuracy, especially on difficult text, where there was a positive difference of six percent between pretest and posttest scores.

Examination of running records, audiotapes of oral reading, and writing samples also revealed David's progress. Although his reading continued to be slow and labored, he was now more proficient at self-correcting miscues to gain meaning rather than simply word calling. David also used a wider range of strategies to recognize new words. At the beginning of the tutoring, his main strategies for reading difficult text were rereading and overrelying on phonics, his weakest skill. After six weeks of instruction, he more frequently used context to recognize new words, crosschecked illustrations to predict events, and found small words in big words. David was more willing to talk and write about the stories he read. He related story events to his own feelings and world views. He was now more experienced and confident in writing and editing with the help of computer software. Thus, the positive results of this study supported the Reading Rescue model as a framework for tutoring middle school students.

Recommendations

Most likely, David would have benefited from any program which provided him the opportunity to practice one-on-one reading and writing of connected text under the guidance of a caring tutor consistently for six weeks. However, the following advantages of Reading Rescue intervention made it unique and might serve as guidelines for remedial literacy instruction:

1. Analyzing daily running records of oral reading of connected text allowed the teacher to identify individual strengths and weaknesses. Miscue analysis of the running record determined instruction in words and letters, yet literature was still the basis for reading instruction.

2. Rereading familiar texts provided the student opportunities to read fluently, gain confidence, and review previously learned new words and favorite story episodes.

3. Reading aloud, along with paired and echo reading, allowed David to read with support beyond his instructional level and experience the joy of engaging in good literature.

4. Writing with the aid of word processing software allowed David to make connections between reading and writing processes and to self-monitor the sense and correctness of his own language.

Although this study involves on-going research, the positive results revealed in David's transformation support unequivocally the value of the Reading Rescue lesson framework. This intervention has shown promise to be the "lifeline" that teachers and other caring adults can extend to students like David who have fallen behind in reading. Reading Rescue provides the opportunity for these sinking students to acquire better reading skills, which will allow them to stay afloat during their challenging middle school years.

References

Allington, R. L. "The Reading Instruction Provided Readers of Differing Abilities." *Elementary School Journal* 83 (1983): 548-559.

Allington, R. L. "The Schools We Have. The Schools We Need." *The Reading Teacher* 48 (1994): 14-27.

Children's Writing & Publishing Center [Computer software]. (1988). Fremont, CA: The Learning Company.

Clay, M. M. *The Early Detection of Reading Difficulties*. Portsmouth, NH: Heinemann, 1985.

- - -. *Becoming Literate*. Portsmouth, NH: Heinemann, 1991.

- - -. *Reading Recovery®, A Guidebook for Teachers in Training*. Portsmouth, NH: Heinemann, 1993.

Duffy, G., & L. Roehler. *Improving Classroom Reading Instruction: A Decision-making Approach*. New York: Random House, 1986.

Gambrell, L. B., R. M. Wilson, & W. N. Gantt. "Classroom Observations of Task-Attending Behaviors of Good and Poor Readers." *Journal of Educational Research*, 74 (1981): 400-404.

LaBerge, D., & S. J. Samuels. "Toward a Theory of Automatic Information Processing in Reading." *Cognitive Psychology* 6 (1974): 283-323.

McCormick, S. "What is Single-subject Experimental Research?" *Single-subject Experimental Research: Applications for Literacy* Eds. Newman and McCormick. Newark, DE: International Reading Association, 1995.

McGill-Franzen, A. & R. L. Allington. "Comprehension and Coherence: Neglected Elements of Literacy Instruction in Remedial and Resource Room Services." *Journal of Reading, Writing, and Learning Disabilities* 6 (1990): 149-180.

Morris, D., C. Ervin, & K. Conrad. "A Case Study of Middle School Reading Disability." *The Reading Teacher* 49 (1996): 368-377.

Spiegel, D. L. "A Comparison of Traditional Remedial Programs and Reading Recovery®: Guidelines for Success for All Programs." *The Reading Teacher* 49 (1995): 86-96.

Works Cited

Conley, M. W. "Middle School and Junior High Reading Programs." *The Administration and Supervision of Reading Programs* Eds. Freeley and Strickland. New York: Teachers College Press, 1995.

Lee, N. G., & J. C. Neal. "Reading Rescue: Intervention for a Student 'at Promise.' " *Journal of Reading* 36 (1993): 276-282.

Woods, M. L., & J. J. Moe. *Analytical Reading Inventory*. 4th ed. Columbus, OH: Merill, 1989.

Wood, K. D., & K. D. Muth. "The Case for Improved Instruction in the Middle Grades." *Journal of Reading* 35 (1991): 84-89.

About Janet Hunt

"Step by step, day by day, one student at a time will find a way to meet life's challenges if I do my part to educate and guide with both my head and my heart."

Janet Hunt has taught fourth through sixth grades for seventeen years in various schools in several states. In 1997, she came to Virginia Beach. An advocate of the instructional principles of the Reading Recovery® Program and the Reading Rescue lesson framework, Janet Hunt is currently the Reading Resource Teacher at Hermitage Elementary School in Virginia Beach. In addition, Janet shares her current research and teaching expertise as an adjunct professor in reading education at Old Dominion University in Norfolk, Virginia. She received her B.A. in German from the University of Washington and her M.S. in Reading from Old Dominion University.

The Influence of Brain Hemisphericity on the Composing Process of Twelfth Graders

by Reinholdine Pierson

my interest in brain hemisphericity began in the early '80s; the interest was personal before it became academic and resulted, as many of my interests have, from reading. I've always loved dabbling in the realms of philosophical thought and discussion, and after a discussion on "finding the self," a psychiatrist friend gave me *Prisoners of Childhood*, by Alice Miller. This profound little book about the issue of identity evoked in me an unusually strong and deep reaction. For the first time, I realized that as a sensitive, gifted, and alert child, I learned how to repress my intense feelings because such feelings were unacceptable to my parents. I tried to be what my parents wanted me to be rather than who I was. I also began thinking about how so many of our students may also feel like prisoners. As educators, do we push our students to be who we want them to be instead of merely accepting who they are? who *they* want to be? How does this significant educational question relate to brain hemisphericity? Is there a correlation between general personality traits, self-esteem, and hemisphericity? What effect might this correlation have on education? Is there a correlation between brain hemisphericity and school drop-outs?

> As educators, do we push our students to be who we want them to be instead of merely accepting who *they* are? who they want to be?

The same friend who introduced me to *Prisoners of Childhood* also introduced me to the concept of right-brainness and left-brainness when he suggested, that because I am very right-brained and my husband is very left-brained, we process information differently. Then, when I remembered past discussions with my husband, I realized that when I *thought* I knew what we were talking about, I wasn't even close! So, when it came time to choose a topic for my doctoral dissertation, I began thinking about how individuals process information and wondered if right-brainness and left-brainness had any academic implications. And so, my research journey began.

The concept that the brain hemispheres have specialized functions is now entrenched in many minds. The popularization of the concept can be found in magazines, where simplistic "tests" offer the reader a self-administered "test" to determine his/her brain preference; it can be found in television commercials; it can be found in cartoons in the local newspaper. Despite this mainstreaming of science into pop culture, I was nonetheless intrigued with the role brain hemisphericity might play in learning and thought. The fact remains that the two hemispheres of the brain do tend to have specialized functions, and individuals do tend to manifest a left- or right-thinking mode preference. But, is there a relationship between brain hemisphericity and a student's composing process and his willingness to continue revising a paper?

As an English teacher, I decided to explore the role of hemisphericity in the area of student composition to test my theory that a student's composing process differs relative to a student's hemispheric dominance.

As an English teacher, I decided to explore the role of hemisphericity in the area of student composition to test my theory that a student's composing process differs relative to a student's hemispheric dominance. In order to begin this exploration, I first had to find an instrument that would test brain hemisphericity. After some research, I discovered the Herrmann Brain Dominance Instrument and tested all my students.

For my study, I chose eight of my twelfth graders as subjects. First, I questioned them about their composing processes, their writing preferences, and the specific processes used to compose three teacher-generated composition topics, and one open-ended response statement to a prompt. I observed the students while they generated their papers in the English computer lab over a period of four months. After my period of observation, I was able to conclude that the right-brained students approached the composing process much differently than the left-brained students: right-brained students preferred free-writing and creative writing, while left-brained students enjoyed doing research papers and book reports.

For the purposes of my study I used the following questions to determine specific characteristics regarding my students' composing process:

- When you're given a writing assignment, what is your first reaction?
- Once you understand what it is you are to write about, what is the first thing you do?
- Do you do any prewriting? outlining? clustering?
- What kinds of writing have you done since the ninth grade?
- What kinds of writing do you find most comfortable?
- What kinds cause you the most anxiety?

- What kinds of formal composition instruction have you had since the ninth grade?
- Have any of your teachers ever taught you how to write about literature? If so, how?
- When writing about literature, how do you proceed? Were you instructed to analyze the literature, or were you able to respond freely to literature through some personal association?

From the first "split-brain" studies in the 1970s to the present, much has been said about, written about, and conjectured about the role of hemisphericity in learning and thought. While dominance is distributed in various intensities between the two hemispheres, as shown in the dominance profiles of all the students in my study, each of my students revealed, however, various intensities of brain dominance; but each of my students also demonstrated primary and secondary preferences, which indicated to me that students function in both hemispheres, and that even though two hemispheres work together, one clearly takes the lead.

For example, when I asked my students about their individual composing process, Sarah, Diane, Eve, and Daniel, all clearly right-brain-dominant, used words like "expressing," "imaginative," "picture," and "personal" when talking about their writing. Sarah said she gets "...these little cartoons in my mind, pictures of what I should write about, of how I'm feeling or my ideas." Daniel said his favorite type of writing is "imaginative." Diane said she likes to "...write about feelings usually." Eve said of her writing: "The kind I do the least is the type I like the most which is personal writing."

As part of my study, students were to respond to teacher-generated topics regarding Shakespeare's *Macbeth*, *Beowulf*, and Chaucer's, *The Canterbury Tales*. I gave my students the following teacher-generated prompts:

> Sarah said she gets "...these little cartoons in my mind, pictures of what I should write about, of how I'm feeling or my ideas." Daniel said his favorite type of writing is "imaginative."

Topic for *Beowulf* Paper

After the completion of our reading of *Beowulf*, you are to write a well-organized expository essay in which you clearly show that Beowulf is either a pagan or a Christian hero. Cite references to support your thesis.

Topics for Chaucer Paper

• Write a dialogue between two of the characters on the pilgrimage (for example, the Prioress and the Wife of Bath), either prose or poetry. Be sure to portray the character of each pilgrim and to retain the flavor of the age.

• If you were to set out to be the Chaucer of today, what group of citizens would you assemble to represent today's society and culture and in what setting would you put them? Now, write your prologue.

Topics for *Macbeth* Paper

• Paraphrase Macbeth's arguments in Act I, Scene 7 against the murder of Duncan. Does he present a moral argument against killing Duncan? Just what kind of argument does he present? Your task is to summarize his speech and evaluate just what it is he says and what later convinces him to change his mind?

• Compare and contrast Macbeth's and Banquo's reactions to the Witches and their predictions in Act 1, Scene 3. How does this reaction illuminate certain qualities of Macbeth's and Banquo's characters that point toward their subsequent actions and their consequences?

• Trace the development and downfall of the Macbeths and analyze the elements of each character's personality that contribute to the downfall.

When discussing the teacher-generated topics on which they had to write, the right-brain-dominant students disliked the topics.

When I asked what difficulties Sarah encountered while writing the *Beowulf* paper, she replied, "Trying to get into the paper itself since I don't really like being told what to write." When I asked Diane the same question, she said she had "no real problems, just the fact that I didn't like the subject matter."

Given the same series of questions regarding the composing process, Karl, Drew, and Gary, all clearly left-brained, mentioned words such as "analyze," "outline," "research," "detail," "hypothesis," and "reference." When I asked Karl if he attempted any prewriting, he said, "I usually outline reference material." Drew said he completes an outline before writing a paper and that he feels most comfortable about writing book reports because "a book report has set themes, set ideas, and everything you need to know is right there in front of you." Gary said he prefers research papers because they "are the easiest to find information on," and explained that he even looked for topics in reference material: "I am looking for general or specific topics depending on the paper I'm doing. I am looking for words I can use in my paper."

When asked about his like or dislike of the teacher-chosen prompts, Karl said "they were easy to support" because they were detailed enough to make it easy to write about." Drew replied, "I dropped out of Superior English in eighth grade because there was more creative writing than I could stand. I don't like it because there is no right or wrong." When asked about the topics for the *Beowulf* paper, Drew said the topic he chose was attractive "because I could support it easily from the book and from the class notes and discussions."

Sarah, Diane, Eve, and Daniel had quite different responses when asked about the kinds of writing they preferred. Sarah said, "I don't like it when I have to write stuff like term papers or factual stuff. I like

> **By contrast, Karl (left-brain dominant) responded to the poem by writing an essay arguing against conformity. Rather than relating how he *felt* about the poem, he related what he *thought*.**

to use my feelings to write." Donna said she felt disdain for writing about topics she hadn't picked herself. Daniel indicated that he could "write for hours" if it was a topic "he" liked or could get interested "in." I then wanted to see if literary genre made a difference in the way students responded to their next prompt and to their composing process, so I introduced the poem, "Have You Seen This Child?" (Appendix I) Below is a brief excerpt of my conversation with Sarah, a student who revealed more right-brain dominance:

Pierson: After reading the poem, what was your initial response?

Sarah: The poem really moved me! So real! It made me want to give everyone copies and let them read it, to experience what I was feeling.

Pierson: How did you feel about being asked to write in response to an open-ended assignment?

Sarah: It was kind of hard writing like that because I had so many things that I wanted to say, to express. I thought of so many different ways I could write about it.

Pierson: How did you decide to proceed with this paper? Please detail the steps you took to complete the assignment.

Sarah: I wrote several different rough drafts and began them in different ways. Finally, I had to go through each draft and take out the parts that were easiest so others could understand what I was trying to say.

I wanted to see if Sarah would reveal the same right-brain dominance through writing and so I gave her the following open-ended prompt for "Have You Seen This Child?"

- **After you finish reading the poem, "Have You Seen This Child?" respond to the poem in any manner you choose.**

Again, Sarah's response emphasized much more about how she *felt* about the poem, the child, and the poet. She expressed outrage at society's demand for conformity, writing:

> In the poem "Have You Seen This Child?" the poet is trying to express his feelings on the battle between conformity and uniqueness. When "we" humans are born, we are born to be our own persons. We can express this when we are young. Of course, all this ends by the time we start school. Then, we are forced to conform to society's norms, values, and taboos. The child in this poem represents "us" as humans. The poet describes how the child wanted to say things but no one understood. I feel it's not so much understanding but that no one really listened. The child was changing yet no one had the time, or wanted to take the time to care or help the child.

By contrast, Karl (left-brain dominant) responded to the poem by writing an essay arguing against conformity. Rather than relating how he *felt* about the poem, he related what he *thought*. When I questioned Karl about his composing process he used words such as "I think... I write down a few notes... and I correlate." I noticed his response to the poem, "Have You Seen This Child?" revealed much more analysis—much more thought and much less intuition. He wrote:

> After reading this poem one singular thought came to mind: "conformity is death." This poem made me very sad because I saw parts of me in it, as I think everyone else does. I have found, in my relatively short life, that everyone is forced to conform in one way or another, maybe it is just dressing the same or talking the same or maybe it is something harder like thinking the same or living the same.

When a person is forced to conform, a piece of their personality is chipped off and falls to the floor never to be reattached. In our society, nonconformists are shunned and ridiculed because of their abstract views. The only reason that the conformists are jealous is because they no longer have a personality of their own; they let it be molded by others. Now they are dead, not in a physical sense but an inner sense.

Given my observations of the composing process with eight of my twelfth-grade students, as English teachers especially, we need to be reminded that if in discussing a literary work with our students, we tell them the only interpretation to a given work is ours, and we reward them for accepting that interpretation, we are in danger of stifling any creative inquiry, particularly for students who reveal a right-brain dominance. As educators, we must encourage our students to think for themselves and to form their own judgments; if we do not, we are creating frustrated automatons. We are allowing ourselves to be satisfied with student regurgitation rather than with creative thinking. We are rewarding the best regurgitators by giving them the best grades, while telling the creative student, who approaches the writing assignment from a perspective we had not envisioned, that he/she fails because he/she did not follow the teacher created topic assignment *exactly*.

> **We are allowing ourselves to be satisfied with student regurgitation rather than with creative thinking. We are rewarding the best regurgitators by giving them the best grades...**

After my classroom observations, I am much more aware of the need for educators to understand *how* our students process information. Educators need to be aware that sitting in our classrooms are both left- and right-brained students, and that these students not only have preferences for a particular writing process, they also respond to literature relative to their thinking mode preferences.

Yet, so much remains unexamined. Of the ten students I identified as "extreme left-brained" or "right-brained," four have had emotional problems serious enough to require institutionalization. Two of those four have a voluminous record of in-school and out-of-school suspensions. All four are right-brained; all four have average or above average IQs, ranging from 109-139; all four of them are artistically talented. Certainly, many variables account for these similar profiles—a student's family situation, a lack of self-esteem, even social, philosophical differences relating to societal norms. Even though I cannot make any definitive conclusions, my observations of these eight students did arouse questions in my mind: Could a student's brain hemispheric dominance play a role in social as well as academic success? Could creating school systems and curricula that value both sides of the brain make a difference? If teaching to both sides would make a difference, how do educators develop teaching models to enable this to occur?

Correlation studies are crucial to understanding whether an individual's hemispheric dominance is instrumental in how he/she thinks, learns, and perceives his/her world, and this realization would have wide-reaching teaching implications for education. If it could be demonstrated that semi-literates, with a fourth grade reading level, are predominantly right-brained, could that mean that in the fourth grade the curriculum begins gearing itself to the left hemisphere? Could a more creative, right-brain approach to reading and writing help such an individual? The implications for researchers lie in the development of valid and reliable instruments to identify students' thinking mode preferences rather than merely making generalizations regarding learning styles. In addition, developing a reliable testing instrument suitable for elementary level students would provide early detection of brain dominance and would enable teachers to help students become functional in the less dominant thinking modes. Perhaps increased academic achievement as well as a positive student response to various learning situations and environments would be dramatically enhanced.

> **When a young man comes into my classroom with pink and green hair and an earring in his eyebrow, I think "right brained" rather than "trouble."**

If nothing more is accomplished by my observations and findings than an awakening of awareness and a much needed dialogue among teachers, curriculum specialists, school superintendents, parents, and researchers, a service will have been rendered for all students. How has this experience affected me? When I start each new school year I now see my students in a different light. When a young man comes into my classroom with pink and green hair and an earring in his eyebrow, I think "right-brained" rather than "trouble."

Have You Seen This Child?

He always wanted to say things, but no one understood.
He always wanted to explain things, but no one cared.
So he drew.
Sometimes he would just draw and it wasn't anything.
He wanted to carve it in stone or write it in the sky.
He would lie on the grass and look up at the sky, and it would be only him and
  the sky and the things inside that needed saying.
And it was after that, that he drew the picture.
He kept it under his pillow and would let no one see it.
And he would look at it at night and think about it.
And when it was dark and his eyes were closed he could still see it.
And it was all of him.
And he loved it.
When he started school he brought it with him.
Not to show to anyone but just to have it with him as a friend.

It was funny about school.
He sat in a square brown desk like all of the other square brown desks and
  thought it should be red.
And his room was a square brown room, like all the other rooms.
And it was tight and close and still.
He hated to hold the pencil and the chalk with his arm stiff and his feet on the
  floor, still, with the teacher watching and watching.
And then he had to write numbers.
And they weren't anything.

They were worse than letters that could be something if you put them together.
And the numbers were tight and square and he hated the whole thing.
The teacher came and spoke to him.
She told him to wear a tie like all the other boys.
He said that he didn't like them but she said that it didn't matter.
After that they drew.
And he drew all yellow and it was the way he felt about morning, and it was
  beautiful.
The teacher came and smiled at him.
"What's that?" she said.

"Why don't you do something like Ken's drawing?"
It was all questions.

After that his mother bought him a tie and he always drew airplanes and rocket ships like everyone else.
And he threw the old picture away.
And when he lay out alone looking at the sky, it was big and blue and all of everything, but he wasn't anymore.

He was square inside and brown and his hands were stiff, and he was like everyone else.
And the things inside him that needed saying didn't need saying anymore.
It had stopped pushing.
It was crushed.
Stiff.
Like everyone else.

References

Atwell, Nancy. "Class-Based Writing Research." In *Reclaiming the Classroom: Teacher Research as an Agency for Change,* ed. Dixie Goswami and Peter Stillman, 87-94 Upper Montclair, NJ: Boynton/Cook Publishers, Inc., 1986.

Bertelson, P. "The Nature of Hemispheric Specialization: Why Should There Be a Single Principle?" *The Behavioral and Brain Sciences* 4 (1981): 63-64.

Blackmore, C. *Mechanics of the Mind.* Cambridge: University Press, 1977.

Bogen, J. E. "The Other Side of the Brain." *Bulletin of the Los Angeles Neurological Societies* 34 (1969): 73-105.

Buzan, Tony. *Use Both Sides of Your Brain.* New York: E. P. Dutton, 1974.

Buzan, Tony. *Research on Composing.* Urbana, IL: National Council of Teachers of English, 1978.

Diamond, S. *The Double Brain.* London: The Whitefriars Press, Ltd., 1972.

Edwards, Betty. *Drawing on the Right Side of the Brain.* Los Angeles: J. P. Tarcher, Inc., 1979.

Emig, Janet. *The Composing Process of Twelfth Graders.* Urbana, IL: National Council of Teachers of English, 1971.

- - -. *The Web of Meaning.* Upper Montclair, NJ: Boynton/Cook Publishers, Inc., 1983.

Ferguson, M. *The Brain Revolution.* New York: Harper & Row, 1951.

Gardener, H. *The Shattered Mind: The Person After Damage.* New York: Alfred A. Knopf, 1975.

Gardner, H. "What We Know and Don't Know About the Two-Halves of the Brain." *Harvard Magazine* 80 (1978): 24-27.

Gazzaniga, M. "The Split Brain in Man." In *Perception: Mechanisms and Models,* ed. R. Held and W. Richards, 110-117 San Francisco: W. H. Freeman, 1972.

Guild, Pat Burke, and Stephen Garger. *Marching to Different Drummers.* Alexandria, VA: Association for Supervision and Curriculum Development, 1985.

Hart, L. *How the Brain Works: A New Understanding of Human Learning, Emotion and Thinking.* New York: Basic Books, 1975.

Jaynes, J. *The Origin of Consciousness in the Breakdown of the Bicameral Mind.* Boston: Houghton Mifflin, 1976.

Klauser, Henriette Anne. *Writing on Both Sides of the Brain.* San Francisco: Harper & Row, Publishers, 1986.

Levy, J. "Differential Perceptual Capacities in Major and Minor Hemispheres." *Proceedings of the National Academy of Science* 64 (1968).

Myers, Miles. *The Teacher/Researcher: How to Study Writing in the Classroom.* Urbana, IL: National Council of Teachers of English, 1985.

Nebes, R. D. "Direct Examination of Cognitive Function in the Right and Left Hemispheres." In *Asymmetrical Functions of the Brain,* ed. M. Kinsborough, 56-77 New York: Cambridge University Press, 1978.

Ornstein, Richard. *The Psychology of Consciousness.* New York: Penguin Books, 1986.

- - -. "The Split and Whole Brain." *Human Nature* 1 (1978): 76- 86.

Prince, George. "Putting the Other Half of the Brain to Work." *Training: The Magazine of Human Resources Development* 15 (1978): 57-61.

Rico, Gabriele Lusser. *Writing the Natural Way*. Los Angeles: J. P. Tarcher, Inc., 1983.

Rico, Gabriele, and M. F. Claggert. *Balancing the Hemispheres: An Exploration of the Implications of Brain Research for the Teaching of Writing*. Berkley: University of California Bay Area Writer's Project Monograph, 1980.

Samples, Bob. *The Metaphoric Mind*. Reading, MA: Addison-Wesley Publishing, 1976.

Sperry, Robert W. "Hemisphere Disconnection and Unity in Conscious Awareness." *American Psychologist* 23 (1968): 723-33.

Sperry, Robert W. "Lateral Specialization of Cerebral Function in the Surgically Separated Hemispheres." In *The Psychophysiology of Thinking*, ed. Frank J. McGuigan and Robert A. Schoonover, 209-29. New York: Academic Press, 1973.

Tchudi, Stephen N. *Language, Schooling, and Society*. Upper Montclair, NJ: Boynton/Cook Publishers, Inc., 1985.

Williams, Linda V. *Teaching for the Two-Sided Mind*. New York: Simon & Schuster, Inc., 1983.

About Reinholdine Pierson

"Long after my students have forgotten my literature lessons, it is my hope that they will remember many lessons about life."

Reinholdine Pierson teaches senior English and serves as Academic Coordinator at First Colonial High School in Virginia Beach. She received her B.A. at Upsala College and her M.A. and Ph.D. at Old Dominion University and is active in the following organizations: VBATE, VATE, NCTE, CEL, VCEE, ASCD, and PDK. A frequent presenter on both state and national levels regarding English Education, Ms. Pierson has also shared her expertise by presenting at the Convention of English Leadership. A graduate of the Tidewater Writing Project, Ms. Pierson is also the recipient of the Virginia Teaching with Technology Award and the Virginia Association of Teachers of English Service Award. Ms. Pierson has served as Editor of *Inward-Outward-Upward: An Anthology of Teacher Writing from the Tidewater Writing Project*. Her publications include "The Gift" in *Virginia Writing Supplement to Prentice Hall Literature Transparencies for Writing; Introduction to the Writing Process: Basic Composition*. In addition to her teaching assignment at First Colonial High School, Ms. Pierson serves as Adjunct Associate Professor at Old Dominion University.

Learning and Memory

by Linda Jaglowski

being a teacher for the past twelve years, I have been interested, naturally, in exactly how learning takes place. What has particularly heightened my interest, however, has been the development of my own child. While he was still very young, he learned or remembered certain details much earlier than other children his age. Because I observed that the seven or eight children within his three-year old play group were at different stages of readiness to handle verbal, cognitive, or physical challenges, I began to review research articles dealing with how, why, and when children begin to learn and utilize certain types of information. For example, a relatively new concept in children's development called the "Learning Windows" has received attention beyond scientific circles (Begley "Cultivating the Mind" 28). The "Learning Window" concept holds that because different sections of the brain mature at different times, a child experiences learning windows, time periods in which a child can best learn or refine a particular ability. This concept also seems to have significant implications for a child's education and what educators and parents can do to maximize learning experiences. While children tend to learn best if exposed to appropriate stimuli during these learning windows, an even more recent discovery, CRE-binding protein (CREB) influences how long they are likely to remember (or not remember) what they have been exposed to firsthand. Yet the CREB theory is just the beginning. Experts in neuroscience believe it may very well be the first step in a "staircase" of connecting genes and molecules to thought and behavior. This is particularly important since memory plays a significant role in higher cognitive processes (Stevens 769).

> The "Learning Window" concept holds that because different sections of the brain mature at different times, a child experiences learning windows, time periods in which a child can best learn or refine a particular ability.

Research in neurobiology is a fairly new field. Analyzing brain functions is difficult at best, but with the development of new medical imaging technology and highly sensitive tools, the study of neurological functions has taken off. Although many unknowns still exist, researchers now know enough to draw some important conclusions on how learning works, especially in children. In a developing brain, millions of neurons form electrical connections that enable the child to think (Wartik et al 57). These cells send their signals through axons, some of which reach a length of up to a meter in humans. Wrapped around many of the axons are other cells which form myelin sheaths, which insulate the axon, letting its signal travel a hundred times faster than an unmyelinated axon. This is particularly important since myelinated axons enable the "circuits" to work much faster which, in turn, make certain activities easier to learn.

> The implication for teachers is obvious. To stimulate more language comprehension, educators must find opportunities to interact verbally with children during the "language learning" window of opportunity, which continues from birth to age ten or twelve.

Myelinization is extremely important in children, because as they mature, different regions of the brain become myelinated at different ages. Even more amazing, the brain knows which areas need to be myelinated first. This myelinization process creates learning windows which are only effective, however, if the child interacts appropriately with environmental stimuli.

The implication for teachers is obvious. To stimulate more language comprehension, educators must find opportunities to interact verbally with children during the "language learning" window of opportunity, which continues from birth to age ten or twelve. For math and logic skills, the learning window is from birth to age four, when day care providers and preschool teachers should create counting games and activities to help children learn sequencing. Because circuits for music reside in the brain near those for math, early exposure to music, ages three to four, trains the brain for higher forms of thinking and enhances the ability to reason. To help a child become more coordinated and active later in life, health and physical education teachers should be aware of the gross muscle development window beginning at age four. A learning window even exists where children are more receptive to learning foreign languages. While it may be possible to learn a second or third language at any age, learning is easier when the language is introduced before the age of ten.

Research also shows that a child's experiences until age ten will determine how much of the child's cortex will be devoted to each part of the body (Begley "How to Build a Baby's Brain" 56). Research indicates a direct connection with the development of the central cortex of the brain and sensory motor development; for example, if a child uses his hands frequently, as in drawing, then more neurons will be devoted to the muscles in his hands and fingers. The more a muscle is used, the more neuron connections will be established. By the same token, the less a muscle is used, the fewer the connections that are established to the motor cortex. Therefore, it will be more difficult to develop these muscles later.

These theories raise interesting yet troubling questions. If teachers and parents do not catch an all-important "learning window," does that mean a child will never become a world-renowned pianist or doctor? On one level, no. The brain retains the ability to learn throughout life. However, becoming aware of the learning windows, a child may be better equipped to learn a new skill. For example, the window for learning fine motor skills ends around the age of ten. If a child learns to play a musical instrument before that time, during the optimum learning years of three to ten, he will be much more skilled with less practice, and his ability will stay with him longer (Begley 75). Unfortunately, the converse is sobering. Children whose neural circuits are not stimulated before kindergarten may never be what they might have been.

Broadening this concept to educational curricula, another promising frontier is the relationship between memory and learning (Wartik et al 58). When the brain gains a piece of knowledge, what occurs in its cells? How can curricula design capitalize on this scientific knowledge? Researchers have identified some of the key molecules of memory and the location in the brain where different kinds of memories are processed and stored. In addition, memory research is providing a growing picture of how the brain works and how the interaction of genes and molecules ultimately produces the elusive universe of thought, emotion, and behavior (Seigfried 1). Scientists now understand that information embedded in an emotional context, those events which have a strong, affective component, stimulate neural circuitry more powerfully than information alone. For example, events or activities that are extremely traumatic or extremely pleasurable tend to be etched in memory longer.

> These theories raise interesting yet troubling questions. If teachers and parents do not catch an all-important "learning window," does that mean a child will never become a world-renowned pianist or doctor?

Causality, a key component of logic, is also best learned through emotions; an understanding that one thing causes another creates synapses, the communications links between nerves and cells, that will eventually support a more sophisticated understanding of the relationship between cause and effect (Begley 75). What then can educators learn from this relationship? The implications of this research for educators deal with the two types of memory: explicit (or declarative) and implicit (or nondeclarative). Explicit memory is the kind commonly used for passing tests in school, involving recall of facts and events, or recognition of people, places, and things. Implicit memory is generally unconscious, involving skills and habits such as riding a bicycle or tying a shoe. In both types, scientists have found similar chemistry underlying the transformation of a temporary memory into a lasting memory (Seigfried 9). These studies show that forming a long-term memory, whether explicit or implicit, requires brain cells to make new proteins. The new proteins forge long-term memories by strengthening synapses.

Incorporating these learning strategies may also improve something else in the classroom: delight in learning.

With short-term memories, synapse strengths are modified temporarily by the activation of various chemicals such as serotonin, a neurotransmitter released during behavorial sensitization, a simple form of learning (Alberini 1100). In contrast, long-term memory involves the production of new proteins, a process requiring gene activation. Cyclic AMP response element (CRE binding protein) attaches CRE sites on genes. Researchers believe that CREB initiates recall by stimulating genes whose protein products then activate additional genes (Tully 244). Other studies reveal that long-term memory results only when learning occurs with rests. With repeated rest intervals between study sessions, a longer-lasting memory that requires protein synthesis is formed (Tully 110).

Understanding the molecular mechanisms of learning and memory has been a major area of investigation in neurobiology. However, experts believe the memory question may be "solved" in the next decade through the discovery of cellular mechanisms that set synaptic strengths for certain types of memory (Stevens 770). The real challenge will be to convince parents and educators that stages of brain development affect learning and that a good start in life will do more to promote learning and long-term memory than anyone has previously imagined.

Again, what are the implications for educators? Perhaps a radical shift in our thinking. For example, perhaps foreign languages should no longer be the exclusive domain of high school but should be offered in elementary school, and even preschool, when the window of learning is open. Music and physical education would be required daily with planned activities that best fit the age and window of the child. The traditional lecture method would be replaced with hands-on learning strategies that studies show actually improve memory (Shakarian 22).

Incorporating these learning strategies may also improve something else in the classroom: delight in learning. "For the first time in any health class, I really enjoyed learning," exclaimed one of my seventh-grade students. What if this were true for all students in all disciplines?

References

Yin, J.C.P., M. Del Vecchio, H. Zhou, and T. Tully. "CREB as a Memory Modulator." *Cell* 81: (1995): 107-115.

Works Cited

Alberini, C.M., Ghirardi, Metz, and Kandel. "C-EBP Is an Immediate Early Gene Required for the Consolation of Long-term Facilitation in Aplysia." *Cell* 76 (1994): 1099-1114.

Begley, Sharon. "Your Child's Brain." *Newsweek*. 1996.

- - - . "How to Build a Baby's Brain." *Newsweek Special Edition*. 1997. "Cultivating the Mind." *Newsweek Special Edition* 28 (1997).

Shakarian, Diana C. "Beyond Lecture: Active Learning Strategies that Work." *JOPHERD* 22 (1995).

Seigried, Tom. "What Memories are Made of" *Dallas Morning News*. 1995.

Stevens, Charles. "CREB and Memory Consolidation" *Nueron* 13 (1994): 769-770.

Tully, Tim. "Mice, Flies Share Memory Molecule" *Science News* 146 (1994): 146, 244.

Wartik, Nancy, and Lavonne Carson-Finnerty. *Memory and Living* New York: W.W. Norton, 1993.

About Linda Jaglowski

"We once believed that intelligence was a static quotient fixed at birth. Today, we know that we have multiple intelligences that change, grow, and can be significantly developed."

> —MARIE PUETT

"When he was 75 years old my father told me, 'As long as I'm alive, I will continue going to school and take different classes to learn something new and keep my mind young. You are never too old to learn.' "

> —JOHN FAY

Immediately after graduating from Virginia Commonwealth University, Linda Jaglowski taught health and physical education for two years in Richmond, Virginia. After traveling throughout Europe as an exchange student, and then throughout the United States, Mexico, and Canada, Ms. Jaglowski resumed her teaching career in 1986 at Kempsville Middle School. For the past two years, Linda has been teaching at Kemps Landing Magnet School in Virginia Beach where she currently serves as curriculum team leader. Linda is an active member of the American Alliance for Health, Physical Education, Recreation, and Dance as well as the Virginia Beach Association for the Gifted and Talented and the Parent Teacher Association. Recently securing three research grants, Linda Jaglowski continues to pursue her research interests in health, physical education, and brain research.

Who Needs Magic?
The Power of Applying Theory to Practice

by Beth Holland

ames, Shannon, Bobby, and Chavon sit, waiting patiently for me to begin their reading lesson… waiting for the magic where I, a Reading Resource teacher, transform struggling first-grade readers into competent readers. Mrs. Johnson, their teacher, notes in her lesson plans that the boys all need help with the vocabulary words from the current story and the short *a* sound. I tap into my creative side and try to make the skills lesson as engaging and meaningful as possible for such dry, isolated material. After the lesson, they leave with smiles on their faces and look forward to returning the next day. Why then, instead of feeling I have met my objectives, do I feel like a failure? It's hard to be honest, even with myself; there is no magic. Despite all my teaching energy and good intentions, most of these students will remain at-risk students for most, if not all, of their educational careers. There must be a more effective way to help these students connect with the literary world. This confession became the impetus for my training as a Reading Recovery® teacher.

Reading Recovery® is an intensive, year-long "on-the-job training" class, which starts teachers on a lifelong journey of understanding the reading process. Before I began the training five years ago, I thought I understood reading; I had a Master's degree, after all. What I didn't realize was that recently, much new research had been published, a result of thirty years of work by a New Zealand cognitive psychologist, Dr. Marie Clay. She is the founder of Reading Recovery®, a world-renowned early intervention program to help students read.

In the Reading Recovery® program, the lowest twenty percent of the first-grade population is serviced at each school. Students are taught individually in highly structured, daily thirty-minute lessons using pieces of their own writing and engaging literature that is personally relevant. Reading and writing are taught as a process rather than a hierarchy of skills. For example, greater than 80 percent of

> After the lesson, they leave with smiles on their faces and look forward to returning the next day. Why then, instead of feeling I have met my objectives, do I feel like a failure? It's hard to be honest, even with myself; there is no magic.

these at-risk students can accelerate their skills to the average of their class in twelve to twenty weeks. Teaching is based on systematic observation, reflection, and problem-solving.

By December of my training year, Reading Recovery® felt like an obsession; I constantly kept thinking about ways to incorporate these strategies into every lesson; I kept thinking about the dramatic changes I would soon experience with my students. Sharing this knowledge and enthusiasm with my colleagues, we all became addicted to Reading Recovery®. The only other time I had noticed similar "addictive" behaviors in myself was when I had been obsessed with tennis and, before that, with bridge. I would come home and replay points and entire matches in my head, both asleep and awake. What could I have done differently to achieve my goal? What had I missed that was important? What would I do next time to achieve the same or a different result?

My Reading Recovery® training taught me that finding the answers to these very same questions makes an effective teacher, particularly a teacher of at-risk students. Because at-risk students lack experience with printed text, become impulsive and inattentive at times, and have difficulty comprehending and applying new knowledge, the at-risk student must be taught those concepts which we can assume the average student gleans from his repeated literary experiences, such as the way a book is organized or how a story unfolds for the reader. To meet their needs, a teacher must apply current theory to everyday teaching and must break down the reading process as far as it can go to meet her student where he is, instead of where she assumes him to be.

> The only other time I had noticed similar "addictive" behaviors in myself was when I had been obsessed with tennis and, before that, with bridge. I would come home and replay points and entire matches in my head, both asleep and awake.

Every year since that realization, I have been immersed in the work of Dr. Clay. I have learned she is responsible for contributing to and publishing much of the brain research and learning theory as it relates to reading. In fact, she was one of the first to link some of the brain research of psychologists such as Bruner and Vygotsky to an explanation of how children learn to read. My exposure to this theory, at both a theoretical and practical level, has forever changed the way I teach reading. Now I understand why I felt that teaching isolated vocabulary words and the short *a* sound were so futile and empty because Clay describes reading as a "message-getting, problem-solving activity" (Clay, *Becoming Literate* 6). Instead of isolated skills and/or words, students need to be taught strategies for problem-solving the message.

As teachers, our main goal, whether we teach at the primary or college level, is to ensure that our students use a balance of informational sources available to them. The three sources of information available from a text at any level are meaning, either carried by pictures and/or storyline; structure, a reader's understanding of the syntax of the English language; and visual, relating to conventions of print (i.e. text layout, punctuation) and phoneme/grapheme correspondence (Clay, *Reading Recovery®* 42).

The visual cues — the role of phoneme/grapheme correspondence — is perhaps one of the most controversial topics in reading research. To ensure that a student possesses the strategies necessary for accessing visual information through visual cues, analogy is the key. According to Clay, "the human mind works often by analogies and will relate something new to something already known and familiar. Reasoning by analogy is probably our most fruitful source of hypotheses about any intellectual problem" (Clay, *Becoming Literate* 335).

> To meet their needs, a teacher must apply current theory to everyday teaching and must break down the reading process as far as it can go to meet her student where he is, instead of where she assumes him to be.

How can this strategy of analogy be reduced to a set of behaviors to be taught? Goswami and Mead suggest we use a developmental hierarchy of "how words work." This hierarchy is based on easily heard breaks within words since children have an easier time seeing what they already hear (153-162). Onset, the first part of a word, and rime, characterized as the vowel bearing part, are probably two of the most important puzzle pieces to complete the picture of how readers most effectively "take words apart" in text to problem-solve. For example, using the word *struck*, *str* would be the onset and *uck* the rime. In order to use analogy, going from the known to the new in taking apart unidentified words, a child must be able to break known words into usable parts or chunks. Problem-solving would involve questions like "Do I know a word that starts like that? (the onset) or "Do I know a word that ends like that?" (the rime) which would lead a child from the known to the new. For example, *straw* or Ch*uck*.

Awareness of the breaks, however, is not enough. The child must have enough practice with this technique, so that this break becomes an automatic recognition. This understanding of "automaticity" in learning is a critical one as we try to teach a child within his zone of proximal development (Clay, *Becoming Literate* 65). The zone of proximal development is the teaching/learning zone where work is neither so easy that the child needs no teacher help, nor so hard that he requires constant teacher help.

For me to teach in a child's "zone" to move him through the stages of word manipulation, I have to be certain that he has had numerous opportunities to practice breaking a word into onset and rime, so that the process will require little or no attention. He will then be ready to take on the new learning required to change either the onset or rime of a known word in order to problem-solve a new word to read or write.

> **As the group leaves, Nicolette announces, "I wish I could stay here all day long."**

The following scale of word manipulation is based on Goswami's work and is arranged from easiest to hardest (Wright Group 56). A level of automaticity should be reached at each stage before teaching the child the next manipulation. It is easiest to teach each task if the teaching is based on an example from text that needs to be problem-solved. Magnetic letters work well for concrete demonstrations of the manipulation of word parts. For example:

•**Changing onsets** of a known word using the initial consonant – e.g. known word: *cat*, new word: *fat* (For example, my child blocks on the word *fat* in a story about a worm sandwich... Would you like a fat worm? I might take magnetic letters for *cat* and *sat*, words he knows, and change the onset consonant to get the new rhyming word, *fat*. What I'm teaching here is the pattern of rhyming words for use in problem-solving, not specifically the word, *fat*.)

• **Changing onsets** of a known word using a blend or digraph – e.g. known word: *red*, new word: *shed*

• **Changing rimes** of a known word with the last consonant – e.g. known word: *cat*, new word: *cap*

• **Changing rimes** of a known word with inflectional ending – e.g. known word: *play*, new word: *play ing*

• **Adding an onset to a known rime** – e.g. known rime: *and*, new word: *sand*

• **Changing rimes** of a known word by changing the vowel – e.g. known word: *cat*, new word: *cut*

• **Change base word** with different endings – e.g. known base word: *a*, new word: *away*

• **Analogy** – onset of one word with rime of another-e.g. known words: *stop-day*, new word: _stay_

What does the use of analogy look like when attacking words on the run while reading text? Last week, Josiah was reading John Burningham's *Mr. Gumpy's Outing*, a story about a man who takes a boat ride and allows some children and animals to join him if they promise to behave. One page of text went like this:

One day Mr. Gumpy went out in his boat.

"May we come with you?" said the children.

"Yes," said Mr. Gumpy, "if you don't **squabble**."

While thinking about the story and keeping sentence structure in mind, Josiah attacks the word _squabble_, using the following thought process:

It begins like *squeeze*...**squ**. The next chunk **-ab** is like the spelling pattern in **cab**. It ends like **able**. Now let me put the parts together, squ-ab-ble. It still doesn't sound just right.

I reminded him to reread it in the sentence to see if the meaning and structure of the sentence can help him fix it. He does and immediately adjusts the pronunciation, as he remembers that his mom has told his sister and him not to squabble when they play together.

The above example illustrates the all-important balance that must be maintained between the three information sources: meaning, structure, and visualization. Throughout a student's early journey toward reading proficiency, the balanced use of these cues needs to be renegotiated through teacher prompting, until the balancing act becomes automatic and self-regulated within the child.

It's May now of the current school year, and many of my "Literacy Group" children—groups of five at-risk students with whom I work, in addition to my Reading Recovery® students, have internalized the hierarchical tasks of how words work to problem-solve unknown words. Nicolette reveals this knowledge to me while waiting for the group to join her on the carpet for the reading of our new big book, *Animal Clues*, written by David Drew.

She blurted out, "I know the name of that book. *Animal Clues.*"

"How'd you know that, Nicolette? Mrs. Holland told you, right?" her friend Jasmine questions in a jealous voice.

"Jasmine, I just rhymed it with blue." Nicolette responds emphatically, as if to let Jasmine know she was missing the obvious.

From this exchange, it is apparent to me that Jasmine is easily able to substitute onsets, the word manipulation necessary to go from _blue_ to c_lue_. She, however, has not reached the level of automaticity with this task that Nicolette has, where this manipulation can be used for independent problem-solving. As we progress through the reading of the book which requires reading clues to guess the name of animals or bugs, we come to the clue, "here is my silk" (Drew 15). Though we are reading it together orally, I drop my voice at _silk_ to see what problem-solving I hear. I hear some attempts, but realize some support is necessary. I think quickly of a known word they all possess, towards analogy. I write _will_ on the board, (the known), and follow it with _sill_, soliciting the pronunciation of this new word from the group. Next I change the last letter of the rime and write the problem word, _silk_. Some of the students get it and some don't, when Nicolette then chimes in with the easiest analogy that had eluded me. "Just write milk up there, Mrs. Holland, and we'll all get it."

As the group leaves, Nicolette announces, "I wish I could stay here all day long."

Since it has always been important to me that my students enjoy coming to my reading groups, I was interested in why Nicolete liked being in my class. When I inquired, she responded, "Because we get to read lots of books!" That's when I was sure that "Literacy Group" was the perfect name for the at-risk groups I teach because I have been able to actively incorporate problem-solving in teaching my students how to read.

I no longer tense up when a child encounters an unknown word, or utter the words, "sound it out," knowing that this is a fruitless plan of attack. Going letter by letter is most difficult for emergent readers and is not used by proficient readers. Good readers use the largest, known chunks of words, along with analogy to problem-solve a new word (Cunningham 3). I now see an unknown word not as a roadblock to reading but as an opportunity to teach a new strategy to a child.

> **In a child's mind, reading appears to be the first task in school that separates the "cans" from the "cannots." It is critical to a child's attitude toward future learning that the reading experience be as successful as possible.**

In the past, we, as teachers, have made the mistake of having children memorize all the words in a particular word family. Doing this, we then defeated the purpose of using learning analogy to problem-solve; if a child knows one word in a pattern, such as **cat**, he should be able to get to new words **mat**, **sat**, or **_that_**, using what he knows about the way words work. Visual analysis becomes, then, not knowing all the words in a story so that it can be accurately read, but, instead, knowing enough words to use as anchors and being able to problem-solve the unknown words using meaning and structure as checks for the resulting attempt. This way, given an appropriately challenging text, a reader can practice problem-solving and improve with each reading experience, be it independent or teacher scaffolded.

> With the job market clamoring for problem-solvers and for those who are not afraid to risk, is it possible that this early training in using analogy as a problem-solving technique could set students on the path for more marketable traits in later life?

In a child's mind, reading appears to be the first task in school that separates the "cans" from the "cannots." It is critical to a child's attitude toward future learning that the reading experience be as successful as possible. Some children mistakenly assume that good readers just know all the words through some sort of "luck of the draw." Donovan was an example of this kind of student. For each word he encountered that he didn't already know, his self-esteem was lowered just a bit more. It took much persuasion from me and some good teaching to show him that good readers don't know all the words; they just know the "tricks" for solving the unknown words. As each lesson would begin, Donovan would be focused, cooperative, and positive, but as soon as he encountered a problem in reading or writing, he would shut down. He would get angry, and the lesson would be over, whether our session was finished or not. I continued to teach him "tricks" for figuring out a problem. And as he began internalizing some of the strategies, I noticed less tension in him when he hit a problem. He began using some of the strategies that, in turn, boosted his self-confidence.

Donovan is now ready to discontinue my program and join his other classmates as a better than average reader. During the reading of the book, *Pot of Gold*, he reads,

> The elf took Grumble to a big tree. You'll have to dig...
> (He hesitates for a few seconds and says keep-deep, using the known word <u>keep</u> to get to <u>deep</u>.)...deep to get it (*Pot of Gold* 6).

His smile said it all when he reread and realized he was successful. His mother echoes his success when she writes in response to the survey question, "What changes have you seen in your child's self-esteem?" His mother replies, "Donovan can now understand better and solve problems instead of shutting down." According to Cooper, author of *Literacy: Helping Children Construct Meaning*, a student should effectively be able to handle a specific number of unknown words in a reading selection. He refers to Nagy when he suggests that readers may be able to "tolerate text in which as many as 15 percent of the words are not fully known; students do not have to know all of the words in a text to read it with a high level of comprehension"(29).

With the job market clamoring for problem-solvers and for those who are not afraid to risk, is it possible that this early training in using analogy as a problem-solving technique could set students on the path for more marketable traits in later life? As Clay says, "reasoning by analogy is probably our most fruitful source of hypotheses about any intellectual problem" (Clay, *Becoming Literate* 335). Furthermore, Clay maintains that "if a child is composing his own messages in daily writing and working towards independence, it is hard for him to avoid being phonologically analytic" (293). In fact, most children learn about the correspondence through writing, whether it is shared, interactive, or independent. If we, as teachers, are providing opportunities for children to write daily, using developmental spelling on topics of their choosing, then our teaching time will be better directed to "how words work" as a path to analogy, rather than to isolated letter/sound activities, such as worksheets or flash cards.

> So, who needs magic when we can apply theory to learning and teaching and have it be successful? Have these recent learning experiences answered all my questions about the reading process? Quite the contrary!

So, who needs magic when we can apply theory to learning and teaching and have it be successful? Have these recent learning experiences answered all my questions about the reading process? Quite the contrary! I'm now left with new questions about how to be a more effective teacher and how to reach every student, not just most of them. Could it be that our search for the "magical" reading series, the "magical" piece of technology, or the "magical" number of planning minutes has been in vain? Instead, could it be that the real power in ensuring all children exit the primary grades as competent readers is in providing all of our primary teachers with extended time to be immersed in current theory, with time to reflect, and with the support needed to apply that theory to their classrooms?

My ability to teach my students that reading is a "problem-solving, message-getting activity" (Clay, *Becoming Literate* 6), can also be credited to the students I've taught over the last five years. For though the goal, to be able to read, is the same for each child, the path taken is never exactly the same. A child with a repertoire of problem-solving strategies will improve and extend his reading proficiency with each reading experience as will I—with the knowledge of how children most effectively learn to read—improve and extend my teaching proficiency with each lesson I teach.

References

Bruner, J. S. "Learning how to do things with words." In J. Bruner and A. Garton (Eds), *Human Growth and Development*, Oxford: Oxford University Press, 1978.

Vygotsky, L. S. *Thought and Language*, Cambridge, Massachusetts: M.I.T. Press and Wiley, 1962

Works Cited

Burningham, J. *Mr. Gumpy's Outing*. Canada: Holt, Rhinehart and Winston, 1970.

Clay, M. *Becoming Literate: The Construction of Inner Control*. Portsmouth, New Hampshire: Heinemann Education, 1993.

_ _ _. *Reading Recovery®: A Guidebook for Teachers in Training*. Portsmouth, New Hampshire: Heinemann Education, 1993.

Cooper, J. D. *Literacy: Helping Children Construct Meaning*. New York: Houghton Mifflin, 1997.

Cunningham, P. *Phonics They Use*. New York: Harper Collins Publishers, 1991.

Drew, D. *Animal Clues*. Australia: Maurbern Pty. Ltd., 1990.

Goswami, U., and F. Mead. "Onset and rime awareness and analogies in reading." *Reading Research Quarterly*. 27 (1992): 153-162.

Irish Folk Tale. *Pot of Gold*. Glenview, IL: Scott Foresman, 1976.

Nagy, W. E. "Teaching vocabulary to improve reading comprehension." Newark, DE/Urbana, IL: *International Reading Association/National Council of Teachers of English*. 29 (1988).

Wright Group. *Guided Reading: Level 2- Integrated Learning Workshops*. Bothell, WA: Wright Group Pub. Inc., 1996.

About Beth Holland

"I define reading as a message-getting, problem-solving activity which increases in power and flexibility the more it is practiced. My definition states that within the directional constraints of the printer's code, language and visual perception responses are purposefully directed by the reader in some integrated way to the problem of extracting meaning from cues in a text, in sequence, so that the reader brings a maximum of understanding to the author's message."

—DR. MARIE CLAY

Beth Holland received her B.S. from the University of Georgia and her M.S. from Old Dominion University. She has been teaching in the Virginia Beach City Public School System since 1976 and currently is teaching at Birdneck Elementary. For her outstanding contributions in the field of education, Ocean Lakes Elementary named Beth Holland as both Teacher of the Year and Reading Teacher of the Year. When not teaching at Ocean Lakes Elementary, Ms. Holland serves as a frequent presenter at both local and state reading conferences and develops staff development courses for the City of Virginia Beach. Most recently, she has been published in *The Running Record*, a national newsletter for Reading Recovery® teachers.

When the Dust Has Settled, What Remains?

by Pat Vakos

Silently seated on the carpet, eighteen eager kindergarten students restlessly await the teacher's permission to take out their bears. Earlier in the day, each child had proudly entered the classroom clutching a stuffed animal. With her pigtails swinging, Alex looked up at her teacher and declared that her bear "Amy" had been to every doctor's appointment since she was born, or, at least, to all she could remember. Not to be outdone, Taylor loudly proclaimed that his bear had been around the world twenty times when it had been accidentally left on an airplane! Now, each child waited quietly to begin the language arts lesson. They had waited all week for this lesson because they were told they could bring to class any prized stuffed bears they owned. The lesson would be about the letter <u>B</u>, and students were already familiar with the big book story about the big brown bear, <u>Brown Bear, Brown Bear</u>. During the lesson they shared stories of their own bears, the ones on their beds, the bears in their favorite story books; some even rehashed the classic of "Goldilocks and the Three Bears."

The first child to leap up proudly from the rug and display her large floppy white bear was Alex: "This is my bear, Amy. <u>B</u> is for Bear. Amy has been with me since I was in the hospital with a broken leg. Amy goes everywhere with me and is my friend," Alex exclaimed. One after another, the children told tales about their bears. The teacher, overjoyed by their excitement, said that tomorrow they would continue their study of the letter <u>B</u> by trying to list foods that start with <u>B</u> such as broccoli, bacon, beans, biscuits, bread, bananas, bologna, beef, butter, and brownies. The teacher would even supply a feast for the children.

> With her pigtails swinging, Alex looked up at her teacher and declared that her bear "Amy" had been to every doctor's appointment since she was born, or, at least, to all she could remember.

Meanwhile, across town in a high school classroom, students are learning about the Reformation. Notes are given in a two-column format for students to copy. The teacher, using an outline on the overhead, discusses the notes with the students and then shows a fifteen-minute movie on Martin Luther. One of the students, Nick, attentively watches the teacher, wondering if it will snow in Wintergreen by the weekend and if he should take a chance and rent a snowboard now. Another student, Alena, copies the notes as she replays in her mind what happened in physical education between Khenia and Vanessa. Will she have to pick sides again? Why does Khenia joke Alena to the point of fighting? she thinks. Will the teacher notice her note writing if she looks up at the board periodically? And, John. John is being John—going insane! He can't sit still any longer listening to the constant verbiage from the teacher and he thinks about inventing an "emergency" to go to the restroom. "No," he thinks to himself, "he won't let me go. I went yesterday during the notes on Calvin. Guidance counselor! That's it. I'll look distressed like I'm about to have an attack of something... No, he won't let me leave, ever."

> One of the students, Nick, attentively watches the teacher, wondering if it will snow in Wintergreen by the weekend and if he should take a chance and rent a snowboard now.

As educators, why do we, so creative in our elementary school teaching, expect our high school students to learn via lecture? Hardly the most creative method. I began my teaching experience in Virginia Beach teaching junior high geography in the same school that I attended in ninth grade! In fact, I was teaching in the same classroom where I had taken Algebra I. Many of the teachers I had known as a student were still there, and my approach to teaching and students was identical to that which I had experienced and seen in those same halls. I began lessons as I had been taught: an outline from notes extended across the blackboard for the students to copy diligently, fill in, and memorize verbatim for the test every Friday. But I felt bothered. After all, I was a product of a changing view in education that began to surface in the sixties. In 1967, Edwin Fenton advocated various teaching techniques to maximize student learning. Fenton bases his theory on the premise that student retention is directly related to student interest and to the methodology used to present information to the student. His inductive and nondirective methods—letting students discover for themselves—have been copied and revamped for the last thirty years, longer than I have been teaching! If the student believes the material is worth knowing and the teacher links the material together for easy mental "recovery," learning will be greatly enhanced. It is no wonder that students quickly forget isolated facts: students need to link and visualize in order to retain information.

So, how do we make our classes more accommodating for visual learners? I was not only armed with Fenton's, *Teaching the New Social Studies in Secondary*

Schools, but with the radical methodologies of social studies methods classes of the late sixties. Yet why was the only sign of life in my classroom when a student took out a four-inch metal hairpick, or when I accidentally stepped into the garbage can? What had happened to the excitement? How do educators account for the vast differences between younger and older students? Are students really that different from elementary to high school? And so I began to rethink how I presented material to my students, and how I could begin incorporating more student discovery, more visual learning, and more critical thinking activities within each lesson.

If educators admit they oftentimes have difficulty with oral presentations of complicated material, why don't we recognize that our students also might have difficulties? Even though I consistently posed this question, I still did not fully understand the ramifications for the visual learner until my own second-grade daughter was diagnosed with central processing disorder. Alexandra lacked the ability to process oral information consistently, so that at the end of second grade, her oral memory was that of a four-year-old. After years of ear infections and tubes in her ears, she could not filter out surrounding noises. She was not hearing impaired; she was, however, a visual learner. It was only after much research that I knew what was best for my daughter's education. But then I had to ask myself, how many children do we teach that are like my Alexandra? Based on what I had learned with my own daughter, I would guess that more of our classrooms consist of visual learners than we could possibly ever imagine, so I began to pay closer attention to how I presented information in my own classes.

To illustrate the concept of "visualizing" information, for example, I begin with the concept of "imperialism." Students might memorize the definitions of "imperialism: domination by one country of the political, economic, or cultural life of another country or region" (Ellis 27). However, in order to visualize this meaning, students need to be presented with examples of imperialism, perhaps documents such as Rudyard Kipling's "White Man's Burden," or art work such as George Harcourt's "Imperialism Glorified," as well as the creation of graphic organizers that illustrate statistical charts, graphs, and tables to show causes, effects, and trends. Then, students are better able to draw connections between this information and conclude that "imperialism" actually has varied applications and impacts throughout history. These kinds of graphic organizers aid students in linking together materials for further analysis and evaluation. To encourage further the

> It is no wonder that students quickly forgot isolated facts: students need to link and visualize in order to retain information.

visualization process regarding imperialism, I might present readings from *All Quiet on the Western Front* and excerpts from *Diary of Anne Frank* to create mental images of the horrors of trench warfare in World War I, and the inhumanity of the Holocaust of World War II.

In addition to these techniques, I also use laminated pictures and time lines in my classroom. When teaching the five characteristics of civilization, my class first lists and generates definitions of each — organized government, organized religion, written language, division of labor, and class structure. Students are then divided into groups and assigned an early civilization to research. Provided with laminated pictures, poems, and writings from the civilization, students become archaeologists and use these "artifacts" to present evidence to the class of the presence of each characteristic in their civilization; students also complete large graphic organizers to be displayed in the classroom. The pictures I use often come from discarded history books or books purchased cheaply at library sales. This activity does not have to be conducted as a cooperative learning exercise, and, instead, may become an individual learning exercise where each student is given several artifacts to determine which characteristics he/she will illustrate.

As another example, I teach the differences between the Renaissance and Medieval Era by giving students laminated strips with magnetic tape on the back containing characteristics of the Renaissance and Middle Ages. The board is divided into two sections and students determine where the strips belong. Once all the characteristics are displayed, I give each student a laminated picture of a famous work of art from one of these periods. They determine in which "board museum" the Renaissance or Medieval pictures should be placed and then explain to the class why they selected that particular "museum." After presenting all the pictures, the entire class makes a visit to the "board museum." It is so rewarding to hear students comment on the exaggerated arm length of individual subjects as they stretch to the heavens in Medieval art or to hear students discuss the realistic smile of the Mona Lisa. They now have a mental image that will remain for some time.

> If educators admit they oftentimes have difficulty with oral presentations of complicated material, why don't we recognize that our students also might have difficulties?

To help students differentiate between Baroque and Romantic music, first we discuss the differences as a class. Then, we listen to music from both periods; the students identify characteristics of that period and why the music stylistically represents the Baroque or Romantic Era. Visualizing history can be like a drama being played out in the greatest of novels.

So for each unit I teach, I try to find some fascinating story to tell my students so they won't forget the era. When we do the English Civil War and the beheading of Charles I, I close the unit by telling my students the story of what Charles II did when he was asked by Parliament to take the throne of England: "Oliver Cromwell led the forces that had executed Charles II's father. Not to be stopped, Charles II got his just revenge as he had Cromwell's body exhumed and beheaded! Of course, he would have gotten greater pleasure if Cromwell had not been dead when beheaded!" The many fascinating stories from Charles II make history come alive for my students. And students consistently want to know!

> It is so rewarding to hear students comment on the exaggerated arm length of individual subjects as they stretch to the heavens in Medieval art or to hear students discuss the realistic smile of the Mona Lisa.

Another great tool to help students visualize can be found along the Internet. I have discovered that computers in the classroom help me teach my students to listen, discuss, and write about the materials in their notebooks. For some students this is not an easy task and often I have found myself after class copying their work off the board to type for them. So, computers in the classroom are the answer to my dilemma. And I have started using them in study sessions with my advanced placement history students. After school, groups of my advanced placement students use the two computers in the classroom to set up graphic organizers for potential essays and brainstorming sessions. Five to seven students sit around one computer as one student types, and the remaining students discuss the elements of each question. At the end of each study session, they make a copy of the completed graphic organizer for each to take home and study. This is what I want to happen in every class I teach: to shift the focus from teacher-centered to student-centered learning. The students define the problem, determine what elements need to be addressed, supply the information, and analyze the results.

To visualize this process for the entire class, I use the LCD panel, or Liquid Crystal Display, where the computer is connected to the overhead projector, so that students can participate continuously and receive immediate feedback. Since they are able to evaluate and analyze their work as they go, oftentimes student discussion revolves around retrieving the information and typical questions arise: Is immigration a social or political factor in the growth of industry in England? Why would the enclosure movement be viewed as both a positive and negative aspect of the Agricultural Revolution? I find that students utilize their critical thinking skills in seminar-style discussions without the need to record the information. And as Aileen Nonis, author of "Technology and Learning" points out, "...students are active constructors of knowledge as opposed to passive recipients of information" (Nonis 32).

When I asked students to evaluate the technique of using the LCD panel in class, their responses were all very positive: "I liked the lesson on the LCD today. It involved more class participation and less lecturing. I felt that I could contribute more and I hope we can use the machine for class in the future." Another student commented, "The use of this technology in the classroom is better than taking notes because it is more open to discussion, less time is spent writing and more time on thinking." Other comments were: "We get to see what we are doing," and "We better analyze relationships because they are easier to see," as well as, "We see, in a systematic order, what we are discussing." My students confirmed what I suspected—the LCD gave them a visual experience which helped them learn and manipulate information and the visual discussion proved to be a significant cognitive tool to learning.

> But what remains in my students' minds? Like the powdery chalk dust, will the materials taught during that day merely disappear?

Because students have experienced success with the LCD, they are better able to reconstruct questions and are also much more successful when asked to write essays that analyze or explain situations and events in history. With ease, students create graphic organizers that break essay questions into necessary components that merge factual support. My students are now more actively involved in graphing and in using the LCD panel, and the quiet student who also needs to *"SEE"* what the concept means, now achieves greater success in the classroom. For example, if students are given a question that asks them to analyze the social and political structure during the French Revolution and compare it to the social/political structure of the Russian Revolution, they now are able to use the LCD panel to break the question into smaller components: What was the social situation like during the French Revolution? What was the political situation like? What about the social situation of the Russian Revolution? The political situation? Only after students have analyzed parts of the question are they ready to brainstorm common characteristics, identify differences within each part of the question, and then graph the results.

When the last bell rings at the end of the day and silence falls across the classroom, all that usually remains of the day's work are bits of chalk on the floor.

But what remains in my students' minds? Like the powdery chalk dust, will the materials taught during that day merely disappear? Or will the use of visualized lessons result in the seeds of concepts that will continue to grow and flourish?

References

Fenton, Edwin. *Teaching the New Social Studies in Secondary Schools*. New York: Holt, Rinehart, and Winston, Inc., 1967.

Good, John M. *The Shaping of Western Society, An Inquiry Approach*. New York: Holt Rinehart, and Winston, Inc., 1968.

Sherman, Dennis. *Western Civilization*. Vol II. New York: McGraw-Hill Inc., 1991.

Works Cited

Ellis, Elisabeth Gaynor, and Anthony Esler. *World History*, Upper Saddle River, New Jersey: Prentice Hall, 1997.

Nonis, Aileen. "Technology and Learning," *NCSSMST Journal*. Vol 3 November (1997): 20, 29.

About Pat Vakos

"If the student can develop a "mental image" of the subject through a blend of student discovery, student interest, and student-centered education, there will be greater student thinking, understanding, and retention."

Patricia Vakos began her teaching career in 1969 at Virginia Beach Middle School. Currently, she teaches AP European and World History at Ocean Lakes High School, also in Virginia Beach. She received a B.S. in Business Administration from the College of William and Mary, Williamsburg, Virginia, and her M.S. in Social Studies from Old Dominion University in Norfolk, Virginia. An active presenter regarding World History and United States History, Ms. Vakos develops curriculum guides and has published her learning strategies in a professional manual entitled, "Lesson Plan Collection for Content Area Instructional Strategies." Because of her active involvement in planning and conducting inservice training sessions for selected educators in Virginia Beach, Ms. Vakos was named as a Virginia Beach District Trainer in instructional strategies for the Staff Development Office, School of Administration. Pat Vakos has been selected for two state awards for economic curriculum materials and was awarded the Fourth Place National Award by the Joint Council of Economic Education for the development of economic curriculum.

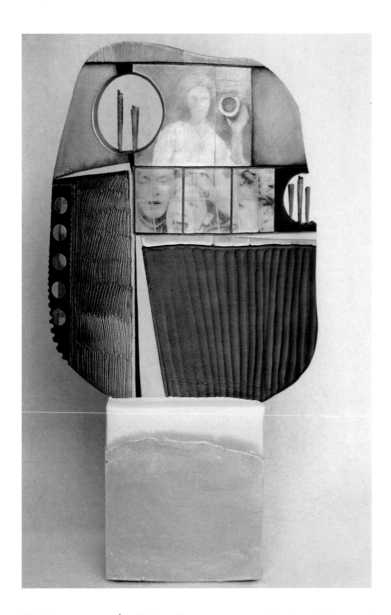

Robert Karl

Under Scrutiny, 1997

Stoneware
and mixed media

"My work spans a concern from inner being to universal ideal. I tend to shun narrative image, representational form, and personal position for a preference for a more subjective thought, mood, and sentiment. Though the journey demands the frequent confrontation with struggle, I prefer poetic form and the voice of harmony to that of bitterness, cynicism, and satire. In this regard, my work reflects inner, outer, and other worlds besides our more familiar one."

Robert Karl

Biographical Information

Having received his B.S. and M.A. in Art Education from East Carolina University, Robert Karl is currently pursuing post-graduate study in the area of Gifted and Talented Education, also from East Carolina University. He received a Fulbright Fellowship from Duke University, an Artist-in-Residence grant and Teacher Incentive Grant from the Virginia Commission for the Arts.

Mr. Karl is the two-year recipient of the Teacher of the Year award at Old Donation Center, the 1986 Outstanding Young Man of America Award, the 1989 Elementary Art Teacher of the Year Award, and the 1993 Presidential Citation Outstanding Teacher Award. He teaches at Old Donation Center in Virginia Beach and is adjunct Undergraduate Art Instructor at Virginia Wesleyan College as well as adjunct Graduate Art Instructor at Virginia Commonwealth University.

Art Education Statement

"Visual art is a language. A highly personal and unique language. And as a language, it communicates. Everyone brings to art his own framework of experience, and, therefore, his own personal language of involvement and response. Art is an expression of the emotion or of the intellect. It is an interpretation of an idea—a language of form, of mood, of shades of meaning. In the educational domain of facts and figures, the arts become an essential dialogue of the soul, a vibrant celebration of the human spirit."

Chapter 4
Student-Centered Learning: Our Subjects, Our Souls

"Like balancers of round stones, outstanding teachers march to a different drummer and do things their colleagues cannot do."

—GERALD DUFFY, "TEACHING AND THE BALANCING OF ROUND STONES"

i recently became intrigued by an article in Kappan *by Gerald Duffy, professor emeritus at Michigan State University. He began by recalling a conversation with a close friend about a place in San Diego where individuals who focus their energies become one with the stones. I was less intrigued with the story itself and more interested in how Duffy would use this analogy to explore that delicate balance that all great teachers are able to establish in their classrooms. Duffy discusses the paradoxical forces that are destined not to balance those round stones and offers the following examples:*

- *Society wants schools to develop citizens who think creatively, but they also want order felt in classrooms. While it seems impossible to develop both creativity and order simultaneously, the best teachers balance these round stones.*

- *Teachers want to be liked by their students, but they must also be taskmasters who require students to do things they think they can't do. The best teachers balance these round stones, too.*

- *High expectations are a key to learning, but too high an expectation causes frustration. The best teachers hit just the right note between expectations and frustration.*

- *Learning occurs best in authentic, lifelike situations, but basic skills require repetition and practice. The best teachers simultaneously develop skills and create real-life learning situations.*

How the best teachers resolve this difficult balance and know exactly how not to tip the stones is difficult to understand, but it certainly involves much more than the skillful use of pedagogy. In the final chapter of A Tapestry of Knowledge, *teachers in the Student-Centered Learning section challenge their students in focused ways that transcend the inherent impossibility of any task. These are educators who definitely know who they are and who thoroughly understand the indispensable message they must give their students. Teachers are constantly challenging the darkness to discover ways to see the light in their students' eyes. The teachers in this chapter make students the focus by promoting the importance of lifelong learning. These articles celebrate that evolution in teaching and learning, one that preserves what has worked in the past with judicious experimentation of new techniques and strategies. We see teachers asking "what if" in the face of an obstacle, and implementing a solution that puts students and subject at the center, solving problems, experimenting with different modes of learning, and taking ownership of their own education.*

Instead of grades as a focus, students, collaborating on meaningful projects, discover how by employing problem-solving skills they can make a difference in their community, by communicating with Virginia Beach City Council members and with Virginia Delegates.

Instead of "I teach-you learn," we all become learners in the case of one classroom where a teacher discovers how to reach her non-native high school students by having them become teachers presenting a colorful, international quilt of ideas, pictures, and conversations.

Instead of a dictator who metes out discipline, students experience shared ownership for classroom management. They "get down to business" with positive discipline, record problems and concerns on slips of paper for the issue bin, and create class agendas aimed at positive change. Students work as teams to improve the atmosphere of their learning environment.

Instead of reading being a reaction to a text, reading becomes a reaction within the text as students use their imaginations to become characters and travel across the country. Students use their characters to learn more about their family stories and to discover that virtually every area in America is a valuable contribution to our country's history.

And, finally, instead of the teacher being too caught up in minutia, one teacher discovers that making a difference in the life of one student makes every aspect of the classroom drama of "motivating the unmotivated" worth it. By examining the learning progress of David, the reader sees what can happen when students become excited about learning and become teams of scientists solving a scientific dilemma.

The students in these classrooms are not as Parker Palmer, teacher and educational activist warns, part of a student-centered setting where "there is sometimes a tendency toward mindless relativism: one truth for you, another truth for me, and never mind the difference"(119). When the students in this chapter move to the center of the classrooms, they learn to think critically, they question, they reflect, they evaluate. Palmer would have us view the classroom less as student-centered and more as subject-centered. Passion toward subject is what moves to the center of learning, not the teacher or the student. And that passion is what creates authentic learning. Such a subject-centered classroom honors "one of the most vital needs our students have: to be introduced to a world larger than their own experiences and egos, a world that expands their personal boundaries and enlarges their sense of community"(Parker 120). A subject-centered classroom also honors teachers—it "invigorates those connections between our subjects and our souls" (120) so that once again the light will dance around learning.

—LEANNE SELF

THAT'S USING YOUR HEAD!
"How was your weekend, class?"

by Carolyn Stamm

Who would guess that an innocent question of mine would lead to seventh-grade students initiating a state law, proposing a local ordinance, appearing on national television, and being recognized through winning state and national awards? That's just what happened, though, when I asked that question to my seventh-grade gifted students from Kempsville Middle School on a crisp October morning in 1994.

Two of my students had competed in a weekend select soccer tournament, and I encouraged them to share their experiences with the class. They told us the opposing team members were wearing shoulder patches commemorating another team member who had recently been killed in a bicycle accident. My students spoke with the opposing team and learned that their teammate had not been wearing a bicycle helmet when a car hit him. This tragic story emotionally moved my seventh-grade class so much that the group decided to tackle bicycle safety as a research project.

"We realized he was the same age as us and played soccer, and that gave us the realization that it could happen to us," stated one of the students.

The class, who began calling themselves the Lifesavers, started researching bicycle injuries. They discovered that 400,000 children are injured and 300 children are killed in bicycle-related accidents every year. A large percentage of these accidents involved preventable head injuries. Eighty percent of fatal bike injuries could have been prevented with a helmet.

"It made me mad because a lot of kids wouldn't have been hurt if they would have been wearing helmets," said one of the Lifesavers.

Startled by their findings, the class resolved to contact local lawmakers to make them aware of the results of their research. The Lifesavers set up meetings with local City Council members and a State Delegate. As a result of their presentations, the Lifesavers convinced the lawmakers to initiate a local ordinance for Virginia Beach requiring children fourteen years and under to wear bicycle helmets.

However, the students then discovered a state law, the Dillion rule, prohibiting cities from making laws that supercede state laws. The Dillon rule, quite simply, does not allow localities to enact ordinances without prior approval from the state legislature. Through research, however, the group learned that Virginia cities may petition the state legislature to pass a law allowing a new local ordinance.

Therefore, the students wrote letters to a variety of sources requesting additional bicycle safety research. After they received information from the National Safe Kids Campaign, I set up a conference call for them with a lawyer from that organization. The lawyer gave my students advice about speaking to and lobbying lawmakers. Other supporters became involved in our project, including the Tidewater Pediatric Society, the Virginia Beach Safety Council, the American Automobile Association, the Virginia Beach Parent Teacher Association, and the Virginia Beach Council for Civic Organizations.

> In March 1995, we were thrilled to learn that the laws were passed and signed by then Virginia Governor George Allen.

In January 1995, selected student speakers persuaded our City Council to support this state law amendment. The Lifesavers, successful in convincing City Council to pass a resolution, then decided it was time to select a sponsor for their bill and lobby the Virginia General Assembly members with a letter writing campaign.

State Delegate Leo Wardrup, from Virginia Beach, sponsored House Bill (HB) 2201 in the General Assembly allowing Virginia Beach to enact a bicycle helmet ordinance. Eight other Virginia representatives signed on to HB 2201 because they also wanted a local helmet ordinance for their constituents. Another delegate, realizing the importance of bicycle safety, sponsored HB 1745, allowing all Virginia localities to enact a bicycle helmet ordinance. The Lifesavers lobbied for both bills with letters and phone calls to state officials.

In March 1995, we were thrilled to learn that the laws were passed and signed by then Virginia Governor George Allen. The Lifesavers were also successful in their request that a state resolution be drafted declaring the first week in May every year as "Virginia Safe Kids Week."

"It is heartening to see this caliber of research coming from our students. They are truly the leaders of tomorrow, and this type of background will help make them concerned and aware citizens of this community," wrote one Virginia Beach city council member. Another city council member stated, "I believe this is an excellent example of how we can teach our kids to access government."

The Lifesavers also heard from many state officials. One Virginia delegate from Clarksville wrote, "You are an inspiration to us all of what active government should be, and I hope you will continue to be involved with your community and your state."

"I imagine many areas throughout the state will follow your leadership," exclaimed another state delegate.

With the prospect of this new ordinance on the horizon, my students realized that the largest group of bicycle riders, young people, needed to become aware of the benefits of wearing a bicycle helmet. Therefore, in the spring of 1995, the Lifesavers presented assemblies to elementary schools and worked with our police precinct in setting up and working at a "Champion Challenge" bicycle race and bicycle safety inspection course. A Virginia Division of Motor Vehicles grant allowed the Lifesavers to purchase and distribute hundreds of free bicycle helmets to youngsters of Virginia Beach.

In June of 1995, the Lifesavers spoke again to City Council and were influential in the passing of Virginia Beach's local bicycle helmet ordinance, the first local ordinance of its kind proposed by children.

"After I talked to the kids, I changed my opinion," conceded our police chief, Charles R. Wall, while testifying on behalf of the Lifesavers during the City Council meeting.

The Lifesavers' enthusiasm continued into their eighth-grade class the next year. They presented new skits to several more elementary schools to increase public awareness. Members of the Lifesavers appeared on Nickelodeon TV's *Nick News* to discuss their project and were subsequently awarded the Governor's Transportation Safety Award, the Virginia State Community Problem-Solving Championship, the National Safe Kids "Safe Kids Check America Challenge" Grand Prize, and the National Safety Council Youth Services Award of Merit. In addition, they won third place in the International Community Problem Solving competition in Rhode Island. To honor the work of the Lifesavers, the Mayor proclaimed a "Bicycle Safety Day" in Virginia Beach. The American Society of Safety Engineers and the Virginia Beach City Public Schools' School Board awarded the group certificates of commendation.

The most recent accolade was the 1998 publication of the Lifesavers Project featured in *What Do You Stand For? A Kid's Guide to Building Character*, by Barbara Lewis.

"It is heartening to see this caliber of research coming from our students. They are truly the leaders of tomorrow, and this type of background will help make them concerned and aware citizens of this community," wrote one Virginia Beach city council member.

One Lifesaver commented, "We didn't just pass this law. We wanted kids to know that they need to ride safely. If we prevented one death and saved one life, then it was worth making a law having kids wear helmets."

Many of my lessons, including this bicycle safety project, center on a strategy based on the educational philosophy of such theorists as John Dewey, Joseph Renzulli, and E. Paul Torrance. The process of *Community Problem Solving* (The Future Problem-Solving Program, 1993) provides a strategic framework for problem-based learning. The students begin by brainstorming possible problem situations that need to be solved in the community. After determining the underlying problem, students then list possible solutions to the community problem. The best solution is determined by selecting measurable criteria and judging the solutions against the criteria. I know the value and effectiveness of this skill when I hear students discuss how they use the problem-solving process in real life situations.

> **Active, problem-solving based learning has empowered my students to become initiators of action instead of receivers of action. By utilizing the strengths of each individual, all students experience ownership in our class projects. They soon discover that middle school students can make a difference in their own community.**

Because information in our society is doubling every fifteen months, students need to learn and practice these problem-solving skills. This technique presents a unique challenge for teachers, and in order to deal with this influx of information, students need skills to cope with change, power to solve problems, and the self-confidence to face and control their futures: "Teaching children how to think—how to examine the world in constructive ways—provides them with strategies for facing the unknowable future" (Community Problem Solving 3). Students need to know **how** to think, not **what** to think; they need to incorporate new information into their existing knowledge base.

The role of facilitator, a listening "guide on the side," is extremely beneficial, given the characteristics and needs of middle school gifted students who discover together that learning is relevant and important.

Active, problem-solving based learning has empowered my students to become initiators of action instead of receivers of action. By utilizing the strengths of each individual, all students experience ownership in our class projects. They soon discover that middle school students can make a difference in their own community. Through modeling, my students incorporate an enthusiasm for lifelong learning in their own lives: "Now adults know we can make a difference in our community," exclaimed Christy Padgett, a member of the Lifesavers.

With the demands and responsibilities of being a teacher in today's society, really listening to students is sometimes a forgotten art, yet listening to my students' responses about their weekends allowed me to capitalize on a teachable moment and make learning relevant and active. All too often, we forget that children have a vested interest in their future and a desire for change: "To change the world, you have to believe that change is possible, and you have to know how to make change work" (Fleisher 5).

The ability to solve problems doesn't just belong to adults. My students go out of their way looking for problems… And I couldn't be happier!

References

Lewis, Barbara. *The Kid's Guide to Social Action*. Minneapolis, MN: Free Spirit Press, 1991.

Works Cited

Community Problem Solving: Preparing Students to Become Active Problem Solvers. Ann Arbor, MI: The Future Problem-Solving Program, 1993.

Fleisher, Paul. *Changing Our World: A Handbook for Young Activists*. Tucson, AZ: Zephyr Press, 1993.

Lewis, Barbara. *What Do You Stand For? A Kid's Guide to Building Character*. Minneapolis, MN: Free Spirit Press, 1998.

About Carolyn Stamm

"I am dedicated to facilitating student projects that transfer learning into solving real life problems. My goal is to facilitate and nurture my students' problem-solving, communication, and leadership skills. These skills are the lamp that illuminates enthusiasm in education and empowers students to shape their own futures and to make a real difference in the world."

Beginning her teaching career in Colorado in 1980 and completing her Master's degree in Gifted Education from the University of Virginia, Carolyn Stamm moved to Virginia Beach. She taught sixth grade at Old Donation Center for the Gifted and Talented where she was recognized as Teacher of the Year in 1991. She then worked as a Gifted Education Resource Teacher at Kempsville Middle School where she was again named Teacher of the Year as well as finalist for the Virginia Beach Citywide Teacher of the Year in 1996. Listed in *Who's Who Among America's Teachers* and receiving the Governor's School Fine Arts Outstanding Educator Award in 1994, Carolyn and her students have won numerous awards including third place in the 1994 International Future Problem-Solving Championship and International Community Problem-Solving Championship. Publishing several articles in *Gifted Child Today*, Carolyn serves on the State Board of Directors for the Virginia Future Problem-Solving Program and currently teaches at Kemps Landing Magnet School in Virginia Beach.

ESL Students Learn through Teaching: A Problem or a Challenge?

by Nikki Galantis

the personalities of my students were wide-ranging: My Ukrainian boy was quick-minded, clever, and constantly trying to cut a deal with me involving break time, graded papers, or parental notification. My soft-spoken Bangladeshi girl was attempting to contend with her beauty and the boys' hovering admiration, which often made her feel uncomfortable. My quiet, tall Serbian boy had been imprisoned in Serbia for a year. In his eyes I sometimes saw sadness from bad memories of the turmoil in his country. Other times there twinkled a slice of amusement at the innocent mischief which usually took place in an American classroom where everyone appeared to be safe and equal. It was quite a challenge to keep this diverse group interested, on-task, and constantly learning every day for two and a half hours. But what? And how?

How often have you been enthusiastically presented with an innovative teaching tool from other educators which was supposed to be helpful to you and beneficial to your students? How often have you believed that this educational instrument held an assurance of a brighter future of learning in the classroom, that it promised to keep your students alert, enthusiastic, and eager to learn anything introduced to them? Ideally, this tool sounded so commendable, so educational, so professional, but what about in the real world? What about in the **CLASSROOM**? Would this tool really meet learning objectives?

Quite a few years ago, just such a tool was purchased for our English as a Second Language Department. It was called *The Magnetic Way* and was supposed to inspire our students to learn English more quickly. *The Magnetic Way Program* contained one 24" x 34" magnetized board and five kits. Each kit contained more than 100 colorful magnetic cut-outs of varying sizes (for depth perception) which pertained to different categories. The categories of the kits were the country, the street, the indoors, people in action, and the supermarket—all with assorted items from cars to buildings to people and supermarket items. It really was a colorful potpourri of people, places, and things that could create fascinating scenes

> **It was quite a challenge to keep this diverse group interested, on-task, and constantly learning every day for two and a half hours. But what? And how?**

for discussion and learning. We had an inservice by an exuberant salesman of *The Magnetic Way* who gave us ideas of how to use the kits to help our students overcome the shyness involved in communicating in another language, to reinforce grammar skills, and to reach new horizons in attaining vocabulary. It was evident that the students were going to enjoy looking at the creations that I would put together. Unfortunately, I had an idealistic picture that would prove to be a burdensome task, and it would soon give way to more pressing "book-learning."

> It was evident that the students were going to enjoy looking at the creations that I would put together. Unfortunately, I had an idealistic picture that would prove to be a burdensome task, and it would soon give way to more pressing "book-learning."

When I first began using the magnetic board, I was enthusiastic about creating a picture and asking questions about it. As time went by, creating the pictures became a frustrating chore that was postponed while I graded papers, kept records, and worked with groups that needed my help. After all, what was more important, getting those papers graded and reinforcing skills or some cute little picture? The same scene stayed up on the magnetic board for weeks like the bulletin boards constantly nagging to be updated. About the only change that took place on the magnetic board was that people and things started getting rearranged in bizarre orders. People were flying in the air, cars were upside down, cats were driving buses, and chickens were cashiers behind store counters. Obviously, the students had an interest in the board. How could I tap into that interest in a positive way?

ESL Background Information

In Virginia Beach, non-native high school students are referred to the Technical and Career Education Center for intensive ESL classes when their language proficiency prohibits them from being successful in a mainstream classroom. Our LEP (Limited English Proficient) students attend a half-day at the Tech Center and spend the other half-day at their home schools. Being at the Tech Center gives these teenagers a comfort zone where they can be with other ESL students who are having similar communication and cultural adaptation problems. Being at the home school gradually immerses them in the sometimes frightening routine of high school. In the low-proficiency classes are students who are able to understand little or no English and are not able to speak it at all or students who are able to produce some English verbal routines but cannot use the language with understanding. Intermediate level ESL students usually make themselves understood by using a combination of simple speech, gestures, and an occasional word from their native language; they know "survival English." High-proficiency students have little difficulty communicating their ideas in English but still need instruction with basic grammatical structures.

The year I decided that I had to figure out a better way to use *The Magnetic Way* and painlessly create a different picture every week was the year I taught high-proficiency students. I was blessed with two huge classes of students from China, Taiwan, the Philippines, Korea, Puerto Rico, Thailand, Zaire, Vietnam, Panama, Japan, Venezuela, Serbia, Peru, The Ukraine, and Bangladesh. This was not only a colorful tapestry of cultures but an unusually enthusiastic, energetic, and highly-motivated collection of students as well. Because of my challenging multicultural class, I came up with an idea! I'd let this eclectic group of students use the cut-outs to create their own pictures for the magnetic board. That would give them practice using their imaginations and get me "off the hook." I will admit that the idea was a bit self-serving at first, and, of course, I realized that I needed more English-related objectives.

Even though "whole language" has become the educational catchword in recent years, I was an advocate of K. Goodman's work and his ideas that language learning should be easy when it is personally relevant, connected to real life events, and is made accessible to the student; only through active ownership will students become empowered. To incorporate the research that integrates listening, speaking, reading, and writing, into my classes and coupling the research with my need to entertain these energetic students, I decided to have the students create conversations between characters displayed on the board. The conversations could be about anything of interest to them, whether it was fact or fiction. Now the ball was rolling. I'd require my students to use at least five new vocabulary words in the conversations that they would have to learn and teach the class. Since they were teaching new

> I decided to have the students create conversations between characters displayed on the board. The conversations could be about anything of interest to them, whether it was fact or fiction. Now the ball was rolling...

vocabulary words, why not have them also teach some grammar and include the lesson in the conversation? What about the other students who would be listening to the presentations? How would I make certain that they would listen carefully and ask questions if they didn't understand? I'd have the student "teachers" make tests that would evaluate their class's listening and comprehension skills. Yes, things were falling into place. I just needed to organize my plan.

I sat down at my computer and came up with a five-day organized outline of requirements for the Magnetic Board Project. I included points for each requirement so the students would clearly understand their grades upon completion. I even gave extra points for being on schedule which became an incentive for students to develop a sense of pacing and avoid procrastination. I passed out the Magnetic Board Project organizer to each student and discussed each part of the project. The students chose a partner and the dates when they would make their presentations. I displayed this information on a wall chart, and we scheduled a presentation every other Friday in order to give each pair of students ample time to complete their project. The following schedule was used:

> **Day 1** – Students create a **picture** and show the teacher. Any holidays during the week should be included. Teacher advises if more details are needed.
>
> **Day 2** – Students write a **conversation** that includes five new **vocabulary words**. Teacher checks conversation for acceptable content and worthwhile vocabulary.
>
> **Days 3 and 4** – Students make a **test** with varied kinds of questions (matching, fill-in-the-blanks, multiple-choice, and the five WH questions: who, what, when, where, why.) An answer sheet is included, and teacher and students correct errors. Students type the test.
>
> **Day 5** – Students make their **oral presentation** to the class, give the tests, and correct the papers.

It took a while before a good rhythm was established in carrying through this five-day project so if the students had the bare essentials in their picture, I had to spur them to explore the kits and find additional items to make their pictures more engaging and colorful. When some of the conversations were short and stilted, students were instructed to add additional details or generate new ideas. Students delved into the dictionary and thesaurus more than once. If I had previously taught the grammar and realized that some of the class still had not mastered it, I would have the students reteach it. Other times they had to read and teach new grammar to the class. By incorporating this teaching strategy, the students understood more clearly where their grammatical problems were rooted.

With each presentation, a colorful, international quilt of ideas, pictures, and conversations developed. The students began competing with one another to display the best work. Features of the students' personalities surfaced as they decided who their characters were going to be and what they would be discussing. Some conversations were amusing and light, such as the discussion between the Bull, the Chicken, and the Pig about their lives of responsibility in the barnyard. Others were culturally informative, such as the discussion between Mei Lung and Sho about the Lunar Chinese New Year. An example of my cultural awakening occurred during this conversation about Chinese New Year. I learned that the purpose of loud noise and drumming during parades was to frighten the legendary Chinese Demon back into its cave so it did not devastate the people. Additional dialogue included interesting facts about famous people such as Bruce Lee, Joan of Arc, Ferdinand Magellan, Martin Luther King, Jr., and Michael Jordan. My personal favorites were the discourses that revealed more of the students' lives and their feelings. Conversations developed about teenagers arriving home late and their parents "going off." I even learned about social lives through party conversations. "Spin-the-Bottle" and "Truth-or-Dare" are still happening!

> With each presentation, a colorful, international quilt of ideas, pictures, and conversations developed. The students began competing with one another to display the best work. Features of the students' personalities surfaced as they decided who their characters were going to be and what they would be discussing.

Other conversations took a more serious tone as two characters discussed the typical emotions of immigrants in the United States:

Randy: "I'm so homesick here."

Lloyd: "There are a lot of people here who miss their country. Some of them haven't seen their family for about six or seven years. And you have only been here for about five months, and you want to go home?"

Randy: "Believe it or not, that's how I feel! I have been full of grief thinking about my life and my memories. Anyway, I guess I would be better off if I could get a job this coming summer."

Lloyd: "Yeah! Good idea! The money that we would earn would be ample for each of us to help our families and to save for a trip back home."

The happy characters usually tried to cheer up the miserable ones. Yet within these conversations it was clear that being homesick was a common occurrence and that it would probably get easier as time passed. On the heavier side, there was an account of a parent being put into prison unfairly and the shame and heartbreak involved. The students and I looked forward to the publishing sessions on Fridays where we would be listening to ingenious minds at work.

This creativity spawned one of the best learning endeavors of the year. The students enjoyed it, learned from it, and appreciated me more because of it. It also reconfirmed my belief of what an incredible resource our students are.

When I began this project, I had specific objectives in mind. However, by using the magnetic board as a motivational educational tool, my students experienced more success than I ever imagined. The presenters learned the importance of teamwork, organization, and good pronunciation in aiding comprehension. By becoming familiar with the dictionary and thesaurus as resources for their writings, they increased their vocabulary. They tapped their imaginations in a non-threatening way. They learned to be prepared by asking the teacher questions about the grammar or pronunciation of their vocabulary words before they presented, rather than learning of their errors while presenting. They were integrating all the language skills necessary for second language acquisition.

In addition, students listening to the presentations benefitted in many ways as well. Because they knew they were going to be tested, they learned to take notes, to pay attention, and to ask questions; otherwise, they wouldn't be prepared for the test that followed the presentation. Often in a regular classroom setting, ESL students nod and say they understand when they really don't. They've learned to do this for two reasons: they don't want to be perceived as lacking in intelligence or English expertise by their peers, and they have learned the teacher smiles and appears happier when **everyone** understands. Sometimes the grammar taught by students was more easily understood than when I taught it. More often, when the presenters tried to teach it and were confused, I had a better understanding of their confusion and could step in and clarify the grammar more easily.

You may ask how this project can help you. After all, you don't have *The Magnetic Way*. How about this idea? You know how you have those huge bulletin boards that you need to keep fresh and up-to-date? Why not designate a part of the board to be the Student Board and, consequently, the students' responsibility? You could provide the students with a group of pictures in your subject area from magazines, posters, or old calendars. Better still, let them find the pictures or have them create their own drawings or paintings. Students can then post their pictures or art work and related facts on the Student Board and every other week, individually or as teams, make a presentation which correlates with what you are teaching that week. This activity not only revitalizes your bulletin board but also serves as a review or extension of what you are teaching.

The teacher's universal lament seems to be, "I just don't have enough time to do it." The positive result of my not having enough time to create pictures and lessons involving *The Magnetic Board* was that it spurred me to be creative. This creativity spawned one of the best learning endeavors of the year. The students enjoyed it, learned from it, and appreciated me more because of it. It also reconfirmed my belief of what an incredible resource our students are. Yes, **we** teach them, but with a little guidance **they** can share a world of knowledge with us as well as with one another.

My next challenge? Creating a Magnetic Board project for my low proficiency students. **That** should be interesting!

References

Richard-Amato, Patricia A. "Literacy Development and Skills Integration." *Making It Happen.* New York 1996: 62-63.

About Nikki Galantis

"I feel that teaching and learning should be reciprocal between the students and the teacher, and the endeavor should be enjoyable for all."

Having received a B.A. from East Carolina University and an M.A. from George Washington University, Nikki Galantis has been teaching in the Virginia Beach City Public School System for twenty-eight years. Teaching fifth, sixth, and seventh graders, Nikki finds her teaching niche to be in teaching high school ESL (English as a Second Language) students. Traveling internationally every summer of her teaching career helped instill in her an admiration of and respect for cultural diversity. Having lived and communicated in two cultures, Greek and American, she feels a close kinship to the plight of non-native students. As a result of her dedication and expertise, Nikki received the ESL Teacher of the Year Award in 1992.

Getting Down to Business

by Anna Spence

d on't be a dictator unless you are prepared for war! And it's not war I wanted! Knowing that I had been a dictator by raising my voice and speaking to students who didn't seem to hear a word I was saying, I came to realize that my 70's style of classroom management, when merely speaking to a student did the trick to correct behavior, simply was no longer getting the job done with the children of the 90's! As school opened this fall, I wanted to develop a classroom management style that would be different and that would meet the emotional and intellectual needs of each student I would be working with on a daily basis.

This positive approach I wanted to be the driving force that enticed my students to be patient with themselves, their peers, and the adults working with them. In *Positive Discipline, A Teacher's A-Z Guide*, authors consistently emphasize that "the most powerful motivation for change is encouragement" (Nelsen et al 1). Therefore, knowing that improvement can occur only when change takes place, I plunged into a new system of helping students help themselves by initiating class meetings that would address specific issues relating to the students' total learning experience. Through constant research and reflection, I reexamined all aspects of my classroom management style and became frustrated with what I learned. However, this frustration is what encouraged me to change. I realized that in class I was spending more and more time on discipline and less and less on academics. I was concerned. My students' learning was hindered by negative behavior. Children were not responding to instruction in a positive way, test scores were down, and students were not excited about learning. Students no longer sat quietly and followed instructions simply because I told them to do so. Let's face it, the classroom was DULL! I realized the children had changed. Now it was my turn for a "make over"; I knew I had to update my strategies if I wanted

> Through constant research and reflection, I reexamined all aspects of my classroom management style and became frustrated with what I learned. However, this frustration is what encouraged me to change.

to meet their needs and challenge their minds. Of course, there is never a "quick fix" or short answer when a process has to be drastically restructured. First, I had to accept the challenge to acquire the skills needed in order to guide my students in a positive direction. I had to change my role from one of director of discipline to moderator of classroom management. This change would enable me to "empower my students to look at themselves as meaningful, contributing individuals, respected for their ideas and contributions" (Byham et al 8). In deciding to improve their behavior, my students would also improve their learning, take special pride in themselves, and have the satisfaction of a job well done (Byham et al 8). I was convinced that an improvement in the classroom climate would definitely enhance student achievement and boost test scores.

> Let's face it, the classroom was DULL! I realized the children had changed. Now it was my turn for a "make over"...

During the first week of school, my students explored posters and positive quotes I had displayed around the classroom. I realized that I had to provide them food for thought before I embarked on a positive and effective system of classroom discipline. My mission for the class was to produce students who could solve problems and make responsible decisions which would influence our class. Some of the quotes and sayings I used included:

1. "Sharing and caring go hand in hand."

2. "The word *impossible* is not in my dictionary." - Napoleon Bonaparte

3. "Life is like a bicycle. You don't fall off unless you stop peddling." - Claude Pepper

4. "Don't be a carbon copy. Make your own impressions."

5. "A person who is a success never has to prove it."

In class one day, a sheepish Sarah asked, "What is an issue bin?" I noticed she was being prompted by other very interested students to find out what an issue bin had to do with learning in our classroom. I thought to myself, "We're on a great new adventure in which my students will serve as the driving force for what takes place this year in my class." I explained to her, "An issue bin is where you place your questions, problems, praises, and suggestions concerning our class. It is necessary for the entire class to take ownership and be responsible for the situations that affect our lives here at school. The issue bin will enable us to solve any crisis that occurs in room 30."

After responding to various student questions, I led the class in establishing ground rules to govern the issue bin so we'd receive maximum feedback for our class meetings. The simple guidelines that follow were adopted by the class through the process of light voting (McClanahan and Wicks 37), a procedure where the teacher takes a quick hand count to insure acceptance or rejection of an idea. As the book *Future Force* points out, this method of recording responses emphasizes the following guidelines:

1. All questions (social and academic) are important.

2. If students want to discuss an issue, they should be responsible for making suggestions for improvement.

3. Before placing a concern on the board, students must research all pertaining facts and remember that praises should always be from the heart and always please.

4. Students should not hesitate to communicate a concern even if that concern was addressed earlier in the year. Additional practice improves problem solving.

Once the ground rules for the issue bin were discussed, we were off and running. I knew I had to be the leading force in guiding these young students in critically examining their decisions and I needed to do so in a positive effective way. "Caring and support starts with us," I told my class.

I suggested that our class meet once each week at an assigned time and explained that we would always conduct meetings at the same time each week so everyone involved would be prepared to participate. Again, using the process of light voting, this activity would not foster surprises. We decided that the time limit for the meetings would be thirty minutes and that we would meet each Thursday afternoon at two o'clock sharp. Excited about the preparation for our first class meeting, the class developed a simple system that did not involve a long time commitment. This system incorporates the following:

1. Gather slips from the "Issue Bin" poster.

2. Type an agenda and beneath each entry identify the name of the student submitting the issue.

3. Copy the agenda for all students prior to the meeting.

Once the preliminary work was complete, I was ready to conduct our first meeting. I was excited and interested in the students' reactions to the items on the agenda. They were all eager to get this project underway, but what they didn't realize was that they were beginning a process that would become a treasured life skill.

I firmly believe that for children to grasp any concept or strategy it first must be modeled by the teacher. Therefore, though I knew the class meetings were going to take place, I also realized that I had to answer student questions such as how to voice a concern, ask a question, or give someone a compliment in an encouraging manner. I made clear that students had to take into consideration the feelings of the person they were going to discuss; the "Golden Rule" was to be used as our guide in forming all our comments. Questions like, "When can I say something?" "How do we take turns?" "How long can I talk?" and "Will other students speak up about the concerns or compliments?" are just a sampling of what students wanted to know. For the first class I decided questions or topics would be limited to those concerning the entire class. These topics, however, did not pertain solely to behavioral issues; we consistently addressed academic concerns as well. For example, we addressed various topics from oral book reports to incorporating the writing process in writers workshop to lunchroom behavior. As we discussed book reports that first meeting, students were able to get a feel of having their voices heard among their peers. And according to Evelyn Schneider in "Giving Students a Voice in the Classroom," a significant part of moral development comes through dialogue, reflecting on experience, and looking at how our behavior affects others" (Schneider 23).

Working together, students established rules for book reports, and if a student didn't feel comfortable standing in front of the class, he could present their reports using alternate methods. Some of the methods they suggested were use of the overhead projector to dramatize illustrations, the use of props such as masks and costumes, or the permission to stand in the back of the classroom and speak to the class as if they were a tape recorder. One student even suggested that he write his book report backwards and read to the class using a mirror! This type of report offered the student the feeling of safety when he faced his peers. A very clever idea! As a result of this first class meeting, my students learned how to make "I" statements, how to support what they said, and how to criticize an idea without attacking the class member who presented the idea (Schneider 24).

> I thought to myself, "We're on a great new adventure in which my students will serve as the driving force for what takes place this year in my class."

To facilitate this process, I then initiated a Plus/Delta chart, a chart where students organize positive praises (pluses) and constructive criticisms (deltas) on opposite sides of a chart in order for students to organize thoughts they wish to communicate. According to *Future Force*, "this chart enables everyone to consider the pluses — or what went well, and the deltas — what could we change to bring about improvement" in our class (McClanahan and Wicks 38).

Some of the student pluses were proper use of chapter books, selecting appropriate reading levels, and discussion techniques regarding important sections of a book. On the delta side students wanted a time limit of three minutes for book reports and freedom to dramatize presentations by using props. The plus/delta chart proved to be a great tool for bringing closure to our meeting. The first class meeting was over, was an overwhelming success, and now, I was ready to try a meeting using the issue bin.

I opened the second meeting with a phrase that stressed honesty and reminded the students to listen carefully. I followed the agenda exactly. Our first entry was a positive praise for another student and a good starting point for the class. Heather wanted to let the class know how proud she was of Deanna's award by remarking, "Deanna is the best runner in the school and I am proud she is in our class." She was very gracious and invited others to comment. They followed suit with such comments as "She beats me all the time,"

> One student even suggested that he write his book report backwards and read to the class using a mirror! This type of report offered the student the feeling of safety when he faced his peers. A very clever idea!

"Her long legs really move fast," and "I am sure that she is the best runner in the school." During the comment session, Deanna was allowed to sit in the "Compliments Chair" which is only used during meetings. I recorded the comments the same day to give Deanna a copy the following day.

The authors of *Positive Discipline: A Teacher's A-Z Guide* have given several suggestions to help class meetings get off to the right start and cautions teachers to "take the time to teach the perceptions and skills necessary for effective class meetings" (57). They suggest the following:

- Forming a circle,
- Giving compliments and appreciations,
- Creating an agenda,
- Developing communication skills,
- Learning about separate realities,
- Role-playing and brainstorming,
- Recognizing the four reasons people do what they do, and
- Finding nonpunitive solutions (Nelsen, et al 57).

The next entry on the agenda was Matthew, a happy-go-lucky guy on the outside, but on the inside he was embarrassed about being first on the agenda after my introduction. I encouraged him by telling him how brave he was to be our first candidate in the category of self-improvement. I assured him that his fellow classmates would offer him compliments and helpful suggestions for improvement in our learning environment. I patted him on the back as he took his place in the "Compliments Chair." In this situation the person who is sitting in the chair must first receive compliments from the class before suggestions for improvement can be given. Some of the compliments Matthew received were: "Matthew is very friendly," "He has good attendance," "He shares his supplies," "I know that Matthew wants to be a good citizen," and "Matthew is a good artist." Matthew also received a list of positive suggestions about ways he could improve his behavior in class. Matthew internalized the entire process by writing: "My classroom behavior will improve if I... raise my hand before speaking, listen to what others have to say before I blurt out an answer, mind my own business, work well in a group, and respect the opinions of others." After all entries were addressed and discussed for the day, the meeting was adjourned and class resumed for the rest of the afternoon.

> Matthew was very excited to see his compliments and helpful hints in print. He now had a chance to be in control of his social behavior with the help of his peers and was ready to experience success.

Students then tape the improvement check list and the compliments list to their desks as a constant reminder that others care about them and want them to improve. Matthew was very excited to see his compliments and helpful hints in print. He now had a chance to be in control of his social behavior with the help of his peers and was ready to experience success. It was clear that with Matthew encouragement proved to be a very powerful tool. I observed that this power seems to be the fuel that ignites positive changes for students, and subsequently grades begin to rise. The authors of *Positive Discipline: A Teacher's A-Z Guide* state that "the teachers who use a form of class meeting find that the emotional and academic intelligences are escalated and that the greatest reward from this activity is that students are given the skills and attitudes that are needed to be successful" (Nelsen et al 56).

I only need to look to my students for evidence of their academic and behavioral success, and a positive result I recognized from employing these strategies in the classroom was that my students' writing improved. The following writing samples of two students in my fourth-grade class emphasize this improvement. Tyler was a student who had been identified as learning disabled in language arts, and Stacey was struggling with the strategies of bringing her thoughts together on paper. The following entries are from writing portfolios at the beginning of the year. Although

I do not have the statistics to prove it, I am convinced that ongoing encouragement through peer tutoring, class meetings, and positive student-teacher conferencing brought about these great results for these students;

From Tyler: "My pet dogs name is Buster he is my best friend. One day Buster schood up. The window screen and got out. And ran acrust the road and got hit by a Punch bugie. But buster did'nt die but he did have to get some steches."

And Stacey: "Once when I was three year's old we got a littal dog we named her porchse She is a girl She is very nice She never dits anyone and she liks playing with stiks a lot. Some times she sleeps with me in my bed it was fun one time she came with us the my gradma houes in Ohio."

The following two entries are from writing portfolios at the end of the year and reveal noticeable improvement in syntax, in supportive detail, and in the ability to communicate a clear, honest voice.

Again, from Tyler: "Oregon is a grate place. I know I spent my summer vacation there last summer. All though the ride was long and hot but once you got there it was boutifle. There's lots of trees and boutifle lakes. When we go to Oregon we went to see my aunt. After my aunt's we went camping whith my grand mon and grand dad. Then we went home to Virgina." (from "Long Ride")

And Stacey: "If you find a fifty dollar bill you should try to find its owner. If you don't find the person you should SPEND it! The reason I say spend it is because my mom and brother once found a fifty dollar bill blowing around in a parking lot. They couldn't find out whose it was so they kept it. My mom let my brother and I spend the money on clothes and toys. We were lucky to find the money." (from "Great Find")

Reflecting on the year, I realize the beginning of any new process has its rocky spots, so after the second class meeting, I analyzed exactly what transpired among my students. All seemed interested in conducting business, but initially were somewhat silly with some of their remarks. Also, at first, students were shy about discussing one another but became more comfortable as more students shared opinions. The main problem I encountered was proving how beneficial their comments and remarks were to our class meetings and to their emotional and intellectual achievement, a

> The class meetings have enlightened me to the fact that students can take control of classroom situations and find effective ways to solve problems. By working together as a team, students improved the atmosphere of our learning environment.

challenge I will continue to embrace. The class meetings have enlightened me to the fact that students **can** take control of classroom situations and find effective ways to solve problems. By working together as a team, students improved the atmosphere of our learning environment.

Has my class grown from this experience? Of course. This type of learning experience has been an exciting one for all involved, and I am proud of my students and the way they accepted the challenge of self-improvement. I have noticed many positive perks within my classroom; the students now have mutual respect for fellow classmates and listen to their suggestions and concerns. Students now listen with interest when someone is speaking and can recall more details than before. I have also noticed that grades in reading and math have slowly inched upward. As Schneider points out, "If we want to nurture students who will grow into lifelong learners, into self-directed seekers, into kind of adults who are morally responsible even when someone is not looking, then we need to give them the opportunities to practice making choices and reflecting on the outcomes. Responsibility means owning one's failures and successes—small, medium, and large" (Schneider 26). And Kohlberg reiterates, "A significant part of moral development comes through dialogue, reflecting on experience, and looking at how our behavior affects others" (Kohlberg 13). Yes, I feel that all my students have benefited from this form of management.

And, success breeds success! Matthew was on that first agenda, a "guinea pig" so to speak. He hesitated a little at first but used his checklist to set goals and establish priorities. Gradually, Matthew's grades began to improve as did his ability to be a team player, and his focus changed over the course of the year from "class clown" to becoming a significant decision maker.

Because I have had extensive training in Total Quality Management, I continue to refine my classroom practice by making class meetings a regular part of our daily schedule on Thursdays. Students look forward to that time of day when they can offer positive opinions to receive praise from their peers. Now, at the end of the school year, our class handles all aspects of the decision-making process in a positive, effective way. Students have learned, mastered, and internalized skills that will carry into other areas of their lives.

Making a difference in children's lives is what teaching is all about. In what other profession is a person given full rein to direct the learning of young minds? So when my husband asks, "When are you ever going to learn how to do your job and stop working so hard?" I tell him, "Never!"

References

Byrnes, Margaret A., Robert A. Cornesky, and Lawrence W. Byrnes. *Implementing Total Quality Management in the Classroom*. Port Orange, FL: Cornesky & Associates Press, 1994.

Works Cited

Byham, William C., Jeff Cox, and Kathy Harper Shomo. *Zapp! in Education*. New York: Fawcett Columbine, 1992.

Kohlberg, L. *Moral Education, Justice, and Community*. Boulder, CO: University of Colorado Press, 1988.

McClanahan, Elaine, and Carolyn Wicks. *Future Force, Kids That Want To, Can, And Do!* Glendale, CA: 1994.

Nelsen, Jane, Roslyn Duffy, Linda Escobar, Kate Ortolano, and Debbie Owen-Sohochi. *Positive Discipline: A Teacher's A-Z Guide*. Rocklin, CA: Prima Press, 1996.

Schneider, Evelyn. "Giving Students a Voice in the Classroom." *Educational Leadership*. (Sept. 1996): 22-26.

About Anna Spence

"I believe the classroom is at the top of the educational ladder."

Anna Mauney Spence received her B.A. in education from Lenior- Rhyne College and her M.A in curriculum and supervision from Norfolk State University. Mrs. Spence is an active presenter for various educational workshops on the local, state, and national levels, specifically those associated with Parent Teacher Associations. In 1994, Anna served as a presenter at the VASCD Conference in Williamsburg, Virginia, on the subject of "Portfolio Assessment." Ms. Spence has been a teacher with the Virginia Beach City Public Schools since 1973 and is currently serving as Gifted Resource teacher at Princess Anne Elementary School.

Reading and Writing with Flat Stanley

by Becky Walter

the Idea... Every year or so I happen upon a special activity that incorporates reading, writing, speaking, and listening into my language arts program. One year I had truckers mailing students preaddressed postcards from their different destinations. The children really enjoyed getting the cards and tracking the drivers' travels on a big map. During the summer, while I was trying to come up with a suitable encore, I overheard two ladies in a bookstore laughing about all the places they'd taken "Flat Stanley" for photographs. The niece of one of the women had sent her a paper doll with the request that her aunt take this character to visit historic sites in Virginia Beach. Intrigued, I asked them about it and found out it was based on a book, *Flat Stanley*, by Jeff Brown. As I discovered more about Flat Stanley's adventures, I felt sure I had found my encore so I purchased Mr. Brown's book to learn more.

> During the summer, while I was trying to come up with a suitable encore, I overheard two ladies in a bookstore laughing about all the places they'd taken "Flat Stanley" for photographs.

The Execution...

As my new school year began, I read aloud to my classes about the adventures of Flat Stanley. Flat Stanley is an adventure story about a little boy who was flattened when a bulletin board accidentally fell on him. He is involved in many escapades but returns to normal with the help of his brother at the end of the book. Although the reading level of the book is better suited for second or third graders, I have found success in using the various chapters with my fifth graders as part of my "teacher read aloud program," and to serve as an introductory or culminating activity for other units. My fifth graders just love letting their imaginations run away with them as they become part of Flat Stanley's world. Because Flat Stanley has been flattened by a bulletin board, he is able to go where other characters only dream of going. In one of his adventures, Stanley helped solve a robbery at an art museum. Dressed as a shepherdess, Flat Stanley hides inside the frame of one of the pictures. He watches the robbers from his hiding place on the wall and then screams when they get near. Shortly after their encounter with Stanley, the thieves are captured and Stanley becomes a hero. As my students get carried away with Stanley's adventures, we make certain to discuss all the implications of Stanley's actions. John Savage, in his book *Teaching Reading and Writing*, points out that "making inferences is an ongoing part of the comprehension process" (Savage 228). As a class, we were able to practice this skill of making inferences as we discussed the implications of Stanley's brother's jealousy because Stanley seemed to be getting all the attention as a new hero.

We also used these inferences as we made further predictions and generated "what if" questions about Stanley's adventures. Because another necessary competence children need to become good readers is the ability to think and predict what is going to happen. My students and I knew perfectly well what would really happen if someone were squashed flat, so that made it all the more enjoyable predicting the outcomes of Stanley's various escapades. My students had no idea they were learning vital reading skills as they offered suggestions as to what would happen when Stanley posed in the picture frame at the museum to spy on thieves. As far as my students knew, we were just reading and discussing for fun!

After we finished reading the book, I introduced the idea of creating their own flat people modeled on themselves. I collaborated with the art teacher and she assisted me in drawing a flat girl and flat boy the perfect size to fit snugly inside the manila envelopes I purchased for my class. After making several copies of each, and cutting the poster paper into squares, I directed the children to first trace the flat characters and then personalize them. As usual, on our "creation day" the students took my basic idea and stretched it to limits I'd never imagined: two best friends created twins; the skate boarders in the room made skate boards for their characters (and proceeded to have them execute wallrides and 360s). If anyone had ever pointed out to those guys that they were playing paper dolls, the project would have been doomed. The next step involved preparing the envelopes. Students who finished early and those with neat handwriting put the school's address in the return address position.

> **If anyone had ever pointed out to those guys that they were playing paper dolls, the project would have been doomed.**

Now, we were almost ready to send our flat person home. As a class we brainstormed a letter to parents explaining our project and asking for their assistance. We also composed a letter to the person who would receive the flat person. I typed these, and to make sure they did not get mixed up, I sent the parents' letter home first. The next day the students took home their flat person and cover letter in the large manila envelope (Appendix I).

Essentially, my part was now over. From here on, it was up to the parents to get an address on the envelope and mail it out. Just like in Brown's book when Flat Stanley would travel through the mail to visit friends, our flat characters would travel to meet grandparents, friends, aunts, and uncles. After the flat characters were mailed out, the children and I just waited for the results. And what results they were!

> After the flat characters were mailed out, the children and I just waited for the results. And what results they were!

The Response...

My students sent their flat boys and girls to grandparents, aunts, uncles, and family friends. And the responses were absolutely fantastic. As pictures, journals, and brochures began to arrive, I gave my students two responsibilities. They had to create a way to display what they received from their pen pals, and then students were required to present their pieces of writing and personal reflections to the class.

I was able to cover various Virginia Standards of Learning Objectives because as students read the written responses from their grandparents and others, they learned how to ascertain relevant information and present their significant findings to the class by offering supportive examples. Because my students were able to share their presentations with the class, their successful academic performance led to increased self-esteem and improved social skills. Through this class project, my students learned to listen to one another, to appreciate other cultures and family stories, and also gained a deeper appreciation for history, especially since one of the student presentations involved a flat character who visited Native American ruins.

The Children...

The first response to our class project was from two sets of grandparents who lived near each other on farms in Georgia. Unbeknownst to me, one grandfather was a motorcycle buff and the very first picture I saw was of a big, burly, bearded man dressed all in black astride a Harley, holding the little paper doll in front of him. Carefully written on the back were the words "Grandpa with Flat Matt." Other photos showed Flat Matt on a tractor and on the pontoon boat with grandmom. Written commentary included a little about the local history. We quickly mounted the pictures and information on a poster and the real Matt proudly shared his report.

One student with low skills and even lower self-esteem was able to shine because her flat person had visited another fifth grade teacher, her grandmother. That teacher created a scrapbook showing Flat Julie spending a day in another school. We saw pictures of Flat Julie getting her visitor's pass, Flat Julie in P.E., Flat Julie sitting at a desk with her math book dutifully open in front of her. Julie loved sharing the scrapbook with her classmates and absolutely glowed when other teachers and administrators oooed and ahhhed over her book.

> Unbeknownst to me, one grandfather was a motorcycle buff and the very first picture I saw was of a big, burly, bearded man dressed all in black astride a Harley, holding the little paper doll in front of him.

A slight, shy student, who was often the brunt of teasing, shared Flat Tom with MeMaw as she recuperated from a hospital stay. She had even taken a picture of Flat Tom sitting beside a bowl of popcorn and a Green Bay Packers green and gold pom-pom as he watched the Super Bowl with the family. During his presentation, one of the class jocks, thinking to belittle him, asked, "Why do you call your grandmother MeMaw, Tom?" Seizing this opportunity to teach another aspect of the lesson, I took time right then to go around the room and have the children share what they called their grandparents. The class soon realized that MeMaw was no more childish than PawPaw or Idgie or Nana, and that they all enjoyed a great love and respect for their grandparents. After that realization, Tom and MeMaw were able to complete their report without even a hint of derision.

One child who insisted she had absolutely no one to mail her flat person to came up with the idea of representing her own life. We had posters of Flat Mary waking up in Mary's bedroom and eating breakfast in Mary's kitchen. Another student's cousin wrote about life on a ranch in California; she kept a seven-day diary of Flat Nancy's activities, and thoughtfully gave her "city" cousin a vocabulary list which included the definition for "steer."

What I Learned…

During this Flat Stanley project I learned that grandparents especially are great untapped resources in our schools. The written replies we received were thoughtful, complete, and witty, covering more historical facts than I would ever be able to in American history. The brochures, pamphlets, and writings were woven into our social studies curriculum all year.

Because this project was completed the year President Bill Clinton won his second term in office, one grandmother, also a schoolteacher, traveled to

Washington for his inauguration and took pictures of Bill and Hillary. Somehow she superimposed Flat Julie on their pictures so that it looked like the figure was standing alongside the President and First Lady. "Inauguration" just happened to be one of the vocabulary words in social studies in the chapter on our first president. That's one abstract concept Julie and her classmates learned.

One father stationed in Panama sent pictures of Flat John at the Panama Canal, and we received a brochure about the results of shipping in Panama. Because much of the cause and effect of social studies involves transportation and the shipping of goods to and from the various ports around the world, the experiences of Flat John made social studies concepts more meaningful to my fifth graders.

What the Children Learned...

In his book *Integrating Language Arts and Social Studies*, Richard D. Kellough points out that many researchers (Clay, 1967; Durkin, 1966; Holdaway, 1979; McGee and Richgels, 1989; Morrow, 1989; Taylor, 1983; Teale, 1982; Teale and Sulzby, 1989) have studied literacy learning from a child's point of view. Teale and Sulzby, in particular, describe "young children as active learners who construct their own knowledge about reading and writing with the assistance of parents and other literate persons" (Kellough 185). The conclusion of these scholars is that reading, writing, speaking, and listening are all vital aspects of a language arts program. It is the incorporation of these four language modes into my fifth-grade language arts program that is the basis of my lesson planning. Since I also teach social studies, I have the fertile ground to till because this adventure with Flat Stanley incorporated all four language modes in an interesting, fun way.

Once the responses started arriving, children were encouraged to devise an attractive display, and when those displays began to receive favorable notice, students made certain their flat characters got mailed. By supplying the students with markers, crayons, and poster paper, I encouraged bold graphic displays as a means of effective communication. Ten- and eleven-year-olds are amazingly creative, and once they had an idea of what to do, we enjoyed a wide variety of posters. Students learned that all informative writing does not have to be essay form. With this enterprise, my fifth graders practiced letter writing and learned that asking for information often results in a posi-

> The class soon realized that MeMaw was no more childish than PawPaw or Idgie or Nana, and that they all enjoyed a great love and respect for their grandparents.

tive response. They learned to display material effectively and to deliver information orally. My students celebrated reading for knowledge as well as pleasure. Finally, my students discovered that every spot in America made some contribution to our country's history. Flat Stanley became famous all over our school and provided interesting reading for staff, parents, and students.

When I revisit this project next year I'll begin in September. My students will create their flat characters to use throughout the entire school year—they will not only learn elements of characterization but will create imaginative stories through writing. Why can't a Flat Julie, a Flat Matt or a Flat Karen travel to the parts of the world we will be studying in history? Or the settings we will explore in literature? Next year... who knows where Flat Stanley might travel...

Appendix I

Dear Parents,

Our class read the book, *Flat Stanley*, by Jeff Brown which is an adventure story about a little boy who was flattened when a bulletin board accidentally fell on him. As Flat Stanley, he is involved in many escapades, but in the end, with the help of his brother, he returns to normal.

The children have drawn and created themselves as "Flat." We are asking each child to mail his/her "Flat Person" to a friend or relative who will take the character around the community and perhaps record a journal entry about what they do. Snapshots would be great, too. Since we are studying American history, if the "Flat Visitor" could collect a brochure or pamphlet about some interesting sight during his stay, it would make this an educational experience as well as a fun one for the entire class.

The adventures of Flat _____ will be shared with the class during the week of _____. A letter of explanation is enclosed to send with the "Flat Person."

Appendix II

Dear _____,

Our class read the book *Flat Stanley* which is an adventure story about a little boy flattened when a bulletin board fell on him. I have drawn myself as a "Flat Person" and would appreciate your taking me places with you and documenting where we've been with photos, brochures, a journal, etc. We are studying American history this year, so if you have an interesting sight in your community, it would be great if Flat _____ could bring these items back when he/she returns from his/her visit with you. Please return Flat _____ with the accompanying material so that I can share them with my class during the week of _____.

Thank you for helping me with this class assignment.

Works Cited

Brown, Jeff. *Flat Stanley*. New York: Harper Collins, 1964.

Kellough, Richard D. *Integrating Language Arts and Social Studies for Intermediate and Middle School Students.* Englewood Cliffs, NJ: Merrill, 1995.

Savage, John F. *Teaching Reading and Writing Combining Skills, Strategies, and Literature.* Boston: McGraw-Hill, 1998.

About Becky Walter

"Students love hearing a good story; they love to participate; and they all want the teacher to think they are special."

Becky Walter began her teaching experience in 1963 in Decautur, Georgia, after receiving her B.A. in English from Queens College, Charlotte, NC. Currently, Becky teaches fifth grade at Ocean Lakes Elementary in Virginia Beach. Holding a Postgraduate Professional Certificate K-4; Middle Education 4-8; English, Becky Walter is also an active member of the National Educational Association, the Virginia Education Association, the Virginia Beach Education Association and the Tidewater Reading Council. A published writer, Becky received the first place award for nonfiction in the Sigma Tau Delta Literary Contest in 1993. In 1994, Ms. Walter also received her Professional Writing Certificate as a graduate of the Tidewater Writing Project.

Motivating the Unmotivated:
A Classroom Drama

by Camilla Walck

david was absent again, his fifth absence in the past two weeks. As I began to mark his absence in my grade book, I heard someone call out to David as he shuffled into my classroom two minutes late. I looked up and saw David leaning over my desk requesting the assignments he had missed. Although I handed him the assignments, I doubted I would get them back. David rarely did his work. Paper and pencil were always borrowed from a classmate. But then, David wasn't the only one who came to class improperly prepared.

Before I began teaching, I would never have pictured the scene before me. I visualized my classroom as being full of eager learners, ready to tackle the task of the day. As I looked up at David and the other students, I realized the monumental challenge before me. I had to find an approach to renew their desire for discovery. The question was, what? I was teaching environmental science to tenth-through twelfth-grade students. Most students in environmental science had already failed one or more science courses, so this course represented a last chance for meeting the science requirements for graduation. Many of the students had been labeled low achievers, while others possessed learning disabilities. Unfortunately, nearly all had simply never been motivated to succeed.

> **"The problem is fundamental. Put twenty or more children of roughly the same age in a little room, confine them to desks, make them wait in line, make them behave."**

As Tracy Kidder, author of *Among School Children*, points out, "The problem is fundamental. Put twenty or more children of roughly the same age in a little room, confine them to desks, make them wait in line, make them behave" (86).

I had always hated classrooms like the ones Kidder describes, classes that followed a repetitive routine, and could recall from my own high school science classes few actual laboratory experiments and endless note taking. My students hated this type of learning experience too and used the word "boring" all too often to describe the atmosphere that pervaded most science classes. Their words reinforced Sylvia Rimm who confirmed that it was the word she heard most frequently from underachievers (Rimm 53). If science was perceived as boring, the problem had to be in how it was presented.

Science must be hands-on and interactive, and I realized I had to be committed to that goal of having students actively involved in my lessons. I would teach my students indirectly, because it has been proven that "indirect teaching behaviors appear to generate more positive attitudes to school and school work" (Bennett 56). To achieve this, I would have to keep "grabbing" their attention; I would have to incorporate a variety of techniques — lecture, discussion, debates, and student-centered activities such as group projects and labs. Lessons must allow students to take ownership of their learning; after all, the challenge of discovery is what will lead to true knowledge.

> ...I soon began seeing a fire of enthusiasm kindling in all members of the class. The students were sharing ideas, discussing presentation techniques, and leading each other on toward self-discovery.

As I prepared for my next unit of study, "Biomes of the World," I focused on getting my students actively involved in understanding various communities of organisms. To do this, I wanted my students to work as teams of scientists. I began my motivational lesson by telling the students I had won one million dollars in the Virginia Lottery. I indicated that I would spend this one million dollars to save one, and only one, biome. It was up to each group of scientists to persuade the class that their biome should be saved. To offer convincing evidence, students needed to research their biome and discover the unique and essential features that make it critical to mankind. Each group would then present its findings to the class. David exclaimed, "A million dollars! Wow, you must be rich." This exclamation was the first spark I had seen in David all year, and I soon began seeing a fire of enthusiasm kindling in all members of the class. The students were sharing ideas, discussing presentation techniques, and leading each other toward self-discovery. I informed the students that their presentations must be videotaped documentaries or newscasts of their assigned biome. David was instantly excited by this idea. He and many other students had never produced their own videos before. This was to be their masterpiece, and each student played an integral part in its creation.

Each group constructed a backdrop that depicted scenes from their biome. To ensure that all students were involved, I prepared a sign-up sheet for each group. The sheet listed categories of research for each biome, and each student was responsible for two of the requirements. The individual groups decided how they would incorporate the research into their presentations. It was fascinating to listen to students discuss and debate student assignments. Never did I interfere, because students were learning to cooperate and collaborate. As they discussed the requirements needed, I noticed the group began to recognize the individual talents of all members. Consequently, the students had no problem assigning the various roles of the project. David's enthusiasm took flight and he was assigned the job of writing two commercials for products from his group's biome, the desert. David discussed his requirements for the commercials with his group, while I noticed his intense interest in discovering products he would be able to find in his biome. My goals were now becoming David's personal and intellectual goals. At that moment, I realized that learning must always become a process of guided self-discovery.

David's group decided to do a newscast. Students brought in background music for their video and numerous extra props to enhance their presentation. Several groups met on their own time to practice their scripts. The most rewarding moment for me occurred when David walked into my class two minutes early with the backdrop he had constructed for his commercials. I was shocked! His backdrop was a desert scene with various desert animals in front of a beautiful desert sunset. "Look at this. I worked on it last night," David said. "I know we already created our backdrop, but I wanted my own for my two commercials. I didn't know there were so many different animals living in the desert." I looked around my classroom and was astounded by the energy going into the lesson. Research books were being brought in, ideas were being shared, and new knowledge was being gained. Most of all, the students were not just learning the assigned material, they were going deeper into the subject than I ever expected! Science certainly didn't look "boring" anymore.

On the day of the video presentations, the students participated in group and individual evaluations. The class made the final decision which biome should be saved. David's biome didn't win, but he didn't seem to mind. He asked questions after some of the presentations and actively participated in the entire lesson. Each student was given a grade for both their assigned research presentation and the group video. The overall grade for each student was based on both their presentation and a written test. I had each group develop four questions based on their presentations. I merged student questions with questions from my biome lectures, fifteen-minute snapshot mini-lessons that introduced a different biome each day, and, during my introductions, students posed questions actively.

> **I sat back in my desk and enjoyed the moment a little longer. It might seem trivial to some, but to me the comments will never be forgotten.**

After much reflection, I must say the lesson was a success! While all students seemed to enjoy the lesson, the effect on David was metamorphic! Not only had he become an active participant in his group's presentation, he continued to come to class each day and actively communicated with me and the other students on a regular basis. I'll never forget the conversation I overheard as David and Robert left my classroom: "I never liked science before this year. All we ever did was take notes and watch videos," David said. "Yeah, science is fun this year," Robert added as he followed David out of the room. I sat back in my desk and enjoyed the moment a little longer. It might seem trivial to some, but to me the comments will never be forgotten. I was proud of the change that I saw in David's attitude, and it was evident that David, as well as many other members of my class, were now motivated to learn. The joy of discovery had been rediscovered by my students and by me!

> I am the first to admit, the challenge for teachers today involves making an extra commitment. Successful teachers must have the courage to be creative and flexible to lead students toward self-discovery.

What have I learned from this experience? I will continue to create lessons that incorporate interactive involvement and inject variety to my presentation. I am the first to admit, the challenge for teachers today involves making an extra commitment. Successful teachers must have the courage to be creative and flexible to lead students toward self-discovery. It is easy to follow the well-traveled road. But I am reminded of those lines from Robert Frost's prophetic poem: "Two roads diverged in a wood, and I—I took the one less traveled by / And that has made all the difference."

I am committed to the other road, and the difference is why I became a teacher.

Works Cited

Bennett, Neville. *Teaching Styles and Pupil Progress.* Cambridge: Harvard Univ. Press, 1976.

Ford, Carolina. *The Less Traveled Road: A Study of Robert Frost.* Cambridge: Harvard Univ. Press, 1979.

Kidder, Tracy. *Among School Children.* New York: Avon, 1989.

Rimm, Sylvia B. *Underachievement Syndrome: Causes and Cures.* Wisconsin: Apple Publishing, 1986.

About Camilla Walck

"The lesson lies in learning, and by teaching I will be taught. There is nothing hidden anywhere, it is all there to be sought."

—BOOKER REID

Camilla Walck graduated from Old Dominion University in Norfolk, Virginia, in 1994 with a B.S. in Biology. While studying at Old Dominion, Ms. Walck served as treasurer of SVEA and was also a member of the Biology Honor Society. Immediately after graduation Camilla began her teaching career at Salem High School in Virginia Beach where she taught Earth Science. She then moved on to Independence Middle School where she became involved with gifted education as the Gifted Resource Teacher. Ms. Walck now teaches Biology and Environmental Science at Princess Anne High School, the only International Baccalaureate program in the city of Virginia Beach. Teaching only a few months at Princess Anne Ms. Walck has already been selected as Teacher of the Month in 1997. Currently, Ms. Walck is pursuing her Master's degree at Old Dominion University.

Sharon Clohessy

Trevi, 1997

Acrylic

"Visual energy is what I want to create in my art work. Through aggressive strokes of paint, I capture the rhythmic movement of shapes and the interplay of color on my canvas."

Sharon Clohessy

Biographical Information

Ms. Clohessy is the Art Specialist at Rosemont Forest Elementary School in Virginia Beach, instructing grades one through five, as well as instructor at the Center of Contemporary Art of Virginia. She is an active member of the Tidewater Artists' Association and the Virginia Art Education Association. Her work has been exhibited at the Virginia Beach Boardwalk Art Show, Stockley Gardens Fall Art Show in Norfolk, Virginia, the Hermitage Foundation Miniature Exhibit, the Peninsula Fine Arts Summer Exhibit, and the Commonwealth Collects at the Center for Contemporary Art of Virginia. Ms. Clohessy is pursuing a Master's degree from Virginia Commonwealth University because, as she states, "the knowledge and technique I'm experiencing as a student will help me become a more accomplished artist and teacher, a teacher more responsive to the diverse needs of my students."

Art Education Statement

"I want my students to go beyond the realm of production in the art room. Helping students to make real life connections, to promote critical thinking, to engage them in thought-provoking inquiry and discussion—these are my goals as a teacher and an artist."

Mapping the Zeitgeist: A Time Spirit Tapestry

In bursts of resonant color and diverse pattern,
it weaves educational text and chalkboard writing;
a patchwork of ambiguity
organized disarray
freedom within boundaries
subtle yet perceptible
spontaneous yet labored

it is…
inside the classroom peering out at the neighborhood
looking at the exterior of an old schoolhouse
a painting, a notebook page divider, a journal entry,
a school chair, school desk, classroom window and door
a screened-in porch, a fenced-in school yard
an organized classroom, the hustle and bustle of the playground
assembled from dividers, rulers, t-squares, notebooks,
file folders, lockers, and books on shelves, memories and dreams
bits and pieces of this and that found at the end of the day on the art room floor

noise and quiet
stillness and restless movement
imagination and intellect
occur day and night
in both rural and beach schoolhouses
in this tapestry of knowledge

it is…
the sun rising on a new school day,
the ringing of the morning bell,
the meaning-making that imbues the day,
the sunset, the final hug as the last child boards the bus

it is everything that you think education should be
it is everywhere that you think education takes place

with threads of gold forming the foundation of our schools,
our children, our treasures.
It is a celebration of learning.

— Cindy Copperthite

About the Cover

Cindy Copperthite

Biographical Information

A graduate of Longwood College with a B.S. in art education, Cindy is pursuing her graduate degree at Virginia Commonwealth University in art education with an emphasis in curriculum and critical thinking. Cindy teaches AP Art History, Art Appreciation, and Advanced Fine Arts Crafts at Ocean Lakes High School in Virginia Beach where she also serves as Fine Arts Department Chairperson. Cindy also teaches classes in art appreciation and art history to teachers and children at the Contemporary Art Center of Virginia.

Cindy has initiated and developed the pilot course for AP Art History for the Virginia Beach City Public Schools. On three occasions, Cindy has been named one of four finalists for the citywide Virginia Beach Teacher of the Year Award. She has also been the recipient of the Secondary Art Educator Award for Tidewater, Virginia. Cindy is committed to creating visual narratives and whimsical images that speak about the beauty and joy, tradition and innovation, culture and heritage that encompass her life.

Art Education Statement

Philosophy of Learning: to look is one thing, to see what you look at is another, to understand what you see is a third, to learn from what you understand is still something else, to act on what you learn is all that matters.

Philosophy of Teaching: Teach from the heart with love, with passion, with your entire being.

About the Editor

Leanne Self, an English teacher in the Virginia Beach City Public School System for fourteen years, currently teaches Advanced Placement and Honors English at Ocean Lakes High School where she also serves as Department Chairperson. Her teaching awards include 1997 Virginia Beach Citywide Teacher of the Year, 1997 Ocean Lakes Teacher of the Year, and the Presidential Citation Award winner by the Academic Governor's School for the Humanities, University of Richmond. In addition to being recognized by Phi Delta Kappa for outstanding excellence in education, Ms. Self received the Outstanding Scholar Award for Academic Achievement by Virginia Wesleyan College and was selected by the Virginia Association of Teachers of English as recipient of the Foster B. Gresham Award given to Virginia's top English Teacher.

In 1997, Ms. Self was awarded the highest commendations by the Commonwealth of Virginia General Assembly through House Joint Resolution 434 which characterizes Ms. Self as intelligent, animated, innovative, and demanding: "Leanne Self's experience as a student, through her continuing education, no doubt explains her exceptional rapport with students and colleagues, who universally praise her energy, her creativity, and her commitment."

A published writer and poet, Ms. Self develops courses in creative writing and conducts writing workshops for teachers. She serves as a mentor teacher, a university lecturer, a tele-conference presenter, and is frequently a guest on educational forum panels concerning innovative teaching techniques and current trends in English Education. An advocate of reader response theory, Ms. Self was selected to give a major presentation at the National Council of Teachers of English Conference on literature teaching in conjunction with Dr. Robert Probst and Louise Rosenblatt, two of the country's most outstanding authorities on teaching literature.

As a fellow of the Eastern Virginia Writing Project, Ms. Self has served as feature editor for the *English Journal* and Editor-in-Chief of *The First Decade*, an anthology celebrating the anniversary of the Virginia Writing Project. In addition to her current teaching assignment, Ms. Self has most recently been serving as author and Editor-in-Chief of *A Tapestry of Knowledge*, a book that presents a rich mosaic of educators who creatively inspire and challenge students.

Having received a Master's Degree in English Education from the College of William and Mary, Ms. Self continues her studies for her doctorate by attending Lincoln College, Oxford University, England, through the prestigious Breadloaf School of English, Middlebury College, Vermont.

Acknowledgements

Preface

References

Nessel, Denise D., ed. *Awakening Young Minds: Perspectives on Education*. Cambridge: Malor Books, 1997.

Works Cited

Goodland, John I., and Timothy J. McMannon. *The Public Purpose of Education and Schooling*. San Francisco: Jossey-Bass Publishers, 1997.

Palmer, Parker. *The Courage to Teach*. San Francisco: Jossey-Bass Publishers, 1998.

Chapter 1
Reflection: Our Inner Journeys

References

Moffett, James. *Active Voices IV*. New Jersey: Boynton/Cook Publishers, Inc., 1986.

Works Cited

Dick, Susan, ed. *The Complete Shorter Fiction of Virginia Woolf*. 2nd ed. New York: Harcourt Brace & Company, 1989.

Palmer, Parker. *The Courage to Teach*. San Francisco: Jossey-Bass Publishers, 1998.

Chapter 2
Collaborative Teaching: Shared Visions

Works Cited

Palmer, Parker. *The Courage to Teach*. San Francisco: Jossey-Bass Publishers, 1998.

Chapter 3
Assessment: Looking In and Beyond

Works Cited

Kirby, Dan, and Carol Kuykendall. *Mind Matters: Teaching for Thinking*. New Hampshire: Boynton/Cook Publishers, 1991.

Rose, Mike. *Possible Lives: The Promise of Public Education in America*. New York: Penguin Books, 1995.

Chapter 4
Student Centered Learning: Our Subjects, Our Souls

Works Cited

Duffy, Gerald. "Teaching and the Balancing of Round Stones." *Kappan* (1998): 777-780.

Palmer, Parker. *The Courage to Teach*. San Francisco: Jossey-Bass Publishers, 1998.